EVER A VISION

EVER A VISION

*A Brief History of
Pittsburgh Theological Seminary,
1959-2009*

Donald K. McKim

*William B. Eerdmans Publishing Company
Grand Rapids, Michigan / Cambridge, U.K.*

© 2009 Donald K. McKim
All rights reserved

Published 2009 by
Wm. B. Eerdmans Publishing Co.
2140 Oak Industrial Drive N.E., Grand Rapids, Michigan 49505 /
P.O. Box 163, Cambridge CB3 9PU U.K.

Printed in the United States of America

14 13 12 11 10 09   7 6 5 4 3 2 1

Library of Congress Cataloging-in-Publication Data

McKim, Donald K.
Ever a vision: a brief history of Pittsburgh Theological Seminary, 1959-2009 /
Donald K. McKim.
p.   cm.
Includes bibliographical references and index.
ISBN 978-0-8028-7133-6 (alk. paper)
1. Pittsburgh Theological Seminary — History.   I. Title.

BV4070.P689367M39   2009
230.07′35174886 — dc22

2009027388

www.eerdmans.com

*To all the saints of God
who have loved and supported
Pittsburgh Theological Seminary*

Contents

Foreword, by William J. Carl III	ix
Preface	xi
1. Two Presbyterian Traditions (1794–1958)	1
2. Two Become One (1958–1959)	11
3. New Beginnings (1959–1962)	21
4. Expansion and Change (1962–1970)	35
5. The Round Table (1971–1978)	75
6. Transition and the Search for Excellence (1979–2006)	151
7. Forming Pastor-Theologians (2006–2009)	225

CONTENTS

Postscript: Ever a Vision!   233

Appendix A: Strategic Plan for
    Pittsburgh Theological Seminary, 2008   235

Appendix B: Historical Roll of Professors   243

Appendix C: Deans of the Faculty   246

Appendix D: Board of Directors, 2008-2009   248

Index of Names   250

Foreword

In summer of 1973, I visited former president of Pittsburgh Seminary Clifford Barbour and his wife, Betty, in their lovely home on Sevierville Pike just outside Maryville, Tennessee, which also happens to be my wife Jane's hometown. We were packing up to move north, where I would soon begin studying Homiletics with David Buttrick while working on a Ph.D. in Rhetoric and Communication at the University of Pittsburgh. With a lovely view of the Smoky Mountains in the background, Dr. Barbour held court, regaling Betty, Jane, and me with entertaining stories about the consolidation of Western and Pittsburgh-Xenia seminaries into one school in 1959. It was fun sharing some of these swashbuckling tales with the presidential search committee over thirty years later — anecdotes that no one on the committee had ever heard!

After arriving in Pittsburgh on a hot, muggy August day in 1973 and moving into the basement of what was then Fisher Hall, one of the first persons I met on campus was Don McKim, the author of this book. Don was one of many Ph.D. candidates who had come from all over the country and around the world (including our next-door neighbors from El Paso, Texas, on one side and Korea on the other) to study with the likes of Ford Battles and David Buttrick.

I'm glad that my wonderful predecessor, Sam Calian, asked Don to write the sequel to James Walther's *Ever a Frontier.* Don is clearly the right person to do it. Don is an accomplished scholar, theologian, church historian, teacher, author, and editor. Even though he has been away from Pittsburgh Seminary for most of his distinguished career (he is now back as a member of the PTS Board), he has always had, like me, a fondness for this place. So this excellent book is a real labor of love.

Having known both Clifford Barbour and Bill Kadel (under whom I served while teaching here during the mid-1970s), it was fascinating to read Don McKim's account of their presidencies. Don tells it like it is, pulling no punches. Soon after returning to Pittsburgh in the fall of 2005, I received a call from Bill Rea, who had written the famous Rea Report referenced frequently in this book. Its publication was a turning point for the seminary at a crucial time in its history. So Jane and I drove to Ligonier to visit with Mr. Rea, who was at the time in his mid-90s and nearly blind. Like Dr. Barbour, he told us many behind-the-scenes stories about those stormy years in the 1970s when I was a lowly graduate student and instructor who had no idea how tense things really were on campus. Oh, we saw it in little flare-ups when we would occasionally attend faculty meetings. But the depth of the fissure was unclear to us. We were just here to get the best graduate education we could find from some of the finest professors in the land.

During the very successful Calian years, the Western/Pittsburgh-Xenia political alignments continued but over time began to subside. When I arrived in the fall of 2005 and took over in February 2006, the faculty was ready to come together in a new way to train pastor-theologians for the church. We are learning each day how to live together, eat together, worship together, and teach together, because everyone is here in the name of Jesus Christ. We are moving into a very bright future where real friendship in Christ means we have the right to disagree, knowing that mutual respect and affection are not at stake — something we are modeling for both students and pastors and, through them, for the whole church. Now, turn the page and read this intriguing story of how we got here.

WILLIAM J. CARL III, PH.D.
President
Pittsburgh Theological Seminary

Preface

Before his retirement in 2006, President Carnegie Samuel Calian asked me to write this brief history of Pittsburgh Theological Seminary. I am delighted to do so!

My association with Pittsburgh Seminary goes back to my early days in Wampum, Pennsylvania, north of Pittsburgh. The main pastor of my youth, Rev. John E. Karnes, was a graduate of the seminary, and I visited the campus with him while still in high school. Other visits followed while a student at Westminster College (New Wilmington), particularly with my professor, Dr. Jack B. Rogers, a graduate of Pittsburgh-Xenia Theological Seminary. When choosing a seminary, I chose Pittsburgh for my Master of Divinity work (1971-74) and stayed on for my Ph.D. degree from the University of Pittsburgh in the joint seminary program with the seminary (1980). In the meantime, LindaJo (PTS '77) and I met in the seminary library and were married in the seminary chapel. I have gratefully served on the Board of Directors for a number of years. So it is with deep respect and great gratitude that I offer this brief history to all interested in Pittsburgh Theological Seminary from 1959-2009.

This book, *Ever a Vision*, supplements *Ever a Frontier: The Bicentennial History of the Pittsburgh Theological Seminary*, ed. James Arthur Walther (Grand Rapids: Eerdmans, 1994). The collection of essays in this volume is essential background for the story of Pittsburgh Theological Seminary, formed in 1959 as the consolidation of Pittsburgh-Xenia Theological Seminary and Western Theological Seminary. In this book, the story continues with the "vision" the seminary has held forth for five decades.

PREFACE

I have approached this work as primarily an institutional history. It is mainly organized around the presidencies of those who have led the seminary for fifty years. The Minutes of the Board of Directors have been the prime documentary source, as the notes attest. Conversations with a number of persons have also been valuable, especially Henry C. Herchenroether Jr., longtime seminary board member and counsel. I solicited comments through a questionnaire from a number of alumni, and I would like to thank those who responded. It is not possible to include all their comments. The ones I have quoted I have done so anonymously, but with appreciation.

I would also like to express deep appreciation to Mary Ellen Scott, who has long volunteered as an archivist at Pittsburgh Seminary and whose friendship I have enjoyed for many years. Other staff members at the seminary's Barbour Library were extremely helpful, including Dr. Sharon Taylor, David Brennan, Patricia G. Beam, and Karen Baughman. Administrative staff who assisted were Linda Smith, who has served the seminary since 1968, and Melissa Logan. Vice-President for Academic Affairs and Dean of Faculty Dr. Byron H. Jackson and his predecessor, Dr. John E. Wilson Jr., have also been most supportive and I owe them much. My friend since our graduate school days together, President William J. Carl III, is always a welcome conversation partner and provides strong and caring leadership in these challenging times for Pittsburgh Seminary. I thank him for our friendship and for writing the foreword to this book.

The idea for the book and the invitation from former president Sam Calian was a surprise, but a most welcome one. In the providence of God, I had succeeded Sam Calian as professor of theology at the University of Dubuque Theological Seminary in 1981 after he became president of Pittsburgh Theological Seminary. His friendship and support have always been especially appreciated. Thanks are also due to William B. Eerdmans Jr. and the Wm. B. Eerdmans Publishing Company for this publication.

Pittsburgh Theological Seminary is a seminary of the Reformed theological tradition serving the ecumenical church. Its rich heritage as a Presbyterian institution through its long number of predecessor seminaries is a treasure whose riches continue to be shared. The seminary has served the church through the last fifty years, during tumultuous and unsettling times in American culture. Its struggles have been

Preface

many, both externally and internally. This book gives a bit of a snapshot of both the difficulties the seminary has faced as well as the strong leadership and ministries that it has continued to carry out through these decades in continuing faithful service to the gospel of Jesus Christ and to the whole household of Christian churches. The vision which has moved it into its future with confidence during these years is that which led those who began "Service Seminary" in 1794 and those who came after to continue the institutions which have flowed together to form Pittsburgh Theological Seminary. The vision takes many shapes and forms. But perhaps at its simplest we can say it is that "the knowledge of God is the service of God." In knowing God, we serve the one to whom all glory belongs and who calls women and men to be the people of God in this world. The seminary's vision is to help enable our "chief end": "to glorify God and enjoy God forever"!

This book is dedicated to all those who have been a part of Pittsburgh Theological Seminary in various ways. No words can encompass the whole story of those who have supported the seminary as administrators, faculty, staff, students, alums, directors, and committed church members who pray for the seminary and support it financially. These "saints of God" are those God has used to carry out the ministry of this seminary and those whom we trust God will continue to use as the seminary lives out the vision.

To God be the glory!

DONALD K. MCKIM

CHAPTER 1

Two Presbyterian Traditions

(1794-1958)

Pittsburgh Theological Seminary came into existence on December 17, 1959, as the consolidation of Pittsburgh-Xenia Theological Seminary of the United Presbyterian Church of North America and Western Theological Seminary of the Presbyterian Church in the United States of America. Each of these institutions had a long and venerable history within its denomination. Each institution was located in Pittsburgh, and each institution prepared pastors for the Presbyterian ministry in separate denominations.

Predecessor Institutions

Pittsburgh-Xenia Theological Seminary

The history of the two institutions and the two denominations is complex. Pittsburgh-Xenia Seminary's history extended back to 1794 — the date used now by Pittsburgh Theological Seminary to establish its claim as the "oldest" of the theological institutions of the Presbyterian Church in the USA.[1] On April 1, 1794, The Associate Presbytery of Philadelphia voted to establish a theological seminary in what is now Beaver County, Pennsylvania, along the banks of Service Creek. Service Seminary opened its doors

---

1. Princeton Theological Seminary was established as the first denominational seminary of the Presbyterian Church in 1812.

in a two-story log building to three students in fall 1794 under its first professor, the Rev. John Anderson (1748-1830), who was named professor of theology on April 21, 1794, by the Associate Presbytery of Pennsylvania. Anderson had recently come from Scotland to serve Associate Presbyterian churches in the New World. The log cabin seminary was close to the two churches Anderson served, near the current town of Aliquippa, Pennsylvania. It averaged six students per year, with the enrollment never exceeding ten. But the little seminary served its denomination.

In 1819, Anderson resigned his professorship due to ill health and old age. A new seminary began in Philadelphia, and the Service Seminary was moved to Canonsburg, Pennsylvania, where the Rev. James Ramsay, an American-born student of Anderson's at Service Seminary, became professor of theology in 1821. In 1828, the Philadelphia seminary and the Canonsburg seminary merged. Ramsey continued as professor of the united seminary, which used buildings at Jefferson College in Washington, Pennsylvania, until its own building was erected in 1834.

The seminary moved to Xenia, Ohio, in 1855 when the condition of the Canonsburg building and the size of the student body allowed the Associate Synod to vote to relocate. The major event of 1858 was the union of the two church bodies, the Associate Church and the Associate Reformed (Presbyterian) Church (ARP). Both of these denominations had their roots in Scotland, and both faced the challenges of securing qualified ministers for their churches in America. The Associate Reformed denomination had established a seminary in Allegheny, Pennsylvania, in 1825 called Pittsburgh Seminary, then Allegheny Seminary, and then Pittsburgh Seminary again when the city of Allegheny became part of the city of Pittsburgh in 1912. Another ARP seminary, New York Seminary, was established in 1805 and then reorganized at Newburgh, New York, in 1829.[2]

When the two denominations merged in Pittsburgh in 1858, the church became the United Presbyterian Church of North America. It

2. See Wallace N. Jamison, "Associate and Associate Reformed Seminaries" in *Ever a Frontier*, 69-97, for the full story of these seminaries. For the basics, see Addison H. Leitch, "A Brief History of Pittsburgh-Xenia Theological Seminary," *The United Presbyterian* (February 16, 1958): 3-5. Cf. George Swetnam, "Star in the West," *Pittsburgh Perspective* 4:4 (December 1963). For the history of the United Presbyterian Church, see Wallace N. Jamison, *The United Presbyterian Story: A Centennial Study 1858-1958* (Pittsburgh: Geneva Press, 1958) and, in brief, Roy E. Grace, "Who are the United Presbyterians?" *Presbyterian Life* (October 5, 1957): 12-14.

had four seminaries: Xenia, Allegheny, Newburgh, and Oxford, Ohio — which was transferred to Monmouth, Illinois, in 1857 and was called the United Presbyterian Seminary of the Northwest. This seminary had no building of its own and met in a local church and at Monmouth College. The four seminaries served 57,789 communicant members in 660 congregations in the new United Presbyterian Church.

Difficulties befell Newburgh Seminary and it was discontinued in 1878. The Monmouth Seminary struggled, and after sixteen years it merged with Xenia Seminary in 1874. This left Allegheny and Xenia as the U.P. church's two theological institutions.

Demographics and shifting population led to a decline in Xenia's student body, and the seminary was forced to move from Xenia to St. Louis in 1920. A missions-minded body within the church, the New World Movement, offered $400,000 to the seminary to move to St. Louis (an amount never paid in full). The seminary retained its old name. This strategic location was to help prepare pastors for service in the midwestern and western part of the country, while Allegheny/Pittsburgh Seminary prepared leaders for the east.

But midwestern churches were not able to support the seminary well enough, and by 1929 the seminary's deficit was over $100,000. The stock market crash in that year only made things worse. The only workable option was to merge with Pittsburgh Seminary, in Pittsburgh — which Xenia's move to St. Louis had sought to avoid a decade earlier. So in 1930, the Pittsburgh-Xenia Theological Seminary of the United Presbyterian Church of North America was formed through the merger of Xenia Seminary with Pittsburgh Seminary.[3]

Four faculty members from Xenia and Pittsburgh Seminaries were selected as the faculty of the newly merged seminary. The president and professor of New Testament exegesis was Dr. John McNaugher, who had served on the faculty of Allegheny (Pittsburgh) Seminary since 1886 and had been president of the faculty since 1909. He served as president of Pittsburgh-Xenia Theological Seminary from 1930 until he retired in 1943.[4]

---

3. See Wallace N. Jamison, "The United Presbyterian Seminaries," in *Ever a Frontier*, 97-116, for an account of this period. Cf. Leitch, "A Brief History," 4-5.

4. For the McNaugher presidency, see Robert L. Kelley, Jr., "Pittsburgh-Xenia Seminary," *Ever a Frontier*, 117-23.

In 1943, Dr. George A. Long, pastor of the Homewood United Presbyterian Church and a longtime member of the Board of Directors, became the second president of Pittsburgh-Xenia Theological Seminary. During his term in office, the size of the student body more than tripled. This put pressure on the seminary buildings, which had been in use since 1899. Since the time of the merger in 1930, the relocation of the seminary had been envisioned. In 1950, the General Assembly of the United Presbyterian Church received a request from the Committee on Theological Seminaries, initiated by the Pittsburgh-Xenia board, that "the Church, with all possible speed and diligence, provide adequate facilities for the theological training of its leadership."[5] A committee was formed, and within one year the denomination's congregations and individuals had pledged over one million dollars to finance the seminary's relocation. Eleven locations in Pittsburgh were studied, including the Lockhart-Mason property in East Liberty. This ten-acre site, across from Peabody High School, was close to several strong church congregations and also the University of Pittsburgh. Charles Lockhart had been the largest single contributor to the existing seminary building when it was constructed in 1899. In March 1951, the twelve heirs of his son-in-law, Henry Lee Mason, gave the family estate at 616 N. Highland Avenue to the seminary for its new home.

Ground was broken in East Liberty in September 1952, and in the summer of 1954 Pittsburgh-Xenia Seminary moved to the new campus. A week of dedication events was held in September during which 2,000 persons viewed the new facilities, including an administration building and dormitory for single men.

The academic year 1954-55 was the seminary's first in its new facility and Dr. Long's last as president. The administration building was named in his honor and the dormitory, McNaugher Hall, in honor of President McNaugher.[6]

In 1946, Dr. Addison H. Leitch had joined the Pittsburgh-Xenia faculty to teach philosophy of religion and religious education. In 1949, he was transferred to the chair of systematic and biblical theology and was

---

5. Cited in Kelley, "Pittsburgh-Xenia Seminary," 125, from the Minutes of the General Assembly of the United Presbyterian Church in North America," 813.

6. See Kelley, "Pittsburgh-Xenia Seminary," 123-28, for "The Long Presidency."

also appointed the first dean of the school. In 1955, Leitch succeeded Long as president.

Leitch was an extremely popular — and often-quoted — figure in the denomination. Under his leadership, the faculty was enlarged and strengthened, and the Fulton Memorial Hall for married students was dedicated in 1957. By commencement of the next year, Leitch announced that the seminary was free of debt and that the facilities were worth $3.5 million.

Western Theological Seminary

The history of Western Theological Seminary was not nearly as complex as Pittsburgh-Xenia's. From 1812 until 1825, Princeton Theological Seminary was educating pastors for the Presbyterian Church. In 1825, the General Assembly voted that it was "expedient forthwith to establish a theological seminary in the west."[7] A seminary to be called "The Western Theological Seminary of the Presbyterian Church in the United States" was established on May 27, 1825. It was to be similar to Princeton in design and control. A Board of Directors was elected for a one-year term. The Board agreed on all things — except a location. Political wranglings ensued for the next two years. Some thirteen sites for a new seminary were suggested, from Indiana to Pennsylvania, including ten sites in Ohio. In 1826, the Board voted to recommend to the General Assembly that the bid of "Alleghenytown" (Pittsburgh) be accepted for the site of the new seminary. But such disagreements emerged that the Assembly voted to postpone a decision for a year.

When the topic was considered the following year, the third pastor of Pittsburgh's First Presbyterian Church, Dr. Francis Herron, was moderator of the General Assembly. He asked to be released temporarily from the chair of the moderator in order to give a strong argument for the selection of Alleghenytown. After his speech, the call for a vote was made. The Assembly approved the Alleghenytown location — by two votes![8]

---

7. Cited by William Wilson McKinney, *Early Pittsburgh Presbyterianism: Tracing the Development of the Presbyterian Church, United States of America in Pittsburgh, Pennsylvania, from 1758-1839* (Pittsburgh: Gibson Press, 1938), 213, from the Minutes of the General Assembly of the Presbyterian Church in the United States of America, 1825, 267. Cf. Howard Eshbaugh and James Arthur Walther, "Western Seminary," *Ever a Frontier*, 133.

8. McKinney, *Early Pittsburgh Presbyterianism*, 217-19.

The new seminary struggled in its early years, despite the efforts of Dr. Elisha Pope Swift, pastor of Second Presbyterian Church in Pittsburgh and founder of the Western Foreign Missionary Society, and Jacob Jones Janeway of Philadelphia, who was appointed Western Seminary's first professor but resigned in 1829. Dr. Luther Halsey, a professor of Natural Philosophy at Princeton College, was appointed by the General Assembly in 1829 and served until 1837. Notably, the Board of Directors appointed as his assistant John Williamson Nevin (1803-1886), who had been teaching at Princeton Theological Seminary while Charles Hodge was in Europe. Nevin taught at Western until 1839 and went on to have a distinguished career as a theologian at Mercersburg Seminary, where he became, with Philip Schaff, one of the architects of the "Mercersburg Theology" that stressed for the Reformed tradition the centrality of Christ and his presence in the Lord's Supper.

The early seminary classes at Western emphasized biblical studies — the desire being that "every student who finishes an entire course in the Seminary shall have critically read the whole New Testament in Greek and most of the Hebrew Scriptures, besides being well grounded in Jewish and Christian Antiquities and the canons of criticism."[9] Second-year students studied theology, particularly the Presbyterian Confession of Faith (the Westminster Confession), as well as other aspects of Reformed theology, while third-year students focused on church history and church government. In addition, a student was required to keep physically and mentally fit for "the religious service to which he was dedicating his life."[10] Ten of the students lived together, sharing expenses, and could do so for one dollar per week. A seminary building was constructed and opened for the spring term of 1831, though it was unfinished. It stood at the center of a top of a hill in Allegheny that later became known as Monument Hill.

Difficulties in raising funds for the seminary led Halsey to leave Western to teach at Auburn Seminary and Nevin to move to Mercersburg. In explaining his resignation, Nevin indicated that his salary had been in arrears by a full year and "latterly the measure of this

---

9. Cited in McKinney, *Early Pittsburgh Presbyterianism*, 221, from the Western Seminary Faculty Minutes, 1829. Cf. Eshbaugh and Walther, "Western Seminary," 136-37.
10. McKinney, *Early Pittsburgh Presbyterianism*, 222.

failure has been steadily on the increase. The arrearage is now upwards of two thousand dollars."[11]

In addition to the financial difficulties, Western was involved in a property dispute with the city of Allegheny that eventually reduced its holdings from eighteen acres to one acre. The theological split in 1837 between "Old School" and "New School" Presbyterians heightened the seminary's financial difficulties.[12] The split lasted until 1869. Princeton and Western Seminaries were recognized by the courts as the legitimate Presbyterian seminaries of the Presbyterian Church. Yet in the midst of the difficulties, the seminary grew to nearly 150 students in the decade before the Civil War.

Disaster befell the seminary on January 23, 1854, when a fire destroyed the old building. Some library books were saved, but students lost all their possessions. Citizens of the city, looking at the burning building on the hill, exclaimed that "the preacher factory is on fire!"[13]

The seminary used space donated by First Presbyterian Church of Allegheny and Second Presbyterian Church of Pittsburgh while rebuilding continued. Property at the corner of Ridge and Irwin Avenues (now Brighton Road) was purchased and became the home of Western Theological Seminary until the 1959 consolidation. The seminary building was soon paid off, and housing was built for professors, along with a library building.

In 1858, New School Presbyterian churches divided over the issue of slavery. In 1861, Old School Presbyterian churches divided along with the nation in the Civil War. In the south, the two Presbyterian branches joined to form the Presbyterian Church in the United States (PCUS). Western Seminary, which was part of the Old School church, managed

---

11. Cited in McKinney, *Early Pittsburgh Presbyterianism*, 231, from *Presbyterian Advocate and Herald* (October 30, 1839).

12. The moderator of the General Assembly in 1837 when the split occurred was Dr. David Elliott, professor of theology at Western Seminary. See William W. McKinney, "Changes through Controversy," in *The Presbyterian Valley*, ed. William W. McKinney (Pittsburgh: Davis & Warde, 1958), 249-50.

13. F. Dixon McCloy commented that this statement reflected "the growing industrialism of the community." See Frank D. McCloy, "The Mount of Sacred Science," in *The Presbyterian Valley*, 372. McCloy heard the story from Dr. Henry A. Riddle, who was president emeritus of Western, who had heard it from both his father and grandfather, who were Pittsburgh residents at the time of the fire (n. 26, p. 584).

to avoid significant theological disputes. The rift in the northern Presbyterian churches was healed in 1869 at a General Assembly in Pittsburgh at which Melanchthon W. Jacobus, professor of Oriental and Biblical Literature and Exegesis at Western Seminary, was the moderator.

Since seminary salaries were low, a number of the professors at Western also served local Pittsburgh Presbyterian churches. Notably, Jacobus, Samuel Jennings Wilson, and William S. Plumer became prominent pastors as well as professors. In 1864, Archibald Alexander Hodge, son of Charles Hodge, was called to Western Seminary to teach theology. From 1866 he was also pastor of the North Presbyterian Church of Allegheny. In 1877, Hodge joined the Princeton faculty to succeed his father.

A number of dedicated professors formed the faculty core of Western Seminary into the twentieth century. Benjamin B. Warfield taught at the seminary from 1878 until 1887, when he too moved to Princeton and became one of the stalwarts of the "Old Princeton Theology" that Charles Hodge had embodied. In 1903, David Schaff, son of Philip Schaff, began to teach church history. He taught until 1926, and today's Schaff Lectures are named in his honor. The "remarkable" James H. Snowden taught at Western from 1911 until 1928. Snowden was a brilliant man who loved philosophical discussions and theological argument. When he was seventy-six, Snowden debated Clarence Darrow in Pittsburgh's Carnegie Music Hall on the question, "Is Man a Machine?" Snowden evidently caused Darrow to lose control of himself, and afterward Darrow said, "The reverend doctor is a very learned gentleman."[14]

Western Seminary escaped the extremes of the Fundamentalist-Modernist controversy of the early twentieth century. The seminary added new buildings and faculty members, including William F. Orr, who taught systematic theology from 1936 until 1957, and then New Testament language and exegesis until 1974. Later, long-serving faculty members included Theophilus Mills Taylor (1942-1962), Frank Dixon McCloy (1944-1967), Walter R. Clyde (1945-1975), and David Noel Freedman (1948-1964).

---

14. See Dwight R. Guthrie, "The Philosophical Theologian" in *The Incomparable James Henry Snowden: His Life and Achievements,* ed. William Wilson McKinney (Pittsburgh: Davis & Warde, 1961), 190.

Two Presbyterian Traditions (1794-1958)

The seminary observed its 125th anniversary in 1951 and later that year inaugurated a new president, Dr. Clifford E. Barbour, who came to the seminary from a pastorate in Knoxville, Tennessee. In 1952, the Board of Directors voted to remain at the Ridge Avenue location amid three-way talks on church union among the Presbyterians (PCUSA), United Presbyterians (UPCNA), and "Southern Presbyterians" (PCUS). Those talks did not produce union. But the Presbyterians and the United Presbyterians continued to talk, and in 1958 the Presbyterian Church in the U.S.A. and the United Presbyterian in North America merged — in Pittsburgh, Pennsylvania.

CHAPTER 2

Two Become One

(1958-1959)

The Uniting Church

The merger of the Presbyterian and United Presbyterian denomination formed the United Presbyterian Church in the United States of America (UPCUSA). The formal proceedings took place on May 28, 1958, in the Oakland area of Pittsburgh, which the magazine of the new denomination, *Presbyterian Life,* described as "home of the Salk polio vaccine, the University of Pittsburgh, Carnegie Tech, and the Pittsburgh Pirates."[1]

A series of special events were held for twelve days in connection with the union ceremony. These included the last General Assemblies of the two uniting churches held on Tuesday, May 27, as well a centennial observance of the United Presbyterian Church of North America, a Memorial Day Convocation of Presbyterian Women, a Union Commemorative Pageant at Pitt Stadium, and popular and special Assembly meetings for the 1,200 commissioners and 2,000 out-of-town guests and area visitors.

The merger event featured ministers and members of the two denominations coming from respective churches and meeting to walk together to Pittsburgh's Syria Mosque, where the consummating worship service and sacrament of the Lord's Supper were held at 10:30 a.m. At 9:50 a.m, as the *United Presbyterian* magazine recorded it,

---

1. "Pittsburgh — Presbyterian Heartland," *Presbyterian Life* (May 17, 1958): 13.

The Presbyterians (900 ministers and ruling elders) came along Fifth Avenue from the Bellefield Presbyterian church, four blocks to the east, and the United Presbyterians (300 ministers and ruling elders) came from the First United Presbyterian church, two blocks to the west, to meet at the intersection of Bigelow boulevard and march up Bigelow to the Mosque.[2]

The meeting occurred at 9:58 a.m., as moderators and stated clerks joined hands and proceeded to the Syria Mosque in a driving rain. The United Presbyterian Church in the United States of America was formed with 3,102,572 members, including 11,573 ministers in 9,462 congregations. Later that day, the Assembly elected Dr. Theophilus Mills Taylor of Pittsburgh-Xenia Seminary as the first moderator of the General Assembly of the new church.[3]

The Consolidated Seminary

Formation

When Xenia Seminary moved to Pittsburgh in 1930 and merged with Pittsburgh Seminary, its campus was only three blocks from Western Theological Seminary. The "differences" in the two denominational traditions prevented cooperative efforts between the two until after World War II. When Pittsburgh-Xenia Seminary moved from the north side of Pittsburgh to its East Liberty campus, its former buildings on West North Avenue were set to be sold.

The situation in the newly formed UPCUSA was simple. As *Presbyterian Life* put it:

> The United Presbyterians had one theological seminary in the United States — Pittsburgh-Xenia — located on a handsome, new ten-acre campus of colonial design in the city's suburban East End. The U.S.A. Church had nine seminaries, one of which

---

2. "We're Together Now," *The United Presbyterian* (June 22, 1958): 2.
3. See "The United Presbyterian Church U.S.A. is Formed at Pittsburgh Assembly," *Presbyterian Life* (June 15, 1958): 28, and the magazine's coverage of the Uniting Assembly; cf. *The United Presbyterian* (June 22, 1958): 5.

Two Become One (1958-1959)

Seal of Pittsburgh Theological Seminary

was Western, located in handsome, weathered Gothic buildings on the north side of Pittsburgh.

The two schools had both been founded in the late eighteenth century — the first two such institutions on America's western frontier. Both had their traditions of training and service and strong-minded bands of alumni and friends. Should one be merged with the other? Should one be closed? Should both be moved somewhere else?[4]

The Board of Directors of each seminary appointed members to a "Committee on Conversations" in November 1957, when merger talks between the denominations were being held. The committee's purpose was to explore a combination of the two institutions in light of the pending merger of the denominations the schools represented.

---

4. "The Area's Two Seminaries Hold the Key to the Heartland," *Presbyterian Life* (May 17, 1958): 12. At the time, the faculty and student body of Pittsburgh-Xenia numbered 248; Western numbered 113.

13

At the same time, President Barbour of Western and Leitch of Pittsburgh-Xenia were meeting. President Barbour reported,

> Dr. Leitch and I began a couple years ago having occasional conversations for the purpose of getting acquainted not only with each other but with each other's institution, so that, should union be determined and merger indicated, we would be able to move forward with better understanding of the elements involved which might be related to the two seminaries. During these several years, we had developed a good friendship and a happy relationship. We have also developed a pretty clear understanding of the problems and the potentials.[5]

On May 20, 1958, Barbour told the Western Board of Directors,

> This report for this particular year ought not to close without some comment concerning the union of the WTS with P-XTS. Both Boards of Trustees have taken the same action indicating a desire to develop out of such a merger a sort of theological university. Steps have been taken to provide a study of the resources, problems and potential of such a plan; and probably a report from that study will be presented to the two Boards at their annual meetings in May 1959. The Board of Trustees and officers and staffs of the two institutions have given evidence of an earnest desire to bring about such a merger in such a way as to strengthen the whole program of theological education and to serve the best interests of the Church.[6]

The idea of a "theological university" was presented in the *Presbyterian Life* account as "containing schools for undergraduate study, postgraduate study, and specialized training in Christian education, inner-city and industrial work, and theology of the laity." Barbour was quoted as

---

5. "President Barbour Writes," *Western Watch* 9:2 (May 15, 1958): inside cover. Cf. "The Area's Two Seminaries Hold the Key to the Heartland," *Presbyterian Life* (May 17, 1958): 12 for mention of these meetings and a picture of the two presidents.

6. Cited in Henry C. Herchenroether Jr., "Pittsburgh Theological Seminary 1959-1999" (August 1999). Herchenroether served Pittsburgh Seminary and its predecessor institutions for over fifty years as a board member and legal counsel. This account and a discussion with Mr. Herchenroether have provided much insight into this period.

Two Become One (1958-1959)

saying that "Everybody we've talked to is enthusiastic about this idea" and that both he and President Leitch hoped that a "first-class theological university will be the fruit of plans now in progress."[7]

This was also the language that was approved by the 171st General Assembly on May 22, 1959, when it approved the Report on Theological Education in the Pittsburgh Area through its Special Committee on Consolidations:

> The Boards of Pittsburgh-Xenia Theological Seminary and Western Theological Seminary are agreed that the ideal for theological education in the Pittsburgh area would include the emergence of one great theological foundation (or university of theology) which would have several schools including at least a theological granting the 'B.D.,' a graduate school of theology, and a school of Christian education or a vocational school.[8]

The General Assembly also approved the committee's report to ratify the actions of the Boards of Directors of both seminaries:

> That the Pittsburgh-Xenia Theological Seminary and the Western Theological Seminary be consolidated to form a Theological Seminary, to be located in Pittsburgh and to be known as 'The Pittsburgh Theological Seminary of The United Presbyterian Church in the United States of America.'[9]

The constitution of the seminary was passed by the Assembly, and the date for beginning unified operations was to be "the opening of the 1960-61 academic year." A thirty-six member Board of Directors was recognized, and a joint interim committee was constituted to operate the seminary until all the legalities and recommendations were completed. On December 17, 1959, Judge William McNaugher of the Allegheny County Court of Common Pleas (and the grandson of former

---

7. "The Area's Two Seminaries Hold the Key to the Heartland," *Presbyterian Life* (May 17, 1958): 12. Theophilus Mills Taylor of the Pittsburgh-Xenia side, writing in the Western Seminary journal, said that "the possibilities for such a school are limitless." See "The Future of Theological Education in Pittsburgh," *Western Watch* 9:4 (December 15, 1958): 2.

8. *Minutes of the 171st General Assembly of the United Presbyterian Church in the United States of America* (1959), 111 (May 22, 1959).

9. *Minutes of the 171st General Assembly* (May 22, 1959), 112.

Pittsburgh-Xenia President John McNaugher) signed the court order to approve the Articles of Consolidation. So Pittsburgh Theological Seminary became a seminary of the United Presbyterian Church in the United States of America.[10]

Early Issues

The language used for the coming together of Pittsburgh-Xenia and Western Theological Seminaries in 1959 was "consolidation." It was carefully distinguished from a "merger." In a merger, one of the present corporations would be designated as a "surviving" corporation while the other would cease to exist. In a "consolidation," however, a new corporation is established, and the two corporations that are consolidated both cease to exist. A brochure of the time was titled "1 + 1 = 1" to indicate that each of the former institutions lost their identities in the interest of the new institution that was formed: Pittsburgh Theological Seminary. The subtitle of the brochure was "The Mathematics of a Dream."[11]

A whole host of issues emerged as the two theological institutions prepared for a full life as a consolidated seminary. During the fall of 1958 and spring of 1959, a faculty member from each seminary taught a course on the other campus: Gordon Jackson taught "Foundations for Christian Education" at Western and Robert Clyde Johnson taught "Kierkegaard and Contemporary Existentialism" at Pittsburgh-Xenia. A combined faculty retreat was held in October 1958 to discuss curriculum and other matters. The two student bodies met in November for a community service. The Elliott lectureship featured the two schools meeting together.

The Western faculty was reported as "unified" and featured "rapport and a spirit of give-and-take which have enabled the total program

---

10. In 1983, the United Presbyterian Church in the United States of America merged with the Presbyterian Church in the United States (PCUS) to form the Presbyterian Church in the USA (PC[USA]), thus ending the split that began with the Civil War. The PC(USA) is the denomination with which Pittsburgh Theological Seminary is now affiliated.

11. The brochure is mentioned in James Arthur Walther, "Pittsburgh: Where the Streams Meet," in *Ever a Frontier: The Bicentennial History of the Pittsburgh Theological Seminary*, ed. James Arthur Walther (Grand Rapids: Wm. B. Eerdmans Publishing Co., 1994), 159.

to move ahead smoothly." There was "general faculty agreement that the new seminary will be a good and useful one no matter how the physical arrangements develop."[12] In December 1958, Pittsburgh-Xenia professor Taylor set the ideal:

> Our one common aim should be to provide for our Church a great theological education center second to none. This center should not only produce an ever-increasing supply of men and women adequately trained to serve mankind and the Church in this generation, but should make articulate and self-commanding our Reformed understanding of the Christian faith to an increasingly skeptical age.
>
> We cannot therefore, be content simply with a makeshift piecing together of the buildings, assets, student-bodies and faculties of two old, existing institutions. While these should be drawn upon freely, they should in no sense hamper, restrict, or limit the new development. While inevitably, and quite properly, the new complex institution will build upon the rich historical heritage of the two former institutions, it must be free to develop its own new and peculiar character. Above all it must truly represent the new United Presbyterian Church in the United States of America, and in so doing any clearly perceptible traces of an older 'Presbyterianism' (U.S.A.), or 'United Presbyterianism' (N.A.) must disappear. It would be folly in the highest degree to allow them to continue competitively. As the Churches have become one, the new theological university must be a new institution representing from the start the new Church which it seeks to serve. Only so can it justify its existence.[13]

A tremendous number of details had to be worked out, of course. On June 25, 1959, the chair of the General Assembly Consolidation Committee, Dr. Herman N. Morse, called a meeting of the Joint Interim Committee of the new Board of Directors. This committee was carefully balanced between members of the former Boards. Committees were arranged to deal with details, and a Joint Plan of Consolidation and Articles of Consolidation were to emerge to be recommended to each

---

12. "Inter Alia" in *Western Watch* 9:4 (December 15, 1958): 24.
13. Taylor, "The Future of Theological Education in Pittsburgh," 3-4.

Board for approval. The joint committee unanimously approved the present Pittsburgh-Xenia campus as the site for the new institution. The three subcommittees appointed were Finance and Property, Educational Policy and Procedures, and Administration and Promotion.[14]

With structures in place, the difficult task of dealing with specific issues began. The name of the new institution was one. The name "Western," besides not being palatable to the former United Presbyterians, also did not match the current reality of Presbyterian theological education — it was no longer a seminary on the "western" frontier of the nation. The name "Pittsburgh," which had been part of the Pittsburgh-Xenia institutional tradition, was not preferable to the former Presbyterians for that reason. But "Pittsburgh" was finally chosen as the most suitable name.[15]

Titles for the institution's chief administrative office and the leader of the Board of Directors posed problems as well. Both predecessor seminaries had "president" as the title for the head of their Boards of Directors. Calling the seminary's chief administrative officer "president" would create confusion. After some contention, the head of the Board was to be called "president" and the chief administrative officer of the seminary to be "president of the seminary."

This was a prelude to the issue of *who* would become the president of the seminary. The two presidents, Leitch of Pittsburgh-Xenia and Barbour of Western, were the two natural candidates. They each represented the tenor and ethos of their institutions and of the predecessor denominations. The person chosen to be president of the seminary would wield great influence in directing the future course of the institution.

Originally it was agreed there would be co-presidents of the seminary. This would not solve the problem of the influence on the seminary; it just postponed facing the issue. Both Leitch and Barbour agreed to the plan. But following the joint meeting of both Boards on November 17, 1959, Leitch resigned from his office, choosing instead to remain on the faculty as a tenured member and professor. This created apprehension on the part of many from Pittsburgh-Xenia who were convinced that a co-presidency was essential. Some directors were opposed to electing Barbour or naming him acting president. Initially,

---

14. Clifford E. Barbour, "President Barbour Writes — ," *Western Watch* 10:3 (September 15, 1959): 1-2.

15. Herchenroether, "Pittsburgh Theological Seminary, 1959-1999," 5.

Clifford Barbour was elected as vice president of the seminary, and the office of the president of the seminary remained vacant. Shortly before Barbour retired, a few years later, he was elected president of the seminary. The constitution and bylaws were later amended to use the term "chairman" (chair) for the head of the Board of Directors and "president" for the chief administrator of the seminary.[16]

The consolidated seminary was ready to operate. It did so on separate campuses for the 1959-60 academic year and came together on one campus in the fall of 1960. Together, the two institutions had assets of $7,300,000. The joint operating budget for the 1960-61 year was $795,651.36. A financial campaign to raise $4,910,000 was quickly planned. There were thirty-six members of the Board of Directors and a combined faculty of twenty-three professors plus three librarians. Projections were for an enrollment of 382 in the student body in 1960. Among the recognized needs for the new institution were additional dormitory space and a dining hall facility, as well as a new library building that could shelve at least 200,000 volumes. Further parking space and utilities would be needed as well.[17]

So two became one. The two denominations became one church. The two seminaries became one consolidated seminary. High hopes were often expressed for the potential of Pittsburgh Theological Seminary to serve the united denomination, if the strengths of both ecclesiastical and educational traditions could be leveraged and melded into an institution that could educate pastors and provide leaders for the new church. The official hopes were expressed in the new seminary's first catalogue by Vice President and Acting President Clifford E. Barbour. His sentiments are worth quoting in full:

> We have a new school in Pittsburgh: The Pittsburgh Theological Seminary. It was constituted by the General Assembly in May, 1959. It has a new Constitution; yet the new Constitution is in line with the documents that gave direction to the activities of

---

16. Herchenroether indicates that the Board's constitution and bylaws had no provision for the office of vice president when Barbour was elected as such. "Pittsburgh Theological Seminary, 1959-1999," 6-7.

17. James Arthur Walther, "Pittsburgh: Where the Streams Meet," *Ever a Frontier*, 160. The combined libraries at the time of consolidation held 102,693 books plus journals and other resources.

the constituent schools, Pittsburgh-Xenia and Western. It has a new Board of Directors, half from each of the consolidating seminaries — new, but with experience in the old.

It has a new campus, only five years old; yet Pittsburgh-Xenia Seminary has been functioning on this campus during the last few years; and the Western staff and student body is looking forward to working on that campus in the opening semester of the new school year. It has a new faculty, but the new faculty is composed of the members of both old faculties. It has a new curriculum, but the new curriculum is not a departure from the assignments made to all United Presbyterian seminaries by the General Assembly. It is a readjustment with a new emphasis on the Division of the Church and the Ministry.

It has a new dream. The new dream is for the achievement of the hopes and ideals of all seminaries but accelerated in its program of development. By its Constitution, the action of its Board of Directors, and the desire of its faculty, the new school will function under the highest possible level of academic standards and will seek to develop into one of the finest theological institutions not only in the country but in the world, for the preparation of men to bring the Gospel of Christ into effective impact on this particular generation. We shall accept as our first responsibility the preparation of men for the pastoral ministry but plan to devise courses of instruction to help meet the needs of the Church for a diversified ministry to include chaplaincies, both service and institutional; workers in administrative responsibilities; sociological services; directors of Christian education; the teaching ministry; and so forth.

The new school will be bigger than either of its constituent schools, and we plan for it to be better, building upon the best of each a future worthy of the heritage and hopes of both. It will be exciting to participate in the achievement of such an ideal and to become partners in this significant enterprise.[18]

The new, consolidated seminary was off and running.

18. Clifford E. Barbour in *The Annual Catalogue of The Pittsburgh Theological Seminary of The United Presbyterian Church in the United States of America 1960-1961* (Pittsburgh: Pittsburgh Theological Seminary, 1960), 5.

CHAPTER 3

New Beginnings

(1959-1962)

September 1959 marked the beginning of the new school year for Pittsburgh Theological Seminary, with classes being held on both the Pittsburgh-Xenia and the Western campuses. Dr. Barbour was serving as vice president and acting president, an appointment to terminate with his retirement in 1961-62. Dr. Gordon E. Jackson of the Pittsburgh-Xenia faculty, who had taught Christian Education, became dean for a three-year term and shifted to the disciplines of pastoral care and counseling.[1]

The tasks of blending the institutions in their various dimensions in the earliest years of the new seminary were not easy ones. This extended from the Board of Directors through administration, faculty and staff, and students. The story of the early years of Pittsburgh Seminary is one of transitional adjustments among the peoples and entities of the institutions. The going was difficult. Theological perspectives as well as institutional and ecclesiastical traditions shaped the people who participated in the initial years of the seminary's existence.

Challenges of the Curriculum

A major hurdle to be surmounted immediately upon the consolidation of the two seminaries was the curriculum. Students who were already

---

1. See James Arthur Walther, "Pittsburgh: Where the Streams Meet," in *Ever a Frontier: The Bicentennial History of the Pittsburgh Theological Seminary*, ed. James Arthur Walther (Grand Rapids: Wm. B. Eerdmans Publishing Co., 1994), 162.

President Clifford E. Barbour

enrolled in Pittsburgh-Xenia and Western seminaries had to complete their prescribed theological curricula, while a new curriculum was needed for entering students of Pittsburgh Theological Seminary. So in the fall of 1960, three concurrent curricula were in place.

In 1959, a subcommittee on the curriculum was formed by the Study Committee on the Consolidation of the Two Pittsburgh Seminaries of the United Presbyterian Church. Its purpose was to recommend a new curriculum for the consolidated seminary. Three significant concerns surfaced:

New Beginnings (1959-1962)

a. The isolation of the fields of so-called academic study from one another and from the so-called practical subjects and concerns.
b. The fact that the present field work practices are in serious need of reorientation and revision.
c. The failure of present curricula to prepare students for the diversity of function that has become the rule rather than the exception in the experience of the settled pastor; and to furnish the specialized training required for the large proportions of the clergy engaged in ministries to special groups.[2]

The concerns of the subcommittee rested on perceptions of changes in ministry in American culture. The influence of urbanization with its attendant problems and challenges was casting aside "a badly dated, even romantic view of the ministry" that was "at the bottom of much of the irrelevancy of the theological curricula in use today." The once-"homogeneous" theological curricula were being thrown into "confusion." There was a need for a theological curriculum to "reflect the best thought of the twentieth century on the meaning of the church." This led, said the committee, to "the need for moving constantly from Biblical and theological study to the curriculum and back again in order to find the means by which the ministers of Christ should be prepared to serve in the modern church and secular society."[3]

On February 6, 1960, at the first regular meeting of the faculty of Pittsburgh Theological Seminary, the faculty approved and sent to the Board of Directors the recommendation that the new curriculum be organized by divisions rather than departments. The faculty recommended, and the Board of Directors approved on February 12, 1960, that curricular divisions be Biblical Studies, History and Theology, and Church and Ministry.[4] The faculty itself was organized into these three divisions as well.[5]

---

2. "Report of the Sub-Committee on Curriculum," Western and Pittsburgh-Xenia Seminaries (1959): 1-2, cited in Robert Ousley Brown, "Curricular Change at the Pittsburgh Theological Seminary: A Critical Analysis of Challenge and Change," Ph.D. diss., University of Pittsburgh, 1980, 56-57. This excellent study provides the framework and much material for the discussions of the Pittsburgh Seminary curriculum that will follow here.

3. "Report of the Sub-Committee on Curriculum," 2, cited in Brown, "Change," 57.

4. The recommendation of the subcommittee on the curriculum had been for four divisions: Bible, Church History and the History of Doctrine, Theology and Philosophy of Religion, and Church and Ministry. See Brown, "Curricular," 58.

5. James Walther noted that "at the outset these divisions met regularly, and a repre-

Courses in the Church and Ministry division were to act as an integrative context, enabling students to bridge the gap between theory and practice and would enable practitioners of specialized ministries to offer courses for students on campus. This was the intention of the subcommittee on curriculum, and it was accepted by the faculty and Board. The basic, three-year Bachelor of Divinity curriculum was to consist of ninety-four total academic hours (seventy-two required; twenty-two electives). The goal was to provide a curriculum that would "furnish thorough training in the Biblical, historical, theological and functional grounding necessary to all ministers."[6]

"Integration" was the key term to describe the organizing principle of Pittsburgh Seminary's new B.D. curriculum. This was made explicit in the description of the curriculum in the seminary's catalogue, where the curriculum is said to reflect "the deep concern of the faculty to fuse into an integrated program of study the traditional classical approach to theological education and the strong contemporary emphasis on the so-called practical courses." The emphasis on integration had a number of facets. The curriculum sought to "discourage departmentalization" and prescribed that the chair of each division was automatically a member of the other two divisions. This was "an attempt to bring together the faculty into an integrated whole." Some traditional courses were moved into the Church and Ministry division — notably Christian Ethics, from "the theological field (though not from theology)." This meant that faculty members might typically teach in more than one division.

Field education (fieldwork) was another area affected. This experience would be part of the student's second-year experience and correlated with courses in the "preaching and teaching offices of the ministry." Small seminar groups would be the context for these courses. The focus would be to "bring together all the student has learned or is learning" and to focus it at the points where the student was "directly related to the institutional church and to the culture." The expectation was that

---

sentative from each division met with the other divisions. Thus there was a unique thrust toward a unified curriculum and teaching strategy. After a few years, however, this arrangement became cumbersome. The divisions continued to exist in the descriptive structure, but the faculty functioned mostly in subject task groups." "Pittsburgh: Where the Streams Meet," in *Ever a Frontier*, 161.

6. "Minutes of the Faculty," Pittsburgh Theological Seminary (February 6, 1960), Paper A, 1, cited in Brown, "Curricular," 59.

as the student comes to grips with the "everyday life of the Church and of the culture," the student would "have to develop a profound sense of relevance" and would be "impelled to explore anew the problem of communicating the gospel to the world."

In short, and in essence, the new curriculum was built around two foci: it focused on "the nature and meaning of the Christian faith which it is our responsibility to communicate" and on "the culture with which we must communicate and the Church through which we communicate."[7]

The Church and Ministry division affected the way courses moved from other divisions were taught. For example, American Church History, taught in the Church and Ministry division, focused more directly on a correlation with American culture. The integration of theory and practice was much more pronounced than previously. Electives were primarily taken toward the end of the seminarian's study, and the attempts to integrate fieldwork with church and culture per se were more pronounced.[8]

Put in the context of American culture in the early 1960s, this was an innovative curriculum emphasizing emerging trends of relating theology and society in significant ways. The curriculum was strong on the traditional subjects: biblical exegesis, systematic theology, preaching, and counseling. But concerns for the "relevance" of these traditional topics to emerging changes in society were also coming to the fore. Pittsburgh Seminary's location in East Liberty and as part of the city of Pittsburgh meant that urbanization was an everyday reality for the school. The urban context provided opportunities for numerous specialized ministries, and training in the skills needed for these forms of service became part of the seminary's concern. The integration of theoretical and practical dimensions was considered vital if seminarians were to be equipped to carry out effective ministry in the developing social contexts of the early 1960s. Dean Gordon Jackson later commented,

> We developed, which was radically new in theological education in the United States, the Division of Church and Ministry. We were the first school to do that. We had our Biblical Division, which was traditional. We had our History and Theology Divi-

---

7. Pittsburgh Seminary Catalogue, 1960-1961, 42-43; cf. Brown, "Curricular," 59-60.
8. See Brown, "Curricular," 60-61, for these points.

sion, which was traditional. And then we had the practical. And now we've developed the Church and Ministry Division which would have at the base of it the theoretical as well as the practically-oriented courses . . . that was rather radical, both for us and for theological education nationally. When the Ford Foundation came to study our school as one among thirty, it proclaimed us at that time probably the most advanced in theological education in curricular development that they had studied.[9]

The curricular expressions and organization of the faculty were meant to be concrete expressions of the "purpose of the seminary" published in the seminary's first catalogue:

> The purpose of Pittsburgh Theological Seminary as defined in the Constitution is to educate suitable persons for the work of the Christian ministry and for other fields of Christian service at the highest possible level of educational competence. For the attainment of this purpose, the seminary shall provide instruction in the knowledge of the Word of God, contained in the Scriptures of the Old and New Testaments, and of the doctrine, order, and institutes of worship taught in the Scriptures and summarily exhibited in the Constitution of The United Presbyterian Church in the United States of America; and shall impart to its students the various disciplines by which they may be properly prepared for service in the work of the Church; and shall cultivate in them spiritual gifts and the life of true godliness; all to the end that there may be trained a succession of able, faithful, and devoted ministers of the gospel and other Christian workers.[10]

The emphasis of Pittsburgh-Xenia on the "gospel ministry" and Western's emphasis on the "pastorate" were joined in the emphasis on educating persons "for the work of the Christian ministry."[11] Dean Jackson underlined this point in his report to the seminary's Board of Directors on May 16, 1961, when he discussed the major new emphasis on field

---

9. Cited in Brown, "Curricular," 67 from an interview with Gordon Jackson, November 20, 1978.
10. Pittsburgh Seminary Catalogue, 1960-61, 17.
11. See Brown, "Curricular," 63, for the quotations from the two seminary catalogues.

New Beginnings (1959-1962)

education in the second year of the curriculum. He indicated that "very careful supervision" was given by both pastor and faculty, the faculty wanting "to bring together theory and practice, centering around the preaching and teaching offices of church and ministry." Thus, said Jackson, "the entire faculty's orientation toward the pastoral ministry" would "come into sharp focus. The pastoral ministry," he said, "is both our primary and our major concern."[12]

Interestingly, the seminary's statement of purpose indicated that the seminary existed to educate "suitable" persons. This term tips off a source of tension between an academic institution — in this case, a seminary — and other institutions — in this case, the church. Should the seminary admit as students those whom the church will find "unsuitable"? What would this mean? The history of Pittsburgh Seminary was to display instances where these kinds of questions became controversial. At the time when the statement of purpose was published, however, President Barbour indicated,

> We have a fine entering class. There are not as many as enrolled in the two schools last fall. We expected this — but, also, we have been responsible for it. We could have had more than twice as many. But our Board and Faculty are convinced that we have a high obligation to Christ and His Church to accept and to train those who are both called and qualified — called by Christ, and qualified by native gifts for the peculiar tasks of the Christian ministry. Many feel called who are not chosen for this particular ministry.[13]

Barbour added that "our interest is in maturity and that we are not 'educating brains.'"[14]

Yet behind this there were also tensions within the faculty about the purpose of the seminary and the nature of theological education. The image of the "theological university" touted at the time of consolidation was

---

12. Gordon Jackson, "Dean's Report," Pittsburgh Theological Seminary Board of Directors Minutes (May 16, 1961).

13. Clifford E. Barbour, "From the President's Desk — ," *Pittsburgh Perspective* 1:3 (September 1960): 2.

14. Pittsburgh Theological Seminary Board of Directors Minutes (November 15, 1960).

still part of the discussion. Along with his emphasis on the pastoral ministry as the focus, Jackson could also later reflect that "we were an educational institution designed for the scholarly pursuit of ministry, whatever the form of that ministry."[15] These early tensions were to continue.

Faculty

Those charged with carrying out the curriculum and educating the students were the blended faculty. In 1960, Dr. J. Gordon Chamberlain came to teach Christian Education and Dr. Gayraud S. Wilmore to teach ethics. Wilmore was the first African American appointed to the faculty. They were followed in 1961 by Arlan P. Dahhrenburg in speech and David G. Buttrick in church and ministry. Also in 1961, George Kehm was appointed as a teaching fellow.

The new professors stepped into a faculty trying to find its way in working together. Several of the former Pittsburgh-Xenia faculty members had opposed the merging of the churches, and tensions developed. Most faculty, however, were able to work together. Clifford Barbour wrote in the first issue of the new seminary journal, *Pittsburgh Perspective:*

> The most exciting and hopeful thing for the Acting President as he has participated in these Board and Faculty meetings has been to note that decisions are made not according to old loyalties but according to new responsibilities and developing opportunities. Men vote on matters to be decided not according to whether it used to be done one way at Pittsburgh-Xenia or another way at Western — but — what is best to do now! Decisions are made not on the basis of old practices, but of new promise.[16]

A year later, at the close of the first academic year, the faculty wanted to communicate to the Board of Directors their sense of the way things had gone during the first year and their resolve for the future. Unanimously, they resolved that

---

15. Cited in Brown, "Curricular," 64, from an interview with Gordon Jackson, November 20, 1978.
16. Clifford E. Barbour, "From the President's Desk — ," *Pittsburgh Perspective* 1:1 (March 1, 1960): 1.

New Beginnings (1959-1962)

The Faculty of the seminary is sensitive to the tensions which have existed in several areas during the past school year and which have impinged upon our life and work in the school. We desire the Board of Directors to know that such tensions have not grown up within the Faculty. The differences that have arisen among us have been mostly of the healthy sort that develop in the normal course of communication among men of conviction.

Indeed, many happy incidents have made us clearly conscious that the Spirit of God has moved among us during the year. Pressures from problems in the Church, strains from multiplied responsibilities for the development of the academic program, and unusual demands upon our time have not unsettled us and we attribute this encouraging estate to the grace of God.

We express our satisfaction at every manifestation of sympathetic likemindedness among members of the Board, and we bespeak their diligence and prayers that our labors together may continue to thrive under God's blessing.[17]

In June 1961, Addison Leitch resigned from the faculty to move to Tarkio College in Missouri. The Board of Directors accepted the resignation "with great regret" on June 19, 1961. Leitch had joined the Pittsburgh-Xenia faculty in 1946.

Campus Additions

The physical space of the new Pittsburgh Seminary was beginning to change. After May 1960, the campus of Western Seminary was not used. Seventeen rooms in McNaugher Hall on the East Liberty campus became faculty offices while a new men's dormitory began to be built. Fisher Hall, named for George Fisher, a Western Seminary Board member, was opened in fall 1961. A dining room area was added at the end of McNaugher Hall which became a focal point for campus fellowship. On St. Marie Street, on the northern boundary of the seminary's original property, an existing apartment building was acquired and named "The Highlander." It accommodated married students.

---

17. Clifford E. Barbour, "From the President's Desk — ," *Pittsburgh Perspective*, 2:2 (June 1961): 2, 10.

The closing of Western Seminary meant the library had to be moved. This took place in June and July 1960 to enable access — though cramped — to the full seminary collection of books. In 1964, the new Clifford E. Barbour Library was opened.

Students Speak

The lives of seminary students from the former Pittsburgh-Xenia and Western Seminaries were full of challenges during the consolidation. Their own varied backgrounds and traditions meant each adjusted differently. When the churches merged and consolidation was announced, the two seminaries provided some opportunities for students — who usually did not have much to do with each other while both seminaries were on Pittsburgh's North Side, except for an annual football game — to get together. It was reported in the final issue of the *Western Watch* (December 15, 1959) that on October 27,

> Ten students from each of the two schools met to discuss the subjects Revelation and Inspiration. This was the first meeting of the program which the seminaries call 'Operation Understanding.' All who attended this meeting realized that differences existed and that these differences ranged from theological position to personality factors; but it was also quite apparent that there was a genuine attempt to understand one another, and out of this attempt there seemed to be a sincere appreciation and mutual respect. The discussion was illuminating and served to attack old misconceptions existing between the two bodies. It was generally positive in tone. If these groups represent the true feelings of both student bodies and the possibilities that remain in them, then there is a real expectation for a basic understanding that will permit the two student bodies to join smoothly.[18]

Fifty years later, students of the time from both former seminaries remembered an awareness of the high caliber of the faculty, which one student called "a diverse and capable faculty, willing to give individual attention to students." Another indicated that what stood out most

---

18. "Student News," *Western Watch*, 10:4 (December 15, 1959): 38-39.

New Beginnings (1959-1962)

over the years was "the personal concern of some of the faculty and their deep faith in Christ." Notably, students believed that the professors cared about the spiritual growth and character of the students and what kind of ministers and pastors the students would become. Most of the professors had served in pastorates and had firsthand experience of pastoral ministry. Personal relationships between professors and students developed, as did friendships among the students. The seminary emphasized worship, with daily chapel services including well-known outside preachers and professors. The emphasis was on the education of good pastors and not on professional training for doctoral programs.

At the same time, students also perceived weaknesses in the seminary. Despite the faculty's rich experience of the pastorate, one student reflected that "the training we received in the practicalities of being a parish pastor was woefully inadequate." Another agreed that "in spite of some fine efforts by faculty and the learning experiences of a student pastorate, I was in for a lot of surprises in my initial pastoral call. I used to joke that the seminary failed to offer courses in unarmed combat and elementary plumbing, which would have been helpful at times." Some felt that many of the professors were not academically up to date because of their pastoral focus. This meant that students were not equipped to identify strengths and weaknesses of contemporary and modern theology. As one student put it, "we did not hear much of the 'other side.'" The "diversity" of the faculty was within rather narrow limits — those of the two Presbyterian traditions from which the seminary was formed. There was almost no racial diversity and no gender diversity on the faculty, and in retrospect some students perceived elements of racism and homophobia among faculty and students.

Prominent in the experience of students, though, was the "blending" process of the two former institutions. One student later said that "the main weakness at the time of the merger was theological and life style differences between the two schools and each trying to take their own traditions and perspectives to extremes." Some felt that "the faculty seemed to be able to blend together more than the students! Western students tended to be by themselves and the same held true for Pittsburgh-Xenia students." One student said that the main campus issues at that time were "smoking in the buildings, the future of Dr. Leitch and how the two student bodies would unite as one."

Stereotypes of students from the other tradition were prominent in the seminary — as they would have been in the two parent denominations before and in the earlier years of their coming together. For some, "there seemed to be an underlying conflict between Western and Pitt-Xenia students. Western students were considered to be too liberal and Pitt-Xenia students seemed to pride themselves on being conservative. This was not the best atmosphere for learning to take place." One student remembered that meetings between the student leaders of the two former schools were "contentious and tempestuous meetings. We at Western were experienced as hardly Christian since we both drank beer and played pool. Those at Xenia were experienced as hardly in the twentieth century since they read Scripture literally and were focused on piety." A Pitt-Xenia student recalled that "each seminary represented a different theological perspective and Christian lifestyle. Pitt-Xenia was heavy on the traditional understanding of Christian faith as well as the classical signs of personal piety (religious language, prayer, witness). In contrast and with exceptions, my perception is that Western was more focused on contemporary theology (e.g. neo-orthodoxy) and with a lesser emphasis on the more pietistic signs of the Christian life." Put more starkly: "From the Pitt-Xenia side, 'How can we faithful Christians possibly work in tandem with those heathen from Western?' From the Western side, 'How can we modern Christians possibly work with those Pitt-Xenia people who are stuck in another century?'" One student said he was told after he graduated in 1960 that "a symbol of the issues was whether the Western pool table and cigarette machine could be placed on the East Liberty campus." The annual touch football game between the two seminaries, played each year at West Park on the North Side of Pittsburgh, was once referred to as "the Presbyterian seminary version of the Steelers against the Cleveland Browns" — a reference to a particularly bitter professional football rivalry.

The obvious challenges of the kinds of tensions that could emerge from the two denominational traditions, the two seminary traditions, the two faculty traditions, and the individual personalities of those in the seminary community continued for a number of years. The "new beginnings" were not completely smooth sailing. As one former student put it, "My dominant memory of seminary is that of an honest struggle on the part of most of the faculty and a partially honest struggle on the part of much of the student body to reconcile the two different Presbyterian traditions — and how difficult that was." Or, to put it another way, the issues of the time "revolved around the question of how to become and remain a united Christian community."

CHAPTER 4

Expansion and Change

(1962-1970)

In May 1961, Clifford E. Barbour announced that the coming school year would be his last. For the year 1961-62, Barbour was named president of the seminary. He was described as possessing "a combination of genial friendliness, steady direction, and a fine balance of firmness and flexibility, all exercised with Christian grace."[1] In summarizing his relationship with theological education in Pittsburgh through the years, Barbour said, "For myself I can say that there has never been an experience in my life where the desire for cooperative endeavor in the cause of Christ has been so exciting and satisfying."[2]

The nominations committee of the seminary's Board of Directors was charged with the task of finding a new president. The faculty preferred a president who was more academically inclined than Dr. Barbour. On November 21, 1961, the Board acted favorably on the nomination of Dr. Donald G. Miller, a Professor of New Testament at Union Theological Seminary in Richmond, Virginia, and a minister of the Presbyterian Church in the United States. He was a greatly respected biblical scholar and teacher but had not previously held an administrative post.[3]

---

1. Pittsburgh Theological Seminary, "Annual Catalogue 1962-1963," 4.

2. "Board of Directors Minutes," Pittsburgh Theological Seminary (November 21, 1961).

3. See *From Faith to Faith: Essays in Honor of Donald G. Miller on his Seventieth Birthday*, ed. Dikran Y. Hadidian, Pittsburgh Theological Monograph Series #31 (Pittsburgh: The Pickwick Press, 1979) for a bibliography of Donald G. Miller. Among his important

President Donald G. Miller

Miller had been born near Pittsburgh, in Braddock, Pennsylvania, in 1909 and educated in the public schools of Pittsburgh and Uniontown, Pennsylvania. He was a graduate of the Biblical Seminary in New York and received his Ph.D. from New York University. "Happily," said the seminary's *Annual* Catalogue:

---

works were *Fire in Thy Mouth* (Nashville: Abingdon, 1954); *The Way to Biblical Preaching* (Nashville: Abingdon Press, 1957); *The Nature and Mission of the Church* (Richmond: John Knox Press, 1957). While at Union Theological Seminary, Miller was a coeditor of *Interpretation*, an important journal for biblical theology. He was also associate editor of The Layman's Bible Commentary.

Expansion and Change (1962-1970)

Dr. Miller offers a combination of Presbyterian background which equips [sic] him admirably for leadership in this merged institution. His mother and his wife were both reared in the United Presbyterian Church of North America. He was ordained and served his first pastorate in the Presbyterian Church, U.S.A., and his major teaching ministry has been in the Presbyterian Church, U.S. Thus he brings a rich heritage of Presbyterianism to this post in the newest, yet oldest, seminary of the new United Presbyterian Church, U.S.A.[4]

The nominations committee reported to the Board of Directors that Miller was said to be "conservative in his theological position, but not an extremist in one direction or another. He feels that somewhat differing points of view in a faculty may be welded into a workable unity so long as these points of view are within the framework of the Reformed and Presbyterian tradition." By a vote of 32-0 (with four members absent), Miller was elected as president of Pittsburgh Theological Seminary.[5]

Dr. Miller began his duties on June 1, 1962. At the fall Board of Directors meeting, he reported that "every effort must be made to strengthen faculty morale."[6] At the same time, a number of developments were occurring to revive the view of a "theological university" which some had held as part of the consolidation vision.

At this meeting the Board heard of developing relationships with the Graduate School of Public and International Affairs at the University of Pittsburgh and an arrangement in which Bachelor of Divinity candidates could take up to four hours at the University of Pittsburgh and receive seminary credit. A joint master's degree program was also being discussed. In a year, the Board of Directors heard from Miller that "plans

---

4. Pittsburgh Theological Seminary, "Annual Catalogue 1962-1963," 5.

5. "Board of Directors Minutes," Pittsburgh Theological Seminary (November 21, 1961). Herchenroether suggests that there was no consultation between the presidential search committee and the faculty, administration, students, or other members of the Board of Directors. He indicates that "there is no doubt the Committee believed it had done its work properly at the time. There is also no doubt that Dr. Miller was the 'academic' to meet the request of the Faculty. Later events showed that the process of his selection created substantial resentment among the Faculty and some students," in "Pittsburgh Theological Seminary, 1959-1999," 11.

6. "Board of Directors Minutes," Pittsburgh Theological Seminary (November 21, 1962).

with the University of Pittsburgh for the beginning of a Ph.D. program are in their final stages now" and that it might begin in Fall 1965.[7]

But as it turned out, by May 1965 financial problems at the University of Pittsburgh had hindered plans to implement a Ph.D. program, according to Miller's report to the Board.[8] In November 1965, the report was that the Ph.D. program had been "taken from the table" with the hope to enroll the first class in fall 1966.[9] At the February 1966 Board meeting, however, it was reported that since the University of Pittsburgh was now becoming a state-related school, any connection with a theological seminary "may require legal interpretation."

Still, hope was held out for a joint Ph.D. program to be established in September 1966.[10] By November, things were worked out, and the chancellor of the University of Pittsburgh, Dr. David H. Kurtzman, signed Articles of Agreement for a joint Ph.D. program to begin in September 1967. At the time this was the only Ph.D. program in the United States shared by a denominational seminary and a major university.[11] The following year, a Master of Social Work degree program was also established with the University of Pittsburgh.

Faculty

Donald Miller was inaugurated as president of Pittsburgh Theological Seminary on April 18, 1963. That year also saw the expansion of the faculty, with five appointments in major positions. The German scholar Dietrich Ritschl joined the faculty as professor of biblical interpretation and doctrine. He was to serve until 1970. Markus Barth, son of the great theologian Karl Barth, was a New Testament scholar who had taught in the United States at the University of Dubuque Theological Seminary

---

7. "Board of Directors Minutes," Pittsburgh Theological Seminary (November 19, 1963).

8. "Board of Directors Minutes," Pittsburgh Theological Seminary (May 11, 1965), 3.

9. "Board of Directors Minutes," Pittsburgh Theological Seminary (November 19, 1965).

10. "Board of Directors Minutes," Pittsburgh Theological Seminary (November 17, 1966).

11. "Board of Directors Minutes," Pittsburgh Theological Seminary (November 16, 1966), 6.

Expansion and Change (1962-1970)

and the University of Chicago before coming to Pittsburgh Seminary. Frederick B. Speakman, a member of the Board of Directors, was on the search committee that nominated Barth and told the Board, "This is a man standing on his own feet, who is no shadow of his father. We found him humble, warm, with a steel-trap mind. We interviewed him for an hour or two longer than we needed, just because we enjoyed it so much." Barth was appointed by a 24-0 vote.[12] Barth taught at Pittsburgh until 1972, when he returned to Europe to teach at the University of Basel.

Edward Farley joined the faculty in 1963 and taught theology until 1969, when he moved to Nashville to teach at Vanderbilt University. Lynn B. Hinds was an instructor in speech until 1972, and Iain G. Wilson was named professor of homiletics and taught until 1968, when he became a pastor in Baltimore.

The biblical studies faculty grew noticeably in the next several years of Donald Miller's presidency. Douglas R. A. Hare began to teach New Testament in 1964 and was joined by Old Testament colleagues Donald E. Gowan and Jared J. Jackson in 1965. Hare served until 1993, including a period as dean. Gowan taught until his retirement in 1999 and regularly afterwards as an adjunct professor. Jackson taught until he retired in 1997. H. Eberhard von Waldow first taught Old Testament in 1966 and did so until 1993.

The latter part of the 1960s saw the arrival of Dikran Y. Hadidian from the Hartford Seminary Foundation in 1966 as librarian and professor of bibliography. He served until 1985. Hadidian was joined the following year by two other Hartford colleagues: the British scholar Robert S. Paul, a specialist in Puritan studies who taught modern church history for a decade until moving to Austin Presbyterian Theological Seminary in 1977;[13] and Ford Lewis Battles, a former Rhodes scholar who was professor of church history and the history of doctrine and the distinguished translator of an English edition of John Calvin's *Institutes of the Christian Religion* (1960). Battles, who was instrumental in establishing the joint

---

12. "Board of Directors Minutes," Pittsburgh Theological Seminary (March 21, 1963). Cf. *Intergerini Parietis Septum (Eph. 2:14): Essays Presented to Markus Barth on his Sixty-Fifth Birthday*, ed. Dikran Y. Hadidian, Pittsburgh Theological Monograph Series #33 (Pittsburgh: The Pickwick Press, 1981), xi-xxv, for a bibliography of Barth's writings until 1980.

13. See *Studies in Church History: Essays Honoring Robert S. Paul on his Sixty-fifth Birthday*, ed. Horton Davies (Allison Park, Penn.: Pickwick Publications, 1983).

Ph.D. program with the University of Pittsburgh and served as its coordinator for a number of years, taught at the seminary until 1978, when he left to teach at Calvin Theological Seminary in Grand Rapids, Michigan, and become the first director of the H. Henry Meeter Center for Calvin Studies on the Calvin College and Seminary campus. When Battles's nomination was made to the Board of Directors, the Board was told that "Dr. Battles discusses and writes in Latin fluently." He was described to Donald Miller as "a little bit of a genius."[14]

Peter Fribley taught homiletics from 1966-1970. Neil R. Paylor joined the faculty in 1968 in Church and Ministry and taught until 1982. Also in 1968, Paul W. Lapp, a noted archaeologist, became professor of Old Testament and archaeology but drowned in Cyprus two years later while on an archaeological expedition.[15] Robert M. Ezzell began teaching homiletics and New Testament in 1969 and did so until his death in 1999. Ronald H. Stone began teaching ethics in 1969 and served until his retirement in 2003.

The strengthening of the faculty through the Miller years featured a number of professors who served for a long period of time and were influential in the seminary experience of hundreds of students. The turbulence of the times, socially and culturally, was reflected in the faculty as well as the student body.

Campus Developments

Construction was common in the early years at Pittsburgh Seminary. Before Dr. Barbour retired, planning was underway for a new library building. Longtime librarian Agnes Ballantyne from Pittsburgh-Xenia resigned in September 1959 as a protest against the consolidation of the two seminaries. James Irvine was appointed in 1960 and served un-

---

14. "Board of Directors Minutes," Pittsburgh Theological Seminary (May 9, 1967). Cf. Miller's "Ford Lewis Battles: An Appreciation" in *Reformatio Perennis: Essays on Calvin and the Reformation in Honor of Ford Lewis Battles*, ed. B. A. Gerrish in collaboration with Robert Benedetto, Pittsburgh Theological Monograph Series #32 (Pittsburgh: The Pickwick Press, 1981), 1-8. This essay reveals that the comment on Battles being "a bit of a genius" was made by one of Battles's mentors, Matthew Spinka (p. 4).

15. On Lapp, further, see the essay by his wife, Nancy L. Lapp, "Archaeology and the James L. Kelso Bible Lands Museum," in *Ever a Frontier*, 255-57.

Expansion and Change (1962-1970)

Dedication of Barbour Library

til 1966. It was Irvine's job to merge the two seminary collections, realizing that a new library facility was on the horizon. Over 100,000 volumes were listed as the library's holdings in the first Pittsburgh Theological Seminary catalog. This was 25,000 more than the library on the East Liberty campus could hold.[16]

Planning for the new library began in 1960-61, but the construction contract was not signed until 1963 when funding was in place. The contract was for slightly under one million dollars. Gifts of $675,000 from the Sarah Mellon Scaife Foundation and the R. K. Mellon Foundation paid for the library's construction and furnishings.

The new library was dedicated on September 21, 1964, and named

---

16. See Stephen D. Crocco, "The Library," in *Ever a Frontier*, 199-200. Crocco's essay covers the history of the libraries in the various antecedent institutions of Pittsburgh Theological Seminary.

in honor of Dr. Clifford E. Barbour. Amid celebration, an item of great interest was the desk donated to the Barbour Library by Karl Barth. Donald Miller reported to the Board:

> On a recent trip to Europe in search of teaching personnel, I was able, with the help of his son Markus, to persuade Karl Barth to let us have the desk and chair on which he has done all of his theological writing for the price of buying him a new desk and crating and shipping the old desk to this country. These were sought after by at least two other institutions in this country, and I am sure that the presence of Professor Markus Barth on our faculty was the deciding factor in our favor.[17]

Barth had inherited this desk from his father, who was a professor of church history. At the desk, Karl Barth had written out his whole *Church Dogmatics* by hand. Pittsburgh Presbyterians had donated money to buy Barth the new desk, which he liked very much.[18] Miller hoped that being able to display the desk in the new library building would "serve as a constant reminder to faculty, students, and visitors of the significant and exciting work of theological study."

Of note was the speaker for the dedication, Martin Niemöller. Niemoeller was one of the heroes of the Confessing Church movement in Germany that had opposed Adolf Hitler. He was a former submarine commander in World War I and became a pastor, suffering imprisonment for his resistance. In his dedication address for Barbour Library, Niemöller drew on his Dachau concentration camp experience, where he lived together with three Roman priests "together as disciples of Christ Jesus."[19] He urged that Christians move out of their own singular traditions and examine what they can learn from others in the faith. For "we cannot and must not become a closed group of society: we owe the gospel to everybody, and therefore we ought to widen our horizon and to come to know as much of other peoples and of other Christians

---

17. "Board of Directors Minutes," Pittsburgh Theological Seminary (May 12, 1964), 3.

18. See Crocco, "The Library," in *Ever a Frontier,* 200. He cites the reference to the desk in Eberhard Bush's *Karl Barth: His Life from Letters and Autobiographical Texts* (Philadelphia: Fortress Press, 1976), 475.

19. Martin Niemöller, "Dedication Address — The Clifford E. Barbour Library," *Pittsburgh Perspective* 5:4 (December 1964): 7.

Expansion and Change (1962-1970)

and of other churches and of their theological work, views, ideas and thoughts as we can." A library such as the Barbour Library — built to house 300,000 volumes — is a key for this task. For, said Niemöller, whoever tries to work in a special field to spread God's saving word "under certain and still unknown conditions" simply "cannot do without a technically most perfect and organized library."[20]

The spacious new facility was off to a propitious start and has served admirably at the center of the seminary campus. In 1964 it had a library staff of seven persons, with plans to expand it further. As will be forever the case, budgets for books continued to present challenges to the seminary's overall financial resources. In June 1966, James Irvine left to take a position at Princeton Theological Seminary's Speer Library and Hadidian arrived. His report to the Board of Directors indicated his interest in the desire to make Barbour Library a premier resource: "The task of implementing the decision to make the Barbour Library a worthy center for study and research and eventually one of the major theological libraries in our country has brought me to Pittsburgh."[21]

Financial challenges for an expanding faculty and campus became prominent as the 1960s continued. The seminary's $10 million endowment was not in itself sufficient to support the seminary's programs. Its primary use was for support for faculty salaries and student scholarships. After the merger of the denominations and the consolidation of the seminaries, support by the General Assembly of the United Presbyterian Church was reduced, due to less financial support from churches — some of which resulted from displeasure by some Presbyterians over the merger and some from the need to provide support in relatively equal measure to all the denomination's seminaries.[22] Over the next decades, denominational support for the seminaries continued to shrink, so that efforts for fundraising from various sources became crucial.

---

20. Niemoeller, "Dedication Address," 8. See the photo of Niemoeller, Clifford Barbour, and Donald Miller in *Ever a Frontier*, 201.

21. Cited in Crocco, "The Library" in *Ever a Frontier*, 202, from Hadidian's 1966-67 report to the Seminary's board of directors. For a description of the library's special collections, the Mason collection and the Warrington collection in Hymnology, see his essay. Cf. Frank Dixon McCloy, "The Founding of the Library of The Pittsburgh Theological Seminary," *Pittsburgh Perspective* 5:3 (September 1964): 4-12.

22. The seminaries were Pittsburgh, Princeton, Dubuque, McCormick, and San Francisco.

Along with faculty expansion and the new Barbour Library, several other notable features of Pittsburgh Seminary history emerged during Miller's presidency. From 1903 to 1926, David S. Schaff was a professor of church history at Western Theological Seminary. In 1965, the first lecture in an annual lectureship in Schaff's honor was held. Professor C. F. D. Moule of Cambridge University delivered the first Schaff lectures on "The Basic Meaning of the New Testament." These lectures were later published — a stipulation of the lectureship — as *The Phenomena of the New Testament*.[23] The next year the lecturer was the renowned philosopher Paul Ricoeur.

Two new residences for married students were dedicated on May 7, 1968. Anderson Hall was named for John Anderson (1748-1830), the founder of the 1794 Service Seminary. McMillan Hall was named for John McMillan (1752-1833), a major figure in early Presbyterianism in "the West" and founder of Washington Academy and Jefferson College. The buildings formed a quadrangle with the two wings of the Highlander apartments and were important additions to the seminary's housing for married students. Funding came from the 50 Million Fund of the United Presbyterian Church. These were Pittsburgh Seminary's first projects financed by the fund.

Plans and construction of the Lewis W. Hicks Family Memorial Chapel also got underway during the presidency of Donald Miller. Lewis W. Hicks (1871-1965) was a member of the Board of Directors of Western Seminary for many years. His son, Wenman A. Hicks (1897-1953), who was elected to the Board on May 16, 1946, died on September 24, 1953. He was vice president of the Board at the time of his death.[24] Hicks bequeathed a large sum of money to Western Seminary to be used for the construction of a chapel. As part of the consolidation of Western and Pittsburgh-Xenia, the funds were transferred to Pittsburgh Theological Seminary.

Lewis Hicks died on September 21, 1965. He had stipulated in his will that a legacy be left to a Presbyterian seminary for the construction of a chapel. The seminary to receive the legacy was to be named by a

---

23. See C. F. D. Moule, *The Phenomena of the New Testament: An Inquiry into the Implication of Certain Features of the New Testament*, Studies in Biblical Theology, Second Series, vol. 1 (London: SCM Press Ltd.; Naperville, Ill.: Allenson, 1967).

24. See the notice of his death in *Western Watch* 5:1 (March 1, 1954): 7.

Expansion and Change (1962-1970)

committee appointed in the will. One way of understanding the reason Hicks had established this plan was that "Mr. Hicks felt uncertain about the possible influence of of old United Presbyterians at PTS. The committee, after an extended review of PTS including very careful observation of Dr. Miller to determine his conservative-liberal status in the denomination, finally designated PTS as the favored seminary."[25]

The architect for the chapel was also to be selected by the committee, which gave it basic control over the style and the design for the building. Consultation with the property committee of the seminary Board and President Miller followed so that the new building would blend architecturally with the existing buildings. The architect selected for the project was Milton Grigg of Charlottesville, Virginia.[26] Grigg was an expert on the architecture of Christopher Wren, the famous British church architect. Originally, the committee had intended to build only a chapel, but President Miller prevailed on the group to include a large auditorium and office space to insure a wider usage of what would be a major investment. The chapel building today serves as a facility for offices and various seminary programs as well as providing the campus's largest assembly area in addition to the chapel sanctuary.[27]

Difficulties emerged in the construction of the facility relating to design and specification for structural steel. These led to portions of the erected steel having to be removed and refabricated, but not at the seminary's expense. When the building was completed, its exterior was in the Georgian style with the heart of the building being

> the chapel itself, cruciform in shape, with pew sections radiating from a rectangular center. Woodwork is a deep plum color with mahogany pew caps and trim, a décor patterned after that of Christopher Wren's St. Clement, Dane Church, London. The

---

25. Herchenroether, "Pittsburgh Theological Seminary 1959-1999," 13. On February 9, 1966, the seminary received the letter indicating the funding for a chapel from the Hicks estate.

26. "The Lewis W. Hicks Family Memorial Chapel," Pittsburgh Theological Seminary brochure. The contractor for the chapel was Martin & Nettrour Contracting Company of Pittsburgh.

27. During the energy crisis of the early 1970s, Hicks Chapel was closed during the winter. Chapel services were held in the former McCune Chapel, described as being done in "chaste Colonial style" (*Catalog Issue of Perspective* 10 [Spring 1969]: 23) which was turned into Williamson Lounge and later the John Knox Room.

walls and ceiling provide a background of eggshell white. Sparkling pewter chandeliers hang from the ceiling whose dominant design is a huge cross extending over the central nave. Intricate plaster moldings add texture and depth to the ceiling. The entire nave is floored with natural slate.[28]

Atop the steeple sits a weathercock, described as "a symbol of special significance in the early reformed churches of Geneva, denoting the 'Awakening of the New Day.'"[29] The architect commented:

> Every structure is a symbol of intangible purpose. This structural allegory combines today's theological thrust with our heritage of Reformed Protestant worship, a philosophy held in common by renowned architect Christopher Wren and John Calvin: the indispensability of God's Word . . . and the Kingship of Christ as the only Son and Head of His Church.[30]

Yet the construction of Hicks Chapel created conflict. In October 1969, the executive committee of the Board of Directors received a petition by students, supported also by some faculty, to suspend the construction of Hicks Chapel. The argument was that the expenditure of this amount of money on a building was unconscionable when it could be better used to help the poor and the socially disadvantaged. After considering whether it might be best to refuse the Hicks bequest, the Board decided to accept it and proceed since the legacy was specifically designated for a chapel and the seminary would not have access to the funds for any other purpose.[31]

Hicks Chapel was dedicated in the spring of 1970, and soon it hosted

---

28. "The Lewis W. Hicks Family Memorial Chapel," Pittsburgh Theological Seminary brochure.

29. James Walther indicates that the "golden weathercock" is "a traditional symbol warning against denial of the Lord," in *Ever a Frontier*, 171. Later, a bitter comment by those who did not like the seminary's theological positions was that the rooster was the rooster that crowed when Peter denied Jesus. In later years, someone shot holes in the weathercock, and it had to be repaired.

30. "The Lewis W. Hicks Family Memorial Chapel," Pittsburgh Theological Seminary brochure.

31. See "Board of Directors Minutes," Pittsburgh Theological Seminary (October 8, 1969).

Expansion and Change (1962-1970)

PTS Biblical Division Faculty with President Miller

a major Pittsburgh Seminary event. The Pittsburgh Festival on the Gospels was held on April 6-10, 1970, as part of the anniversary events to celebrate the 175th Anniversary of Pittsburgh Theological Seminary. A variety of events were planned from spring 1969 to spring 1970 to celebrate the seminary's long and distinguished heritage. The annual Schaff Lectures were delivered on October 20-22, 1969, by Professor Paul L. Lehmann of Union Theological Seminary, New York; and a Conference on Human Values in the 21st Century was held on March 9-13, 1970, to bring together significant leaders in the disciplines of biogenetics, demography, theology, sociology, and technology "for the purpose of stimulating dialogue among the academic, religious and secular communities, on human life and values in the 21st century world."[32]

The Festival of the Gospels was a scholarly gathering on a grand

---

32. "Calendar of Special Events," Pittsburgh Theological Seminary brochure.

scale. Some seventy scholars representing Protestant, Roman Catholic, Orthodox, and Jewish traditions gathered to consider the Gospels of the New Testament under the theme "Jesus and Man's Hope." Formal papers were prepared and working groups held discussions. Many of the papers were published in a special issue of *Perspective*.[33] Evening cultural events including art, music, and films added to the festivities. Donald Miller served as moderator of the event.

Challenges of the Curriculum

Ongoing challenges for the seminary took place not only with the physical plant and faculty but also with the theological curriculum into which new faculty were inserted. Changing times had an impact here, too.

While faculty and administration embraced similar views of the seminary's purposes, the ways by which those purposes would be carried out and enacted became points of contention. This lack of consensus had effects throughout the seminary community. To carry out the task of "integration," as the 1960-61 initial curriculum hoped, would prove to be a difficult task.

Some years later, Donald Miller reflected on the curriculum situation of his early presidency:

> During my first five years [1962-1967], the influences which were operative in forming the seminary curriculum were twofold: first, academic integrity, where the curriculum embodied the customary theological disciplines of language study, systematic theology, history of doctrine, etc., at a very high academic level. Second, theological integrity, whereby the curriculum took seriously the tradition of the church, through the Bible and the history of the church, and sought direction for the future.[34]

Historically, the seminary's faculty had been the major force in curriculum matters. The content and methodology of what was taught rested in the purview of the faculty. As Miller went on to explain:

---

33. See "Jesus and Man's Hope," *Perspective* 11:1-2 (Pittsburgh Theological Seminary).

34. From Brown, "Curricular Change at the Pittsburgh Theological Seminary," 65-66.

Expansion and Change (1962-1970)

> When I was there, the constitution had taken curricular, student, disciplinary, and other matters out of the hands of the president and placed responsibility for them in the hands of the faculty.... The appointment of faculty members, their raises in rank, their tenure, as all curricular matters and matters of student life, were entirely in the hands of the faculty.... Curricular decisions, in my first five or six years, were made by the faculty, acting on recommendations from the curriculum committee. The administration had little or no voice in curriculum matters. Curricular changes were reported to the Board and approved by them, but this was usually a superficial rubber-stamping of faculty action, with little understanding on the part of the Board of what was involved. At long last, the faculty had complete control of curriculum, and deep differences developed at this level which led to a power struggle for each side to get its view pushed through.[35]

Yet within the faculty, the fissures that were remnants of the earlier denominational and seminary traditions were still felt. Miller put it this way:

> The former U.P. seminary had had a tradition of presidential leadership. The former U.S.A. seminary had had a tradition of faculty dominance in administrative matters. The two groups developed into a "them" and "we" contest.... The situation began to clear up after the first two years of my administration by the appointment of quite a group of new faculty members to whom the questions holding over from the merger meant nothing.... Several of the faculty members who had come through the merger period left for other fields of service. This, too, tended to lessen the tensions relating to the old merger problems. After about five years of my administration we were building a strong faculty.[36]

It took time for some of the fresh wounds from merger and consolidation to be healed, but even as the two cultures were coming together other issues emerged to cause difficulties. The seminary faculty voted on

---

35. From Brown, "Curricular Change at the Pittsburgh Theological Seminary," 66.
36. From Brown, "Curricular Change at the Pittsburgh Theological Seminary," 68.

May 2, 1963, to adopt a curriculum for the 1964-65 year that was based on an expanded number of courses to be taught in the Church and Ministry Division to foster more firmly the "integration" of the curriculum that the division was created to establish. The result was to put thirty-seven hours of required and elective hours into the Church and Ministry Division, including courses in American Church History and Culture, Homiletics and Exegesis, Psychological Foundations, Counseling Field Education (one credit hour during each semester of the middler year), Christian Education, Liturgics, Doctrine of Church and Ministry, Ethics and Missions, and Polity and Administration. In addition, time in class and field experiences were given to visiting prisons, courts, union meetings, mental hospitals, and other "real-world" settings, as well as to a sociological study of the church and its context, supervised experience in a ministerial setting, and an experimentation into new forms of ministry. The purpose of it all was to correlate "theory" and "practice," or "academic studies" and the "real world" of social change.[37]

In the 1965-66 curriculum, the B.D. program did not require the simultaneous study of Greek and Hebrew. To this point, both languages were taken in both semesters during the junior year. Now Greek was studied the first year, and Hebrew the second.

In March 1967, the faculty voted to establish a B.D.–Th.M. sequence which would enable students to declare their intentions by the end of the middler year to move into this sequence. If students were accepted for the Th.M. program, they would complete a fourth year at the seminary and receive a B.D. and Th.M. degree upon graduation. If they did not participate in the Th.M. program, they continued with their current B.D. curriculum.[38]

By 1968, relations with the University of Pittsburgh had produced a number of cooperative programs. These were summarized in Dean Gordon Jackson's report to the Board of Directors in May 1968:

Doctorate of Philosophy in Religious Studies
Bachelor of Divinity-Master of Social Work in four years

---

37. This is drawn from Brown, "Curricular Change at the Pittsburgh Theological Seminary," 69; from Faculty Minutes (May 2, 1963), 109; and from the seminary's annual catalogue for 1964-65, 43.

38. From Brown, "Curricular Change at the Pittsburgh Theological Seminary," 70, citing faculty minutes (March 14, 1967), Paper A, p. 1.

Expansion and Change (1962-1970)

Bachelor of Divinity-Master's Degree in Graduate School of Public and International Affairs in four years

Bachelor of Divinity-Master's Degree in Library Science in four years

Master of Education with the School of Education in one year

Relationship to the Doctorate in Education in which the student might opt for a minor in one of our Master's Programs

Our Master's Degree in Advanced Pastoral Studies staffed in part by professors from the Medical School, the School of Social Work, and the Department of Speech of the University.[39]

These curricular changes and the new opportunities indicated the ongoing evaluation of the seminary's curricular program through the mid-1960s. But bigger changes were in the offing. Pittsburgh Seminary was due to be evaluated by the Middle States Association of Colleges and Secondary Schools and the American Association of Theological Schools in March 1970. These periodic reviews by educational accrediting agencies are a standard part of higher education. In the case of theological seminaries, both the state accrediting agency and the body that accredits seminaries must be satisfied that the institution meets all requirements.[40] In 1968, the seminary organized six task forces to prepare the self-study required prior to the site visit. This task enlisted the efforts of faculty, administration, students, and Board of Directors members. The report of the Curriculum Task Force reveals much about changes in the curriculum from 1960-61 through the mid-to-late 1960s.

In 1960 the faculty hoped that a special division, Church and Ministry, could:

a. Integrate the classical studies with each other around a concern for the practice of ministry, and

b. Provide training in pastoral skills.

The integrative and training functions, it was assumed, could be performed inductively as "field education"; would give

---

39. "Report of the Dean of the Seminary," "Board of Directors Minutes," Pittsburgh Theological Seminary (May 1968), 2-3.

40. The American Association of Theological Schools (AATS) is now called the Association of Theological Schools (ATS) and has its headquarters in Pittsburgh.

occasion for students to bring issues from their part-time parish work into the classroom to provide an integrating focus to all their studies. Because field education was open only to Middlers and Seniors, the first year was devoted to a broad introduction to the Bible and Church History, along with an introduction to the sociological analysis of contemporary society.

3.2.20. This curricular concept of 1960 did not work as its planners had hoped. The Church and Ministry Division never became the integrating center of the total Seminary program, and field education never became a focus for inductive learning in the classroom. Yet in the meantime no single formative or coherent concept of curriculum emerged to "put together" the programs which have served the overwhelming majority of students. Many different views about what a seminary should be and do are to be found within the faculty and among students, reflecting the varied views to be found among church members and leaders around the world. Consequently, the adjustments which have been made in curricular programs since 1960 reflect such pressures as efforts to account for obvious failures, attempts to attract better students, changes in faculty membership, changing influence of personalities in divisions, shift of views on the curriculum committee, and student expectations and participation in planning.[41]

This self-study report document acknowledged that the original vision for the integrating work of the Church and Ministry Division had not materialized as hoped. In the midst of this failure, there was no integrating vision that arose to take its place either as a way to insure that the integration occurred in Church and Ministry courses or as an alternative plan to provide a curriculum that could meet the needs of the majority of students. This vacuum was attributed to the varieties of viewpoints about "what a seminary should be and do" within the seminary community, held by both faculty and students. These were reflective of the diversities of views held by "church members and leaders

---

41. From Brown, "Curricular Change at the Pittsburgh Theological Seminary," 70-71, citing Pittsburgh Seminary's "Report of the Self-Study," January-December 1969, submitted to Middle States Association of Colleges and Secondary Schools and The American Association of Theological Schools, February 15, 1970, 23-24.

Expansion and Change (1962-1970)

around the world." Consequently, curricular adjustments through the 1960s were said to reflect the pressures of the divergent viewpoints and were perceived as responses to the mounting pressures on the seminary from a variety of sources, including the personalities and inclinations of both faculty and students. So the need for continuing curricular planning and evaluation was real. By the end of the 1960s, with the cumulative effects of tremendous social changes in American culture as well as the ongoing discussions of the nature of the seminary and its curriculum within the seminary itself, Pittsburgh Theological Seminary was poised to adopt a radically new curriculum for the 1970s and, it turned out, much beyond.

Toward Curricular Change and Presidential Transition

The self-study precipitated by the accrediting visit produced tensions within the seminary community regarding the nature and purpose of a theological curriculum, as well as leadership and governance issues.

Donald Miller's presidency began well. In his first report to the Board of Directors, Miller described his first year as "a difficult but good year" and as a cause for "deep gratitude."[42] A drop in enrollment to a total of 217 students was reported to the November 1963 Board of Directors, but at the same time, Dean Gordon Jackson indicated that "the morale of the seminary is high. President Miller's leadership is quiet and permissive, steady and influential. He 'wears well.'"[43] When a Liberian student from the seminary community was refused service in a local barber shop, Miller visited the barber shops in the immediate community and invited them to the seminary for a luncheon to discuss the problem. Five of the six barbers attended. He "found them sensitive to the problem, but victims of the economic necessity to survive in a community which does not yet seem ready to desegregate at the barber shop level."[44]

---

42. "Report of the President," "Board of Directors Minutes," Pittsburgh Theological Seminary (May 14, 1963).

43. "Board of Directors Minutes," Pittsburgh Theological Seminary (November 19, 1963).

44. "Board of Directors Minutes," Pittsburgh Theological Seminary (November 19, 1963).

By fall 1964, enrollment had increased to 251, with 107 new students entering the seminary.[45] The next year, in a sign of some growing tension, the faculty issued a letter in support of Dr. Miller's presidency.[46] In February 1966, Miller reported to the Board of "a series of faculty exchanges with each other and with interested students with regard to such subjects as the Confession of 1967, the War in Vietnam, and the nature of biblical inspiration," indicating that the "mood of the year has been one of lively encounter with the church's past and with contemporary issues."[47] In assessing the 1965-66 year, Miller described it as

> both a creating and frustrating year. It has been anything but dull. My over-all impression is that the year has been one of the most difficult but one of the most satisfying since merger. I think a number of us feel that God is insisting that ours is the greatest possible potential and He will not let us be satisfied with anything short of full realization. Perhaps this is why the times are both painful and so profoundly hopeful.[48]

In May 1966, the report of a Visitation Study to Pittsburgh Seminary by the American Association of Theological Schools (AATS) was released. The report was made as the consolidated institution completed its sixth full academic year. The visitors from AATS were Dr. Perry LeFevre from Chicago Theological Seminary and Dean Robert Cushman of Duke Divinity School. The team reported that while there was a "commendable degree of morale" in the institution, there were also

> residual signs of the fairly recent merger ... perhaps reflective of somewhat differing views of the aims and standards as well as the role and function of theological education as entertained among the several members of the faculty. This is indicative, per-

---

45. "Board of Directors Minutes," Pittsburgh Theological Seminary (November 18, 1964).

46. "Board of Directors Minutes," Pittsburgh Theological Seminary (November 19, 1965), 8.

47. "Board of Directors Minutes," Pittsburgh Theological Seminary (February 17, 1966).

48. "Board of Directors Minutes," Pittsburgh Theological Seminary (February 17, 1966).

Expansion and Change (1962-1970)

haps, of diversity of perspective, both cultural and professional, rather than simply theological or denominational as such.⁴⁹

The team also found in its study of the constitution and bylaws that there was "a measure of ambiguity and awkwardness with respect to the administrative organization and function of the seminary which seems to us not conducive to maximum educational effectiveness" (p. 4). In particular, it was not clear what practical prerogative and authority was lodged in the office of the dean. There was ambiguity in regard to the leadership of the dean in the educational program of the seminary and the dean's relationship to the faculty. The dean was to have "general oversight of the educational program of the seminary," but, in practice, said the team, the role "takes rather more the character of negotiator than of authorized creative leadership and authority under the general administration of the President and the Board of Directors." This the team found to be "unconducive" to "cogent administration and bold educational planning" (p. 5).

Students were interviewed in this visit. Two groups indicated that there were "no really exciting issues, books, or ideas which were being discussed in a lively way apart from what might take place in the academic program, by the general student population" (p. 9). A third group disagreed. But all three groups agreed that "the most important issue of an intellectual kind in the student population was the issue of extreme conservatism (even fundamentalism) over against a more liberal interpretation of the Christian faith. The general sense too was that a small minority of students were deeply and actively concerned in the area of social ethics, but that this concern was not broadly shared" (p. 9).

On matters of the shape of the Bachelor of Divinity curriculum, the team found that "to the outsider reading the catalog description, the program appears to be balanced. Conversations with students however create the impression that the real thrust of the curriculum is in the areas of the classical theological program — Biblical, historical, and systematic. Even many of the Church and Ministry courses appear to reflect something of this same emphasis" (p. 12). The team's impression was that the

---

49. "A Visitation Study to Pittsburgh Theological Seminary" (March 1966), 4. Further references in the text are to the pages of this study.

emphasis in the curriculum, the way many of the particular courses are taught, as well as some of the difficulties inherent in the approach to the Church and Ministry sequences tend to foster the rather narrow and traditional conception of the nature of the church and the ministry which we found present in student thinking. It is probably a caricature to describe this emphasis solely in terms of preaching and "spiritual" concerns, but such a characterization certainly reflects the tendency of which we became aware. This emphasis also probably reflects the kind of view of the church and ministry which many of the students themselves bring to the seminary (p. 12).

The visiting team was preparing the way for what the seminary's self-study would likewise find as it prepared for the accreditation visit by the AATS in the following years. Attempts at "integrating" the whole curriculum through courses in the Church and Ministry division were not working:

> The Church and Ministry courses appear to be subject to peculiar difficulties of their own. Reasonable as the integration of learning in this area would seem, reports show that it is exceedingly difficult to bring off in practice. Students reported again and again that these courses appear from their viewpoints to be bits of information and theory set side by side, or running on parallel tracks. They seem to feel that on the whole, these courses are not undergirded by a basic body of unifying theory and that the individual faculty members carry on their own parts of the courses rather independently. (p. 13)

The recommendations of the visitors was that

> the faculty might well consider ways of including in the students' educational experience emphases which would help them develop a more contemporary and less traditional view of the nature of the church and ministry both on the theoretical level (as it grows out of a broader and deeper exposure to the cultural and societal and personal structures of contemporary life to which church and ministry must be addressed in our time) and at the vocational level as it exposes the student to the variety of special-

ized ministries such as the chaplaincy, student work, the experimental ministries, the church renewal movements, the development of lay movements, etc. (p. 13)

The visiting team also found dissatisfaction among students with regard to the style of teaching and learning:

> that the educational process is in part an unprofitable burden and that it is constricting rather than liberating. In a very vivid phrase one of the students said: "we have no time to read and think, only to read and remember." Another described his experience as "dump-truck education." A third said he wanted to reread all of the books he had had to read for course, after he graduated, so that he could take time to reflect on them, since he had had no time to do this in his regular course. There was no demurrer from these comments. (p. 13)

The AATS visitors saw opportunities for the seminary in the future. The resources of the seminary and its commitments were strong foundations on which to build, if the seminary would seize the initiative:

> the critical question involved in whether or not these future opportunities may be realized may lie in the willingness of the faculty and administration to examine the present style and *telos* of theological education as it now exists at P.T.S. It appears to the team that the shape of the present curriculum and the general conception of its "end products" tend to leave unchallenged the inherited conception of church and function of the ministry as these are compared or contrasted with insistent and inescapable demands of the shape of things upon the church and ministry of tomorrow. That this is a legacy of most theological schools makes it no less pertinent for each to face with openness its own inheritance of complacency with an unexamined tradition. We think it timely that this faculty join with colleagues in sister institutions in a reexamination of prevailing assumptions about the aims of theological education as the cultural changes of our time force a reconsideration of the matter and mode of their redemptive role in the world and the nature and function of their ministries. (p. 17)

On the issue of faculty recruitment, given the number of factors involved including salary and fringe benefits, teaching schedule, leave policy, and opportunities for scholarly activity, the visiting AATS team found that "in relation to many of these considerations we do not feel that Pittsburgh is in a particularly strong position to attract first rate scholars to their faculty, im [sic] comparison with the major theological and university centers in America" (p. 19). The team suggested the administration and Board review its situation and perhaps create several chairs for distinguished scholars that would be "particularly attractive" and then fill the rest of its openings with younger scholars "who have great promise but who are not yet published and productive scholars" (p. 19).

The issues identified by the AATS visit became increasingly important in the next several years, as the seminary continued to face conflicting views about its nature, purpose, and character as an institution. The social unrest of the times in its various forms, as well as internal seminary struggles over issues of governance, curriculum, and changing conceptions of ministry all were to become points of tension with real and lasting consequences.

In May 1968, President Miller reflected that the academic year had been "a year marked by achievements and by unrest. Both reflect the mood of our time. One dares to hope that the achievements have been creditable and the unrest creative."[50] Some of the "unrest" of the times related to the changing social climate of the period and the cultural forces that were reshaping America in the mid-1960s. The issues of race and the developing Vietnam War were becoming forces that could not be ignored in the seminary. Dean Gordon Jackson highlighted the race issue in his May 1968 report to the Board of Directors:

> The crisis of the city, focused in the crises of poverty, white racism, and black frustration, is one of the more viable parts of the context in which we have tried to do our theological work. Both faculty and students have been struggling with the sense of frustration, the meaning of guilt, and the possibility of irrelevance. Especially since the death of Martin Luther King this highly sensitive community has been agonizing between the poles of theo-

---

50. "Board of Directors Minutes," Pittsburgh Theological Seminary (May 7, 1968).

logical discourse and the cries of human hurt, anger, and need. The faculty has gone about its business of theological work with a sure sense for ultimate concerns but with new and incisive probings into the meaning of those concerns for man's daily round. The students, as might be expected, have turned in a number of directions: some withdrawing deeper into the books; some shielding themselves by things religious; a good many struggling between the two poles of ultimacy and daily concern; and some so worked up that the academic machine almost ground to a halt for them. Within this milieu students have asked pointedly and often why we have no black professors, practically no black students, why we are not more of a social service agency, why we are building a chapel, why our curriculum doesn't reflect more sociological, urban, and psychological concerns, why we cannot seem to attract a strong social ethicist, whether theology is really relevant after all, etc.? These questions come often with a sting, have provided many hours of dialogue among students, with faculty, and with administration. It is my judgment that the tragedy of the American city is making us all better theologians in a very deeply pragmatic sense and it is my belief that the stirrings of God may be found in our midst.[51]

Within the seminary faculty, divisions were emerging over President Miller and his leadership. Whatever the full range of issues with his leadership might have been, it was the issue of curricular change that sparked full-scale debate. As we will see in the next chapter, the new curriculum that would be adopted for Pittsburgh Theological Seminary for the 1969-70 academic year featured much broader opportunities for students to choose elective courses. This reflected societal changes and increased pressures for churches as well as educational institutions to show themselves as "relevant" to emerging American culture. After the "death of God" theology and in the midst of the civil rights movement and the escalating conflict in Vietnam, traditional patterns and values were being questioned in society and its institutions. Pittsburgh Seminary was not immune to these struggles. The necessity to engage in a self-study, which embraced an intense scrutiny of

51. "Report of the Dean of the Seminary," "Board of Directors Minutes," Pittsburgh Theological Seminary (May 1968).

the theological curriculum, pushed the seminary to articulate its understanding of its nature and purpose by the theological curriculum it would adopt. In a sense, struggles in American society between traditionalists and those desiring radical change were mirrored in the curriculum struggle.

Donald Miller conveyed his views in two pieces in the "From the President's Desk" feature of *Pittsburgh Perspective* in 1967, a year after the AATS visitation and its critique of the curriculum and its promotion of a "narrow and traditional conception of the nature of the church and the ministry." In June 1967 he responded to the critique:

> Perhaps a way out of at least some of the theological confusion of the moment might be to realize ourselves with the continuities of history. If we knew better the history of the past, it could well be that much that is called "new" today is but old errors dressed out in new garb. Furthermore, attention to the total pathway by which we have come would be a savory corrective to the tendency to think we had made new discoveries when we are only succumbing to the spirit of the time and reflecting the current temper. To listen to our ancestors might save us from excitedly telling people what they already know, and calling it the Christian faith.[52]

Miller went on to quote T. F. Torrance on the importance of the past for theological thinking and made a similar point by appealing to Philip Schaff's *The Principle of Protestantism*:

> This is not to propose that our fathers knew all that there is to be known: that there is no more "light to break upon the sacred page" than that which they saw; that we should be "cabin'd and cribbed" by their modes of thinking or their results; or that any one of them, or group of them, should be the sole orientation point around which all theological thinking revolves. Historicism of this type has often been a handicap to theology, substituting a survey of other men's thoughts for the rigorous process of doing our own thinking.
>
> I am suggesting, however, that we stand in a stream of conti-

---

52. "From the President's Desk," *Pittsburgh Perspective* 8:2 (June 1967): 3.

nuity with past generations, and that the meaning of the span of this stream where our own generation stands will be obscure without tracing the stream to its source, and that the th[e]ological objects which come floating down the stream will be confusing and valueless unless we explore the banks of the entire stream and look at these objects in their original setting.

Our "now" needs a "then." Our "henceforth" must be guided by a "hitherto." I am not arguing for a binding "historicism" but for a liberating "historical perspective" which will break the pattern of our contemporaneity and free us from the bondage of the moment.[53]

One sees clearly here that Miller was arguing for a "historical perspective" which will take into account the historic witness of the church and its theological understandings. If this were to be translated into a theological curriculum, one would expect a heavy weight on the classical, traditional disciplines and types of courses — the very kind of critique that the AATS visitation team had leveled.

Six months later, in December 1967, Miller's column was more pointed in its critique of the appeal to the "present moment," and he commented directly on the issue of a theological curriculum:

Relevance continues to be the watchword of much popular current theology. So far as I can capture the "feel" of the use of this word, it seems to propose the approach of the "market analyst" in business. It is the function of such a one to determine what the public wants, or thinks it needs, and to produce that. "Success" is determined by the "marketability" of the product. It is not the quality of the product but the number of people who buy it that is decisive.[54]

Miller quoted the sociologist Peter Berger, who defined the problem of the late 1960s as "how to perpetuate an institution whose reality presuppositions are no longer socially taken for granted." This led to a paragraph describing how "radical theologians" had sought to adjust theology to the "reality presuppositions" of contemporary people, and

---

53. "From the President's Desk," *Pittsburgh Perspective* 8:2 (June 1967): 3-4.
54. "From the President's Desk," *Pittsburgh Perspective* 8:4 (December 1967): 3.

then quoting Berger again to suggest that if there really is no "other," who is "out there" (God), then, like Karl Marx, people will find other things to do with their time than to engage in theological concerns.

This led to Miller's direct comments on contemporary, "radical" theology, "relevance," and curricular proposals:

> The "radical" theologians, because of the dramatic nature of their views, will be widely discussed but will likely not take over the church. What seems to be happening, however, in the less radical segment of the church is a loss of nerve which is leading not so much to a drastic "adjustment" to modern reality concepts or a bold laying aside of theology, but the quiet retreat from it, an abandonment by default.
>
> This seems to be influencing theological education at the point of new curricular proposals. To be "relevant," less time must be given to the classic theological disciplines and more to psychology, sociology, political action, etc. Does this not suggest that the theologian, *as theologian,* has little or nothing to offer the world? Hence the increasing desire to identify with other professions![55]

Miller's commitment to the seminary preparing future ministers who were "theologians" and not psychologists, sociologists, or politicians came through clearly. His article continued with the caution that ministers should not venture into areas beyond their expertise (after all, no minister would seek to tamper with another person "medically"), and that "if ministerial training belittles its unique field — theology — and gives a sort of smorgasbord curricular offering in the many fields now proposed, will not the minister finally work himself out of a job?" It is "sacred knowledge" which is the "distinctive, characteristic and formative study of the sacred ministry," said Miller, quoting G. R. Dunstan. He continued,

> Will a theological curriculum do anything more than delay "professional death" if it seeks to bypass the solid discipline of hard-core studies in the languages, history, and theology out of which theologians are made? And if we do not strive to be authentic

---

55. From the President's Desk," *Pittsburgh Perspective* 8:4 (December 1967): 4.

theologians, do we have anything distinctive to offer the world? And if we have nothing distinctive to offer, should we not accept professional death and retire from the scene? Perhaps the day may come when true relevance will be found in the summons: "Let the theologian be a theologian."

This does not mean, of course, that *any* knowledge in *any* field can not be laid under tribute to the gospel, nor made to serve the ends for which the church exists in the world. It does mean, however, that the minister should enter each area of thought or activity with the distinctive contribution of a *theologian*, and it could be that if ministers were better theologians, casting theological light on every area of life through the preaching, teaching, and fellowship of the church, the laymen thus confronted might be better equipped to bring the meaning of the gospel to bear upon the whole fabric of society.[56]

Miller's position had its adherents among some of the seminary's faculty. The tensions that arose over curriculum, however, emerged with an alternative vision supported by other faculty members. The lineaments of the view that challenged the traditional approaches to the theological curriculum can be seen in the two editorials written by Church and Ministry professor David G. Buttrick in the newly named Seminary journal *Perspective* in the Spring 1968 and Winter 1969 issues.

The first of these pieces appeared in the issue immediately following the December 1967 comments by Miller. Buttrick used the occasion of the revamped and redesigned seminary journal to reflect on "change" as a cultural fact of life: "Here we are spruced up with a new cover, clearer type, a larger page. We've put on height and weight and we are bright-eyed with resolve. *Perspective* is changing."[57] He noted the history of the journal, which began when the two seminaries were consolidated and now boasted a circulation of more than six thousand. And the changes needed to continue:

Nowadays we do not choose change: change is imposed — perhaps a *grace*ful imposition. For in our time fond forms are per-

---

56. "From the President's Desk," *Pittsburgh Perspective* 8:4 (December 1967), 56.

57. "Editorial," *Perspective: A Journal of Pittsburgh Theological Seminary* 9 (Spring 1968): 5.

> ishing while new thought and custom labor into life. Scoffers to the contrary, theological disciplines are involved in this revolution, the cultural "happening" that is the twentieth century. Christian thinking today is learning to read and respond to what critic Louise Bogan has labeled "the myth that is forming at the heart of our world." So theology is wrestling with emerging new language, with philosophies *au courant,* with dazzling cosmic models the sciences supply. And biblical scholarship, with revised hermeneutic, is probing revered texts to yield new understanding. Equally active are the practical fields in rethinking Christian ethos, the life-styles and speech-modes that may display our faith in an accelerating age. The problem for most of us, parsons and professors alike, is keeping up when there are too many books to read, too many words to hear, too many thoughts to think through.[58]

From there, Buttrick assured his readers: "to serve you, we will strive to follow the flurry of theological debate and crowd close to the fervor of keen biblical scholarship." And certainly, said Buttrick, "we intend to be less parochial."

This editorial revealed some basic presuppositions of those who wanted the Pittsburgh Seminary curriculum in 1969 to be significantly altered and to engage more fully the changing religious, theological, and social contents of American culture. Since "change" is central to contemporary existence and culture as well as to the whole range of theological disciplines, which are also changing, one could intuit that a seminary curriculum ought to equip potential pastors to deal with these changes, and to do this by providing courses that are directly related to the contemporary cultural scene.

The curriculum issue was pointedly joined by Buttrick in his editorial in the Spring 1969 issue of *Perspective.* Here Buttrick argued that seminaries must adapt to the change in the types of students who now attend — the "secular" student, instead of those who, as in the past, are more "tradition oriented." Since Buttrick's piece is so clear on the issues involved, it is helpful to see it in its entirety:

---

58. "Editorial," *Perspective: A Journal of Pittsburgh Theological Seminary* 9 (Spring 1968): 5.

Expansion and Change (1962-1970)

How hard it is to talk of theological education nowadays. The topic is torn by present controversy. Some men, considering themselves conservers of Christian heritage, rail against the "relevance boys"; while others deplore moribund seminaries in an age on fire with crackling social change. The conflict has been so exaggerated by both sides that only straw men topple. No sane professor involved in theological education could wish to discard essentials in favor of "with it" secular wisdoms. The Church *must* study Scripture, *must* learn "moves" in Systematic Theology, *must* be concerned with Church History and with the genealogies of Dogma, *must* grapple with Ethics and with those disciplines we piece together under the heading of Practical Theology. Nevertheless, theological education seems something of a problem nowadays.

The problem is students! We still admit students who, having grown up in what David Riesman has called "tradition oriented" communities, parochial enclaves, have been somewhat sheltered from worldly corrosions. But, more and more, seminaries are greeting students whose language and life-styles have been secularized. For them, theological disciplines are a struggle; they have prior questions to voice before education can sensibly proceed. Can we teach Scripture if the question of Scriptural authority remains either unanswered or, worse, unarticulated? Can we attend to Church History if there is a silent suspicion that, in an age to come, there may not be a Church? How will students learn of worship or of preaching if these enterprises seem ever so slightly absurd? Or, how will students do theology if they are still wondering sincerely if there is any reality at all beyond the world around us? To pursue classical theological subjects while ignoring urgent questions would be folly, for the prior questions are after all basic to rigorous theological study. Unless seminaries recognize and respond to the secularized student, they may succeed in safeguarding traditional disciplines while failing the evangelical mandate of the Gospel.

Actually seminaries should welcome the problem of the secularized student even if it means a tough coming to terms with the world we live in. Perhaps we will have to rethink hermeneutic procedures (How do secular men interpret Scripture?), to forge a new language for preaching and new forms for praise; perhaps it will mean a reordering of theological method and a reconceiving of Church History. Theological education may have to include in its pedagogy more than a touch of missionary impulse, lest we become what Peter Berger labels a "cognitive minority."

If theological education could begin to devote more time and study to the prior questions, there might be gain. We might graduate men and women who have "fought-it-out" in themselves sufficiently to seed the Gospel in secular soil. Then, when faith that has been grafted into the *Weltanschauung of* the Enlightenment withers, a hardier strain of Christian commitment might grow toward harvest.[59]

The appeal to "prior questions" and the "secularized" students in the context of rapid social and religious change were main elements driving a number of the Pittsburgh Seminary faculty members to seek a radically revised curriculum that would reflect the seminary's contemporary context in an urban setting at the end of the turbulent 1960s.

So lines were drawn on the way to curricular change at Pittsburgh Theological Seminary. By one account, "the discussions rapidly picked up a lot of the old United Presbyterian/Presbyterian disagreements. The Faculty was sharply divided. Some directors, influenced by faculty members, actively supported one side or the other, overlooking the need for Directors to remain outside active management of the institution."[60]

Dissatisfaction with President Miller's leadership continued to grow in some sectors of the faculty. Among the concerns were that the faculty was not involved in decision making, that administratively Miller did not function well, and that Miller was not good at listening to other viewpoints. Increasing desires by students and faculty to participate more fully in the governance of the seminary produced a clash with the administrative style of President Miller, and of the board-of-directors style of management. Vocal protests became more common. According to one observer,

---

59. "Editorial," *Perspective: A Journal of Pittsburgh Theological Seminary* 10:3 (Spring 1969): n.p.

60. Herchenroether, "Pittsburgh Theological Seminary 1959-1999," 15.

Expansion and Change (1962-1970)

the Faculty seemed to be divided into two groups on this governance issue. One group was mostly those Faculty members whom Dr. Miller had been instrumental in bringing to the campus and the other group was mostly the old Faculty members some of whom had deeply resented the way in which the Presidential Search committee had operated in selecting Dr. Miller.[61]

Things came to a head when a joint faculty and Board of Directors meeting was called to resolve the issues. The meeting was marked by formal presentations on curriculum issues, but according to one participant it

> degenerated into an unfortunate argument losing all objectivity and became severely personal with Dr. Miller as the focus. The result was a nasty split in the Faculty. Finally, under the leadership of the senior member of the Faculty, who criticized Dr. Miller for his position in the argument, the Faculty voted against Dr. Miller's position by a very narrow margin and showed a real lack of confidence in his leadership. The Board (some of the directors had been privately solicited by some of the Faculty) could not seem to bring itself to assume its authority to resolve the dispute nor to support the President. Some of the Directors were already committed to a position due to the influence of a single faculty member, making an objective decision by the Board practically impossible. The entire matter of the curriculum change was intertwined with the governance issue and went on for several years.[62]

Pressures on the seminary, from the nearly constant construction in the physical plant for several years to challenges in financing the operating budget and lowered levels of support from many sources, had further added to the difficulties of this period.

The faculty vote against Miller was, in essence, a vote of no-confidence. Some saw that the resulting unrest affected important parts of the seminary in terms of morale, financial support, and drop-

---

61. Herchenroether, "Pittsburgh Theological Seminary 1959-1999," 15.
62. Herchenroether, "Pittsburgh Theological Seminary 1959-1999," 16.

ping enrollment.[63] The unrest at the seminary also penetrated to surrounding churches.

It was all too much. In May 1969, shortly after the joint faculty/Board meeting, Donald Miller announced his resignation, to become effective on May 31, 1970. At the same time, the director of development, J. Rowe Hinsey, also resigned to retire.[64] Miller would go on to become pastor of the Laurinburg Presbyterian Church in Laurinburg, North Carolina.

Students Speak

Students from the era often recall the faculty as a primary strength of the seminary at this time. The expansion of the faculty with the addition of scholars and teachers who were also concerned with the church and with students was perceived as equipping the seminary with a core of dedicated professors. One student said, "At the time I attended, I thought the professors were challenging and good. Only after being out of seminary for a decade or two did I realize how great those professors really were." Another said of the faculty, "They were available to us and willing to talk with us. It was a real and grand experience not recognized until long after graduation!"

Some students from the earlier period of the 1960s recognized the continuing effects of the merger of the seminary faculties. One student said, "The old liberal-conservative split was in evidence." Another saw lingering problems from days past: "An obvious division in the faculty that dated back to the predecessor seminaries. A president who could not deal with the sixties." And "because the seminary was newly merged, there was some bickering between the conservative and neo-orthodox view points. Faculty and students, especially students, were not willing to listen to a different point of view, which I found to be sad, and hampering to one's education."

63. The seminary enrollment figures reported in the catalogs were:
    1966-67 catalog   B.D. program   191   Total 263
    1968-69 catalog   B.D. program   190   Total 285
    1969-70 catalog   B.D. program   182   Total 280
    1971-72 catalog   M. Div. Program 201   Total 315
64. "Board of Directors Minutes," Pittsburgh Theological Seminary (May 25, 1969).

Expansion and Change (1962-1970)

Some PTS Students at Play

Students in the later 1960s also recognized ways in which the seminary's past was influential. One said, "There was still some memory on campus of the fundamentalist/liberal tensions from previous years when the two campuses merged. The student directory still was called the 'fundy-finder' by some students." This "tradition" continued at least through the 1970s at the seminary.

Some students felt a tension over the nature of the seminary. One said, "It felt like there was a struggle going on whether the main task of PTS was to prepare pastors or to prepare scholars. That may not have been a realistic struggle but that is the way it felt as a student in my M.Div. years." One student attributed this to "an apparent lack of vision: Was this a training ground for pastors, or a graduate school preparing people for ministries in academia?" For some, an important concern was "the desire on the part of many students to have help with growing in their personal faith. The response from the faculty was that it was not their business, they were in the business of education." Similarly, another student commented on whether he received adequate preparation for ministry: "On the intellectual level it did well. On the practical level and the development of spiritual life, it didn't do as well."

The Barbour Library was considered first-rate, and many students have spoken of the friendships established during their seminary years, friendships that continued far into the future. Before the acquisition of the Highlander, and later the construction of Anderson and MacMillan residence halls, housing for married students — who were attending seminary in increasing numbers — was problematic. The expanded facilities were very helpful in meeting housing concerns for students with spouses and families. As could be expected, however, there was a gulf between married and single students, and communal efforts to bring the two groups together during this period were not, on the whole, successful.

Students had varying experience with field education at this time. Some felt the seminary did not give enough direct supervision. One student recalled, "My field work was basically unsupervised. I had no experience in youth ministry, yet I was expected to do it under a pastor from another country who had no contact with American youth culture or youth ministry." A similar sentiment was expressed about student internships: "Student internships were not consistent. It was really a crap shoot whether one got an adequate mentoring pastor. I came out of seminary a good preacher and teacher, but not having the foggiest notion of how to be a pastor." Others had good experiences with the congregations in which they ministered and the pastors who were their mentors. One student recalled meeting with the pastor on Sundays, following a day of field education: "I received a lot of practical insight into ministry from those weekly conversations in a local diner." One student, when asked if the seminary provided an adequate preparation for later ministries, responded, "In some respects yes, and in some, no. I learned how to study the Scriptures and to understand theology. However, with regard to the practical aspects of ministry I didn't get much help. I had to learn that by trial and error at the churches I served." In general, responded another student, the professors, "although excellent academicians, were generally not dealing with application of our studies to practical issues in pastoral ministry."

The seminary's urban setting was a positive one for a number of students during this time. As one put it, "The seminary's urban location provided me with my first opportunity to experience the wonderful diversity

Expansion and Change (1962-1970)

of God's creation, especially in my field studies assignments at churches on the North Side." For another student, the presence of persons from various areas was a plus: "We had a diverse population of students: German, Brasilian, South/Central American, Indian, and African (Uganda). There were also some of us from other parts of the United States — not just the tri-state area around Pittsburgh. This helped with expanding our experiences and ideas beyond what we thought to be 'the normal.'"

Some of the issues relating to the seminary's campus life have been touched on, particularly in regard to curriculum concerns. Curriculum change during this period created student frustrations. Among other campus issues were the theological diversity and communication among all parties on campus. Another was, as one student recalled, "the discussion over the lack of community at the seminary. Some students were disappointed that there was not more of a sense of a worshiping/working community of which everyone could be a part."

In later years students recalled the construction of Hicks Chapel, which as we saw earlier was also controversial. In the words of one alumnus,

> Construction of the chapel was another contentious issue. The decision to do it (and to accept the gift which made it possible) was made by the Board of Trustees . . . I recall. But most students — as well as most faculty members, I suspect, and probably even Dean Gordon Jackson himself — thought building a fancy chapel was outrageously poor stewardship, that the old chapel in the Long Administration Building was perfectly fine, and that we ought to not forfeit the volleyball court (which is where the new chapel now stands).

Pittsburgh Seminary's relation to its local community also raised important concerns for the seminary during this period. The incident in which the barber shop refused service to a student from Africa triggered a boycott of the barber shop by PTS students. A Korean student recalled, "I used to walk to an African American neighborhood for a haircut."

Campus security became a concern in this period: "cars were being hi-jacked weekly, stores and churches were set on fire in the immediate area of the seminary, and [there was] a sense that the larger community around the seminary was coming apart." One student said, "I remember the cars stolen off the lot and that I would remove the ignition wire from my car so that it would not get stolen. But alas, no one wanted my wreck!" Concerns over the evolving neighborhood around the seminary grew as the decade progressed. A number of students had some anxiety about "living behind a fence" in "a bucolic environment in the midst of urban distress." One student who attended the seminary for a year in the 1960s and then returned and graduated in the early 1970s commented, "The campus was completely open when I started in 1965 and was fenced, guarded, and locked down when I graduated in 1972."

The social and cultural turbulence of the 1960s affected Pittsburgh Seminary in many ways. The seminary's own internal discussions and divisions on the curriculum issue mirrored and reflected the varying theological viewpoints of the faculty and the emerging concerns in American culture as a whole. As one student put it, "So much of the seminary life was distracted by what was happening in the larger culture. In historical perspective this is both amusing and tragic. This situation meant that the seminary was not very helpful in relating to the preparation of pastors for congregations at that time."

During the 1962-70 period, Pittsburgh students identified a number of social issues that impacted their lives as seminarians. These included civil rights, 1960s-style sexual-freedom issues, the integration of craft unions, disinvestment from South Africa, racial reconciliation, Vietnam, hostility toward "the church" as it had been idealized, social activism of all kinds, the Confession of 1967, drugs, and the assassinations of Martin Luther King Jr. and Robert Kennedy.

As we have seen, the theological splits within the seminary community also showed themselves in reactions to social change and responses to the explosive social situations of the time. One student saw it this way:

> The tension that seems to be an almost eternal one between *evangelical* and *progressive* constituencies of the church existed at the seminary in the middle-1960's. Progressives focused on social justice issues: civil rights, Vietnam, and the confession of 1967. I remember co-leading a Seminary-sponsored sympathy march from East Liberty to Frick Park in Oakland early in the fall of our first year at the same time as one of the great civil rights marches in the South. . . . Evangelicals gathered in secret places . . . for prayer.

Expansion and Change (1962-1970)

Another student later commented,

> This was the period of Civil Rights and the marches and protests that were taking place across the country. There were a number of students who organized groups to join the marches and protests in the South. We were under martial law and curfew when the riots broke out in Pittsburgh. This was a surreal experience for many of us. I must say this struck me because I was well aware that Mt. Lebanon and Fox Chapel were not integrated as well as several other "white" sections of Pittsburgh and the surrounding townships. This did not seem to be the focus of interest for those organizing the run to join the marches in those days. It was too close to home.

Students became involved in the social struggles in varying degrees. One said, "We had major discussions about racism, and were able to do something in maintaining communication between the suburban churches and the Black churches in the turmoil after Martin Luther King's death." Another related,

> The social ferment that was shaking up the country did not bypass the often cloistered existence of the seminary. When I came to seminary in 1967 it was apparent that a certain percentage of the students were simply there for the 4D deferment. The student body tended to be more social activist than not. The Pittsburgh chapter of the Berrigan Defense committee was formed at the seminary by students. We picketed our own Presbytery for using segregated union labor for a building project. (This was after we joined pickets around the U.S. Steel Building.) After the assassination of King we sat on the lawn and listened to the sirens, gunshots and explosions coming from the Hill District.

By mid-1970, Pittsburgh Seminary had endured a turbulent decade in the wider culture and a period of expansion and change on campus under the leadership of President Miller. With Miller's departure at the end of May, the seminary was in for a new period of presidential leadership in a different style. The new leadership would face both old problems and new challenges.

CHAPTER 5

The Round Table

(1971-1978)

The celebration of Pittsburgh Theological Seminary's 175th year came to an end with the conclusion of the 1969-70 academic year. With the resignation of Dr. Miller, the seminary faced a time of transitional leadership. In May 1970, the Board of Directors named Dr. Howard Jamieson, associate professor of New Testament and dean of students, to be acting president. Jamieson had joined the Pittsburgh-Xenia faculty in 1955. Dr. John M. Bald, associate professor of Christian ethics and associate dean, who had come to the Pittsburgh-Xenia faculty in 1957, was named acting dean to replace Dr. Gordon Jackson, who returned to full-time classroom teaching as the Hugh Thomson Kerr Professor of Pastoral Theology.[1]

A New President

The search for a new president was, this time, carried out by a presidential search committee that included members from the Board of Directors and the student body. The process was thus much more "inclusive" than the method used to select Dr. Miller. On November 18, 1970, the Board approved changes to the seminary's constitution and bylaws which attempted to open up the governance of the institution by enabling more faculty and student participation in decision-making. This

---

1. "Board of Directors Minutes," Pittsburgh Theological Seminary (May 18, 1970). Both titles were changed from "Acting" to "Interim."

President William H. Kadel

was a portent of further actions to come. The changes gave representatives of both the Board and the student body positions on all faculty search committees and in Board meetings, as well as at meetings of the Board's executive committee.

When Dr. Jamieson accepted a call to a Presbyterian church in southern California, Dr. Bald became interim president after December 31, 1970. The presidential search committee was at work, searching for suitable candidates. One observer commented that this search was

> hampered by the perception (valid to a degree) that PTS was a place where presidents were treated badly and were not supported by the Board. This reflected the experiences of both Dr.

Barbour and Dr. Miller. This perception was coupled with the perception among the churches and their members that PTS was to some "too liberal" and to others "too conservative." This latter perception was one PTS could not win.[2]

On February 1, 1971, the presidential search committee recommended Dr. William H. Kadel to become president of the seminary, and he assumed office on April 1, 1971. Kadel was born in Gettysburg, Pennsylvania, and was a graduate of Gettysburg College. He received his B.D. degree from Western Theological Seminary in 1938 and served pastorates in Ohio, Pennsylvania, and Florida. He was an Army Air Force Chaplain from 1942-45. Kadel earned a Th.D. from Union Theological Seminary in Richmond in 1951 with a dissertation titled "Contemporary Preaching in the Presbyterian Church U.S. and the Presbyterian Church U.S.A. in the Light of the Preaching of History." This work was 1,491 pages in length and featured a historical overview of Christian preaching from the early church to the present time. In it Kadel also surveyed 800 ministers about the themes and texts of their sermons from October 1, 1949, through March 31, 1950. His survey yielded responses on 2,244 sermon subjects and texts from Presbyterian Church U.S. pastors and 1,740 from the Presbyterian Church (U.S.A.). One of the conclusions Kadel drew from his study was that "there is no adequate reason, from the point of view of the pulpit message, for the continued separation of the Presbyterian Church in the United States and the Presbyterian Church in the U.S.A."[3]

After serving Florida pastorates, Kadel became the founding president of Florida Presbyterian College (now Eckerd College) in September 1958.[4] He led the institution until he became executive secretary of the Board of Christian Education for the Presbyterian Church in the United States in July 1968. Special convocations were held at the seminary throughout 1971 to mark the inaugural year.

---

2. Herchenroether, "Pittsburgh Theological Seminary 1959-1999," 16.

3. William Howard Kadel, "Contemporary Preaching in the Presbyterian Church United States and the Presbyterian Church in the United States of America in the Light of the Preaching of History" (Th.D. diss., Union Theological Seminary, 1951), 1,481. A copy of this dissertation is in the Barbour Library at Pittsburgh Theological Seminary.

4. See "William H. Kadel Meeting and Study Area." The Peter H. Armacost Library at Eckerd College, www.eckerd.edu/librarydedication/?f=rooms.

EVER A VISION

The Chapel Wall

One night in early February 1971, the new Hicks Chapel was vandalized by the spraying of the chapel wall with anti-Vietnam war quotations. A meeting of the Executive Committee of the Board of Directors was held on March 30, 1971, in which the committee met with Dr. Bald, the interim president, and other administrators as well as campus leaders. The convocation and worship committee agreed to present a plan for the decoration of the chapel after the damage was repaired. Everyone at the meeting "indicated disagreement with the act done, but some indicated sympathy with the message and offered the opinion that probably the majority of the students and faculty were likewise in sympathy with the message, but not with the act by which it was placed on the Chapel wall."[5] This incident raised a question for the Board and the seminary community: With an event of this kind, what role would the Board expect the president of the seminary to assume?

Some six months later, on the evening of October 12, 1971, newly installed President Kadel reported to the Board of Directors that

> some unknown person or persons gained entrance to the chapel and repeated the kind of event of last spring by writing with black paint on the wall behind the pulpit in the chapel a message consisting of three words, "Stop the killing." The message was written in large letters covering the entire panel of the wall behind the pulpit. This time anonymous phone calls to various members of the community late at night on October 12 sought to call to the attention of certain persons in the community their act that was performed so that consideration might be given to what steps might be taken before members of the administration and staff and faculty discovered the words the following day. The President of the Student Government and I were two of those called.[6]

Kadel reported that the administrative council of the seminary had met from 9:00 a.m. to 4:00 p.m. the next day, October 13, agreeing that the

---

5. "Minutes of Special Meeting of the Executive Committee held March 30, 1971," Pittsburgh Theological Seminary.
6. William H. Kadel, memo, "Members of the Board of Directors of Pittsburgh Theological Seminary" (October 15, 1971), 1.

wall was to be repainted immediately, and that persons in the seminary community would be asked to pay for the repair. The repair cost $270 — which, Dr. Kadel said, the seminary budget itself could not withstand. Contributions would be optional in the community. In addition, the president was asked to make "an open appeal to the person or persons involved to seek to contact me at my office or home, so that we may talk about this matter." Kadel continued:

> First of all, let me say that no punitive action will be taken. But, it is believed to be necessary that the feelings of the person or persons involved and their sense of why this is the best avenue of communication need to be heard and shared. By way of this memorandum, I am requesting that person or those persons to meet me to discuss this matter. I will be happy to meet at any time and any place that is considered the most helpful. Again, let me emphasize that this is an honest desire to seek for understanding, and hopefully will be valuable to the institution in the future.[7]

The convocation and worship committee was asked to hang the banner prepared following the convocation which bore the words that were written on the chapel wall in the spring.

In an example of the "open community" and "open process" approach that was to be characteristic of his administration, Kadel called the attention of the seminary community to

> the option that is open to every person or group of persons, either formal group or informal group, to have any issue raised and dealt with as an agenda item on any of the political divisions of the seminary. "Open community" means making possible to every member of the community access to points of influence where decisions are considered and made. We would urge members of the community to utilize the processes that are available to deal with any of the issues that are of concern. We do not imply by this statement that the writing on the chapel wall is intended as a denial of the open process, or as necessary because the open process was not understood. We simply want to recall to every-

---

7. William H. Kadel, memo to The Members of the PTS Community, "The recent painting of the chapel wall" (October 15, 1971), 1.

one's attention the opportunities that are theirs to have their concerns properly considered.[8]

Kadel indicated that this matter was being handled administratively, with the Board being appraised of the situation. He pointed out to the Board that the students had quickly acted to seek the repainting of the wall and that "this time, there is a great deal of hostility within the community against the unknown persons who have chosen to do this." Kadel hoped the unknown persons would come forth as he requested so that "we can deal with their problem constructively and redemptively. We are doing everything in our power to see to it that this does not happen again. If it does, then the time for patience may be past." Kadel asked the Board for its support "as the administration seeks to be patient a little while longer with a very difficult situation."[9]

An Open Community

In President Kadel's first report to the Board on May 4, 1971, after having been in office for slightly more than a month, he indicated his commitment to an "open community." He identified his early reading on problems at Pittsburgh Seminary:

1. Organizational relations — thinking toward a single community and open communications among all segments of the community.
2. A search for direction — what are we all about?
3. Financial Resources
4. Trust
5. Faith[10]

A short time later, the chapel wall was painted again. The Board minutes reveal that

---

8. William H. Kadel, memo to The Members of the PTS Community, "The recent painting of the chapel wall" (October 15, 1971), 2.

9. William H. Kadel, memo, "Members of the Board of Directors of Pittsburgh Theological Seminary" (October 15, 1971), 1.

10. "Board of Directors Minutes," Pittsburgh Theological Seminary (May 5, 1971).

The Round Table (1971-1978)

Dr. Kadel reported on the second painting on the Chapel wall. Persons admitting responsibility for the painting met and discussed the matter with him in response to his request and offer of no-reprisals. These persons have assured Dr. Kadel that they will not be responsible for any future such paintings. Dr. Kadel also reported that a banner displaying the words used in the first painting incident is now hanging on the Chapel wall in place of the paintings with the understanding that it will be removed not later than the termination of the United States participation in the war in Viet Nam and may be removed for any use of the Chapel when its presence is considered inappropriate.[11]

The Board also commended President Kadel for "the redemptive spirit and manner in which he handled the whole issue of the writings on the Chapel wall." Yet in the eyes of many, "the event severely damaged the image of the Seminary in the Presbyterian community. Support both financially and by participation of pastors and lay members of the churches plummeted."[12]

At the same Board meeting, President Kadel noted the approval of the seminary's new constitution by the General Assembly of the United Presbyterian Church. He reported on the new structures being put in place to provide governance for the seminary and the constitutive members of each of the councils and committees. These were the Administrative Council; Academic Council (with a By-Laws Committee) and Long Range Planning and Policy Committee. These structures reflected Kadel's interest in a shared governance model for the seminary with input from all the varied constituencies that would move toward consensus-building as the method of the decision-making process.

---

11. "Board of Directors Minutes," Pittsburgh Theological Seminary (November 17, 1971).

12. Herchenroether, "Pittsburgh Theological Seminary 1959-1999," 17. Herchenroether goes on to say that "the Board supported Dr. Kadel in his handling of the Chapel affair, with some misgivings. It was certainly not the time to show a rift between the Board and the Administration so soon after the failure of the Board to support Dr. Miller in his disagreements with the Faculty. As noted before, the history of the problems between the Board and Administration beginning at the time of consolidation was widely known in the denomination and in the general world of theological education and was interpreted as portraying an institution that did not support its Administration."

President Kadel's assessment of the seminary situation in its many dimensions and his commitment to finding ways to work through its problems was evident in his report on the state of the seminary, submitted to the Board on November 17, 1971. His statement is worth quoting in full:

> As I make this report after seven months in office, I have a little more sense of the seminary and am able to make some observations. We have developed an open process and life style where we have people talking to each other and this is good. However, in an attempt to share decision-making responsibilities, it is necessary to spend a lot of time in committee work. Participatory democracy is not the most economical use of time. But I believe it is ultimately the most effective in terms of getting ownership of decisions made and in moving forward with the least possible suspicions and tensions. The trust level is still low. It may be that this is a reality with which we will need to live for a long time. It bothers me no end that a theological institution, an institution of the church, that is preparing ministers of the church for the preaching of the gospel and the development of the community of believers who respond to the gospel and seek to take the gospel to the world as a reconciling and redemptive force find it so difficult to live in the spirit of the gospel. The lack of trust seems to be accepted as a given because there is much that is not worthy of trust in the institution. I for one reject this point of view. It seems to me that Christians are called to love and not to predicate that love on the loveliness of those who are its object. Trust seems to me to work in the same way. Unless we begin to trust each other, even though at times that trust may not be justified, I question whether we can ever build a meaningful trust-level. There are frustrations in the seminary community and these frustrations are caused in large measure by the uncertainty of what we are going to be doing in the future. The frustrations are enhanced by the fact that we are using the participatory democratic process to arrive at those decisions which takes longer. There is a degree of ambiguity in our life. And it is a serious question as to how much ambiguity an institution can afford. It is my hope that we will all be patient, and make those contributions we

The Round Table (1971-1978)

can make, looking forward to the finalization of decisions by mid-April of 1972 of what our program will be like in the immediate years ahead.[13]

To help move the seminary forward in addressing the problems that were apparent to President Kadel, the proposal was accepted that the inaugural year activities would focus not on a person but on the institution. Professor Harold E. Scott, a former Pittsburgh-Xenia faculty member and a well-respected associate professor of homiletics at the seminary, was charged with chairing a committee to work on this responsibility. The first task was to indicate the basic issues that needed to be addressed through the year. Some outside speakers were brought in, and eight questions were asked in an attempt to identify key issues for the seminary as it engaged in the task of theological education at the beginning of the 1970s:

1. May all possible theological and/or social positions live together in the seminary, or may excessive diversity threaten our usefulness?
2. What kind of curriculum should we provide for the training of ministers? Should we emphasize classical disciplines, practical training, or courses that relate theological content to contemporary thought?
3. What is the proper scope of our educational task? Do we merely prepare people for ministry, or do we extend our services to the laity, to in-parish ministers, to other professional groups, etc.?
4. What are our special opportunities with regard to a changing student body? In what ways may the seminary provide for the theological education of Blacks, of women intending ordination, of a growing number of students who enter seminary with vocational or theological uncertainty?
5. To what extent is a seminary responsible for a student's spiritual growth?

---

13. "Board of Directors Minutes," Pittsburgh Theological Seminary (November 17, 1971).

6. What is the relationship of the seminary to churches? Are we servant, or leader, or partner in dialogue?
7. Are we primarily concerned to serve the needs of the United Presbyterian Church, or should we view ourselves as a center for theological education serving an ecumenical constituency in a defined geographical area?
8. Are we merely an educational institution with a particular subject matter, or should our political processes, our business practices and our administrative policies reflect and express our subject matter?[14]

The questions posed here were significant ones for Pittsburgh Theological Seminary and for other theological institutions, particularly denominational seminaries, at this time. In one sense, they are ongoing questions for theological education institutions into the present time. They raise issues of the nature of a seminary community as it includes diversity; the nature and function of the theological curriculum; the scope of the institution's educational responsibility, internally and externally; the ways in which the institution should adjust to changing student bodies; the relation of the seminary to the personal spiritual growth of students; the relationship of the seminary to churches; the role of the seminary as a denominational school in relation to a surrounding ecumenical constituency; and whatever distinctiveness there may be for all the seminary's processes from the fact that the seminary is a theological institution, instead of simply an educational institution.

These basic questions were ones that the predecessor seminaries faced, in various ways, and with which the new, consolidated seminary began to struggle. Now, with the turbulent 1960s having greatly affected American society and culture as a whole, these were questions for the decades of the 1970s that arose in the institutional life of Pittsburgh Seminary. As the leadership style of the new president showed, and the implementation of a new curriculum symbolized, Pittsburgh Theological Seminary was moving into a new era in the early 1970s.

The changes in the seminary's constitution to widen participation

---

14. "Board of Directors Minutes," Pittsburgh Theological Seminary (November 17, 1971).

The Round Table (1971-1978)

by the community in the governance and decision-making process was accompanied by the establishment of a Task Force on Blackness in June 1971 and the authorization to establish a Doctor of Ministry program to begin in 1972.

Symbolic of the new changes emerging in the presidency of William Kadel was the "round table." In February 1972, a gift was received from the women of Shadyside Presbyterian Church to refurnish the president's office at the seminary. The refurnishing was limited to "a new round table, chairs and a credenza" along with a plaque in honor of Shadyside's pastor and seminary Board member, Dr. Howard C. Scharfe. The "round table" — at which all could sit in parity and all viewpoints could be heard and collegial discussion could be engaged in — was a fitting symbol of President Kadel's style and dream for the governance of Pittsburgh Seminary and the ethos of life together in the seminary community.

President Kadel wrote at length about "The Open Process at PTS" in January 1973:

> simply stated it is a way of decision-making. Issues are looked at by representatives of all functional groupings which make up the seminary community (Board, Administration, Faculty, Students; and including Alumni and Friends where appropriate). Others who so choose may observe and share thoughts. Power and authority to make decisions is shared within the community and is lodged at those places where there is the best available information and the greatest competency to analyze the information and decide what is best for the whole life of the community.[15]

Kadel went on to indicate that

> this is not the most efficient system in terms of the economy of time. It requires spending a lot of time together in committees and groups. The autocratic style of administration, in which one person decides everything, is most time saving, but it does not always produce the best decisions. In this day when the trust level between persons is extremely low, the complete centralization of

---

15. William H. Kadel, "President's Message," Pittsburgh Seminary *Panorama* (January 1973): 2.

power tends to produce decisions which are less acceptable to those who are meant to be served by them.[16]

A benefit of the open process, according to Kadel, was that it "eliminates the need for 'hidden agendas.' Sooner or later such become quite clear and must be dealt with openly. Cloak room politics becomes impotent as indeed such procedures should be, and every issue must be addressed, examined and decided in the light of the substance of the issue itself."[17] Kadel appealed to the Christian's baptism into Christ and becoming a part of the body of Christ, the church, as a "good theological base" for this approach. For "the Christian community is a shared community. We share all things — even power and decision-making. Perhaps we have not thought of this enough. We share our faith experiences, our love, our goods. Why not our community life processes?"[18]

Kadel added that "power is always subject to misuse. Decisions will never be the best. There is always a greater chance of error when a person acts singly than when he works with others and has opportunity to test his ideas and feelings." This is rooted in our understanding of humanity — that no one is perfect and everything humans create, or touch will bear the mark of human "limitation." Since all persons have been created in the image of God, "each has much to offer." When each person is taken seriously and given the opportunity to apply human skills to the decision-making process, the community is enriched.

The Pittsburgh Seminary history of "diversity," he said, makes the open process especially hard to live with. For "hurts that in other administrative styles tend to stay hidden come to the surface. Anger and hostility must be dealt with." But ultimately it "leads to a more healthy community." While not all persons find the open process easy to live with, "our experience is that the vast majority of the seminary community is pleased with this style and find it quite desirable."[19]

---

16. William H. Kadel, "President's Message," Pittsburgh Seminary *Panorama* (January 1973): 2.

17. William H. Kadel, "President's Message," Pittsburgh Seminary *Panorama* (January 1973): 2.

18. William H. Kadel, "President's Message," Pittsburgh Seminary *Panorama* (January 1973): 2.

19. William H. Kadel, "President's Message," Pittsburgh Seminary *Panorama* (January 1973): 2.

The Round Table (1971-1978)

Kadel's final word was the full recognition of his position as president of the seminary and the chief executive officer, elected by the Board. He indicated that "the open process is not an abdication of this responsibility. But I trust the process as a way of fulfilling my responsibilities and stand ready at all times to respect the result and to accept accountability for the product of such community participation."[20] President Kadel was firmly committed to the open process in the open community. It marked an administrative style that sought to give community "ownership" to decisions, arrived at by listening to the voices of many, through long periods of discussion and the sharing of perspectives.

Institutional Directions

In May 1972, the president reported to the fall meeting of the Board of Directors that the new constitution was providing "a good direction of sharing power and decision-making within the community."[21] Much was being done and it was reported at that meeting, in reference to Dr. Kadel, that "the game we play around here is trying to see if any mortal man can match his metabolism." At that meeting too, a new dean was called.

After the resignation of longtime dean Gordon Jackson, who wished to return to the faculty, Professor Robert Ezzell, who was an assistant professor of homiletics and lecturer in New Testament, had served as interim dean beginning June 1, 1971. Ezzell had been charged to deal especially with three areas:

1. The establishment of a Community-Oriented Studies Program (COSP) in which students would live in a community setting, be immersed in its urban culture and then reflect on their experiences in regular meetings with faculty.
2. The development of the Doctor of Ministry program.
3. Conversations with other regional theological institutions to foster ecumenical exchange and dialogue. These institutions were St. Vin-

---

20. William H. Kadel, "President's Message," Pittsburgh Seminary *Panorama* (January 1973): 2.
21. "Board of Directors Minutes," Pittsburgh Theological Seminary (May 2, 1972).

cent College (Roman Catholic); St. Francis College (Roman Catholic); St. Cyril and Methodius Theological Seminary (Eastern Orthodox); and the Reformed Presbyterian Theological Seminary (Reformed Presbyterian Church).

The desire to reach out ecumenically was of special concern to a number of the faculty, and in a post–Vatican II context it was now possible to do more ecumenically with Roman Catholic institutions than ever before. Relationships with the Orthodox were to grow in later years, but not much was ever possible in a joint relationship with the Reformed Presbyterian Seminary in Wilkinsburg.

The faculty had agreed, when Jackson returned to the classroom, that a dean from outside the seminary community would be desirable. Before President Kadel took office, the Dean's Search Committee wrote in a letter to the seminary community on March 22, 1971, that "the Committee agreed to receive and honor a student petition asking that the Seminary give top priority to the selection of a Black leader as our future Dean." President Kadel felt similarly about the appointment. The committee considered a large number of applicants and recommended that Dr. David T. Shannon, associate professor of religion at Bucknell University, a Baptist minister, and an African American, be called to the deanship. Shannon was unanimously elected and began his work on July 1, 1972.

Seminary enrollment had risen from 280 in 1967-68 to 337 in 1971-72. Enrollments of African American students had moved from four to twenty-five. The sources for student enrollment were also changing. In 1967, 60 percent of the students were from church-related colleges, with 40 percent from state-related and private institutions. By 1972, the percentages had been reversed, with 60 percent of students from state-related and private institutions and only 40 percent from church-related colleges.[22]

The number of women seeking theological education at Pittsburgh Seminary was also growing. In 1967, there had been twenty-one women enrolled; in 1972, there were thirty-seven, with seventeen in the M.Div. program. In May 1972, a Task Force on Women was established to study women in church and society. In November, the task force's work was

---

22. William H. Kadel, "President's Message," *Panorama* (January 1972): 1.

described to the Board as "to sensitize and educate the seminary community to the concerns of seminary women."[23]

Dr. Kadel reported in November 1972 that he now had a "cautious optimism" about the seminary. He disagreed with the line from the hymn: "Some would say 'change and decay in all around I see.' Yet there is another side — another point of view. It is the point of view of the cautious optimist. It can be stated in words like these: 'Change and positive growth in all around I see.' This is where I am as I make this report."[24] One base for this stance was that

> the seminary community has a clearer sense of the institutional direction for the future. The work, and discussions, of last year produced an affirmation of our primary stance, while not exclusively so, toward the preparation of men and women for parish ministry. The educational program should be such as to develop competently those professional skills which are needed for ministry in our times. Attached to this report as Exhibit A is a summary statement made by Harold Scott, chairman of the Committee of Eleven, the product of his researching all of the input that came during the variety of activities that were carried on during the last academic year. This document represents Harold's "reading" of the data and must be read by members of the Board in that light.[25]

Scott's "Exhibit A" was a summary of the work of the Committee of Eleven, which sought input from the seminary constituencies that it passed along in the form of a "Memo to Wm. Kadel." It was written on October 31, 1972 — Reformation Day — which prompted Scott "to suggest a title for this as 'Ninety Five Theses Minus Seventy-two!!'" The twenty-three points that followed were divided into two parts: "As an institution, Pittsburgh Theological Seminary will be fulfilling its 'Now' mission more adequately when it . . ." and "The type of student who should be graduated from the seminary is . . ."

---

23. "Board of Directors Minutes," Pittsburgh Theological Seminary (November 29, 1972).

24. "Board of Directors Minutes," Pittsburgh Theological Seminary (November 29, 1972).

25. "Board of Directors Minutes," Pittsburgh Theological Seminary (November 29, 1972).

The full text of "Exhibit A" is presented here to show the range of concerns for the seminary at this time and the goals to which the seminary was looking in terms of its institutional identity, purposes, and the ministries it sought to carry out as a theological institution and a denominational seminary. These were set forth both in terms of the seminary's institutional mission and its mission in the "formation" of the students who were its graduates.

As an institution, Pittsburgh Theological Seminary will be fulfilling its "Now" mission more adequately when it

1. Sees theological education as a part of a larger context than campus interests and participants more than those who administrate, study or teach.
2. When it continues to be a mission arm of the church, admitting uncommitted persons to a searching process for personal identity and vocational direction.
3. When it encourages and nurtures what has been called by various names: the spiritual life, the cement that holds together what the Seminary is all about — faith commitment, the creating of "authentic" Christian persons who have a measure of wholeness.
4. When it initiates cooperative projects with those who are direct partners in seminary education and the practice of ministry: e.g. Candidates Chairmen and Ministerial Relations Chairmen.
5. When it seeks to understand the storm that has gathered in the churches; the search for mission of denomination, judicatory and congregation; the frustration of the standard brand churches; the reformation of the ecclesiastical institution; and the strange conservative bent that is having its effect sociologically, psychologically and theologically.
6. When there is an appreciative recognition of the contribution of those who have a stakeholding in theological education.
7. When it continues to listen, to hear and understand the sociological context in which the Seminary is placed, i.e., the mind set of Western Pennsylvania.

The Round Table (1971-1978)

8. When it acts upon its recognition of the *desire* by the judicatories for a greater sense of ownership in the Seminary.
9. When it is able to interpret the overtures — often hesitatingly offered and frequently ill framed — of those who seemingly in the past have set themselves over against the Seminary as hints of a willingness to be partners in the endeavor.
10. When it responds to the hope of some of the stakeholders that the Seminary will help them with some of the crises they face, e.g., how to live with widely divergent ideas.
11. When it involves others besides professional theologians in the training process.
12. When it consciously seeks to develop a trust relationship, to initiate a ministry of reconciliation beginning at the Seminary and spreading out.
13. When a more thorough communications and public relations job is done with the stakeholders in theological education in Pittsburgh.

The type of student who should be graduated from the Seminary is

1. One who is able to teach what the Gospel is and how it speaks to contemporary life.
2. One who has a thorough knowledge of the classic theological disciplines as well as a practicing knowledge of sociology, psychology and behavioral sciences.
3. One who has a basic commitment to the parish ministry, although not all students need to enter the parish ministry.
4. One prepared to be a Teaching Elder as well as a Social Activist, who will also recognize the possibility of positive values of diverse opinions within the church.
5. One who is sensitive to persons where they are at a particular time, who will also have the capacity to hear what people are saying or perhaps are attempting to say, with a knowledge of how to live with people at the point of their need.
6. One who has both desire and ability to communicate with all types of persons, i.e., not only with the economically

deprived but also with the better educated, more sophisticated laymen who in the newer generations make a growing fraction of the population.
7. One who has the ability to implement programs without alienation of various congregational or community elements.
8. One who possesses sufficient knowledge of church polity to know the place and appreciate the value of the judicatory.
9. One who has desire and ability in practicing pastoral skills.
10. One who *really can be* an enabler.

The listing of these goals for institutional direction and the seminary's "Now mission" which is "to develop competently those professional skills which are needed for ministry in our times" is revealing. The seminary was recognizing a place for students who were uncommitted to the church (or Christianity) and were involved in a seeking process. The seminary was seeking to create "authentic" Christian persons who possess a measure of "wholeness." The seminary saw its role as partnering with presbytery committees. The seminary seeks to understand the "storm" in the churches. It recognizes the contributions of those who have a "stakeholding" in theological education. It seeks to understand its context: the sociological context of western Pennsylvania. It seeks to act on letting Presbyterian judicatories participate in seminary "ownership." The seminary wants to be willing to interpret the actions of those who have been seminary detractors as providing "hints of a willingness to be partners" in the seminary endeavor. The seminary wants to help people learn to live with diverse ideas. It wants to involve more than just "professional theologians" in the "training process." It wants to develop a trust relationship and initiate reconciliation — from within the seminary itself, to spread into the church through the seminary's graduates. The seminary seeks "a more thorough communications and public relations job" with "the stakeholders in theological education in Pittsburgh."

This very full agenda indicated the desire of Pittsburgh Seminary to listen to the church, interpret the culture, and participate with others in the tasks of theological education. It is a much more detailed and

The Round Table (1971-1978)

contextualized statement of the ways in which the seminary's mission could be carried out than had ever been previously articulated, even at its predecessor institutions. The vision incorporates important elements of American culture as they emerged through the 1960s and a style of institutional responsibility that was seeking to grow in the early 1970s. The mission goals also reflect, to a large degree, the "round table" approach to leadership embodied by President Kadel himself. As Harold Scott indicated in his note to the president, accompanying the "theses": "Your own involvement in the process was so thorough that you will recognize the material."

The goals for "student outcomes" (in the language of contemporary educational accrediting institutions) are also revealing. Here, the Pittsburgh Seminary graduate is one who "should" be able to relate the gospel to contemporary life; is equipped with knowledge of the classical theological disciplines as well as "sociology, psychology and behavioral sciences"; who is basically committed to the parish ministry (though not all students will enter the parish) and will combine the roles of "Teaching Elder as well as a Social Activist" and who will see the values in the diverse opinions within the church. The graduate is "sensitive" to where persons are at a particular time and will have the capacity to hear persons' needs and to live with them at their points of need. The graduate desires to communicate not only with the "economically deprived" but also with the "better educated, more sophisticated laymen" whose numbers were growing in the population. The graduate can implement programs in non-alienating ways, knows and appreciates the value of the church's judicatories; has the desire and ability to practice pastors skills and is one who *"really can be* an enabler."

These goals for students are also a snapshot of the times regarding the desired skills and character for Pittsburgh Seminary graduates. This combination of the classical and the contemporary in one sense had always been part of the ideal for a seminary graduate. In earlier times, the emphasis would have fallen more heavily on education in the classical disciplines. Here there is a parity between the historic disciplines and the contemporary sciences, since the goal of knowing the classical is to be able to relate the gospel to the contemporary. In parish settings, graduates are expected to combine the historic role of the pastor as the "teaching elder" with the savvy of the "social activist" and will do so by honoring the positive dimensions of "diverse opinions in the church."

"Sensitivity" is a key term — in terms of the graduate's ability to "hear what people are saying or perhaps are attempting to say" (a pastoral counseling/care emphasis) in combination with knowing how to live with people "at the point of their need." The ministries of the graduates are to extend to communication to diverse groups — from the economically deprived to the educated and prosperous is a goal. There is an emphasis on not alienating "various congregational or community elements," knowing the place and value of church government, and desiring to practice pastoral skills. The tenth goal picks up a prominent motif for ministry in the 1970s: "One who *really can be* an enabler." The desire was for pastors to "enable" people to carry out ministries.

Curriculum Changes

Changes in the faculty bylaws and in the seminary's constitution that went into effect in 1971 to enable wider faculty and community participation in the seminary's work, along with the "round table" administrative style of Dr. Kadel and the work of the new councils and committees, all contributed to the "Exhibit A" goals in the "Scott Report" from the "Committee of Eleven," which President Kadel presented to the Board of Directors in November 1972. By that time the change in the seminary's curriculum, which had been the "presenting problem" in the last year of Donald Miller's presidency, had been in place for a year. This "new curriculum" borne out of the earlier struggles was both a reflection of and a prescription for many of the institutional values and "student outcomes" which the Scott Report conveys. The curriculum was an expression of the seminary's attempt to deal with the results of the tumultuous 1960s and to place an emphasis on the open, wide-ranging nature of theological education in America as it was emerging by the beginning of the 1970s. It recognized cultural changes and sought to equip graduates in churches to deal with the changing society by providing a much less structured course of study and enabling students to follow their interests much more easily. The failure of the Church and Ministry division to act as an integrative focus for Bachelor of Divinity students led to a shift in curriculum emphases that sought to be responsive to the changes in the social scene. From a highly structured curriculum, the move was made to a much more wide-open model.

The Round Table (1971-1978)

On November 18, 1970, the Board of Directors authorized changing the seminary's basic degree program from the Bachelor of Divinity to the Master of Divinity. This was the trend of the time and was mandated for member institutions of the American Association of Theological Schools. This change also eased the way for the development of the Doctor of Ministry degree, which Pittsburgh Seminary was later to grant.[26]

In March 1970, the faculty, administration, and Board of Directors of Pittsburgh Seminary received a report from the Middle States Commission on Institutions of Higher Education. This report indicated the contextual situation in American higher education along with a word of advice for what would be the new Kadel administration:

> The outward calm in an academic institution today can be deceptive. Students openly question the competence of professors, the relevance of courses, the integrity of the administration, and even the grounds of faith. Younger faculty are often restless and discontented.... The incoming administration must anticipate the forces of change which lie beneath the surface.[27]

The new Pittsburgh Seminary curriculum that emerged for the 1969-70 academic year was a result of the recommendations of a joint faculty and student Curriculum Committee. It was approved by the faculty on March 13, 1969. The 1969-70 catalogue indicated the changes that were coming. With implementation of the new curriculum on the horizon, it was not possible to change all course descriptions, so the catalogue sketched the main elements in what was being called "an elective curriculum":

> While this catalog was in the press, the faculty adopted an elective curriculum. We were able to stop the presses to describe

---

26. The board of directors also determined that those who had graduated from Pittsburgh Seminary or its predecessor institutions with the Bachelor of Divinity degree (and assuming the person had a prior baccalaureate degree from an institution of higher learning) could receive a Master of Divinity degree "upon a payment fee of $25.00." See "Board of Directors Minutes," Pittsburgh Theological Seminary (November 18, 1970).

27. "Report to the Faculty, Administration, Trustees of Pittsburgh Theological Seminary," Calvert N. Ellis (Chairman), Middle States Commission on Institutions of Higher Education, March 15-18, 1970, p. 1, cited in Brown, "Curricular Change at Pittsburgh Theological Seminary," 72.

briefly the new curriculum, as well as the processes through which it was arrived at, but the course descriptions ... could not be changed in time. They should be viewed as containing the stuff for new descriptions but the course structuring will be different, radically so in many cases.[28]

The degree program was still, at the time, the Bachelor of Divinity degree. What was being envisioned was not merely a makeover of what had been previously in place, but a completely new curriculum. As the catalogue noted, "At this writing the three divisions of the faculty are at work re-thinking their divisional goals and their courses so that the elective curriculum will not be merely a renumbering of courses but will be a new structure at Pittsburgh Seminary to enable men and women to work more effectively in the ministry of Jesus Christ."[29]

The catalogue indicated the backgrounds for the new curriculum and then proceeded to outline its main structures and features.

The student and faculty curriculum committees were at work for months drawing up an elective curriculum. The definitive action of the faculty was itself the culmination of a lengthy process of discussion and debate. Even now detailed points are being hammered out. However, the main structure of the elective curriculum is clearly visible.

A. The Curriculum Structure.
   1. No course shall be more than three hours (a few courses, e.g., Greek reading, may be one hour).
   2. Total hours for graduation will be 78.
   3. Of the 78 hours, 45 are to be distributed according to the following formula: every student will take at least 15 hours in each of the three divisions, the selection of courses and professors to be that of the student in consultation with his adviser.
   4. A minimum requirement of three hours of Hebrew and

---

28. Pittsburgh Theological Seminary, "Catalogue Issue of Perspective," 10 (Spring 1969): 48.

29. Pittsburgh Theological Seminary, "Catalogue Issue of Perspective," 10 (Spring 1969): 49.

three hours of Greek will be retained for every student. (These are the only two required courses.)

5. There will be no comprehensive examinations.

B. Introductory and Advanced Courses

1. The divisions will set up introductory (or A-level) courses to be distinguished from advanced courses. While particular advanced courses may assume prerequisites, no general formula of prerequisites is desired by the faculty.
2. It is probable that each division will offer at least four three-hour A-level courses each semester. A-level courses can be either one-semester course or two-semester course. It is also probable that these courses will be offered on a two-year cycle and announced in the catalog to help students plan their course of study.

C. Field Education

Field education will no longer be a requirement for graduation. It, too, will be elective; and the field education office will continue to assist and supervise students who wish to elect field education for non-credit.

D. Student Load

1. In a typical semester the student's load will be four three-hour courses. This will help the student focus in depth as well as breadth, avoid fragmentation of time, and have the opportunity to be reflective in his intellectual endeavors.
2. In any given semester, one audit course will be permitted over and above the four-credit courses with permission of the instructor. Such audit courses will not count toward the 78 required hours.

E. Faculty Advisers

A system of faculty advisers will be set up to help the student plan his course of study and to assist him at all points in his academic work.

Within this elective curriculum independent study will continue to be stressed. We intend to make as much use as possible of courses numbered 300, 600, 900 and designated Independent Study. Students may request courses in their special interests and needs and pursue them at the truly graduate level by way of independent study.[30]

The new curriculum represented a radical change both in curricular assumptions and in the implementation of a program of study that shifted the number of hours needed for graduation from 90 (66 required; 24 elective) to 78 (only two required courses: Hebrew and Greek).

Early reflections about the effect of the new curriculum were provided by the 1970 Self-Study of the Curriculum Task Force. This group noted that while some new courses had been added, many courses were "the continuations of what had been offered before." Smaller classes had been a result of the new curriculum and this had meant, in some cases, a shift from the lecture method to seminar-style teaching. A kind of circular situation with the new curriculum was also noted:

> The adoption of the elective system has been a response to the valid desire on the part of the students for more responsibility in choosing when they study what, but their choice has been limited by the implicit assumptions of the three divisions about what seminary students ought to study. This in turn reflects the assumptions which controlled the selection of faculty with their particular specializations.[31]

Some early negative reactions to the curriculum were also captured in the Self-Study report of the Curriculum Task Force:

> Lack of distilled educational theory of the curriculum . . . no recognizable image of PTS as distinct from other theological schools . . . no clear stance in matters pertaining to sociology, psychology and media . . . no clarity whether contemporary

---

30. Pittsburgh Theological Seminary, "Catalogue Issue of Perspective," 10 (Spring 1969): 48-49.

31. Pittsburgh Theological Seminary, "Report of the Self-Study" (January-December 1969): 3.4.12, 27-28, cited in Brown, "Curricular Change at Pittsburgh Theological Seminary," 75.

needs of the church and society, or how contemporary theological and social movements influence curricular change.[32]

The report went on to say, however, that

> Such observations, however, imply that there could be either a clear consensus in the Faculty or some authority which could make and enforce a coordinated decision on all of these matters. Even if it were possible to achieve unanimity, the issue still remains: is a tightly integrated seminary curriculum a better preparation for contemporary ministry than the kind of mixed pattern which now obtains? The problem for the Pittsburgh Seminary faculty is discovering or adopting a frame of reference or principle by which it can work together with integrity for effective seminary education.[33]

The outward "appeal" of the new curriculum was its freedom and flexibility for students. This is captured in the 1970-71 seminary catalogue, the first one to present the new curriculum as it had developed:

> Pittsburgh Seminary has a curriculum which gives each student freedom to plan his studies in light of his own background and his own aims.... Each student is free to study what he needs to study when he wants to study it.... The curriculum is designed so that a student can begin his studies in a given area, such as systematic theology, at more than one point.... There is no "one way" to start the study of theology.
>
> You are an individual with your own background, interests and purpose. At Pittsburgh Seminary you are free to design your own program of studies. The entire range of course offerings is open to you, and you are able to engage in independent research and university study. Metropolitan Pittsburgh offers many field education opportunities from which you may choose in light of

---

32. Pittsburgh Theological Seminary, "Report of the Self-Study" (January-December 1969): 3.3.14, 27-28, cited in Brown, "Curricular Change at Pittsburgh Theological Seminary," 75.

33. Pittsburgh Theological Seminary, "Report of the Self-Study" (January-December 1969): 3.3.14, 27-28, cited in Brown, "Curricular Change at Pittsburgh Theological Seminary," 75-76.

your concerns. Pittsburgh Seminary's curriculum sets you free to learn.³⁴

The emphasis on freedom was continued in the seminary's catalogue in the following years. Additional phrasing in the next several catalogues continued to emphasize this theme. Freedom was also granted toward the flexible interplay of degrees as needs and interests changed:

> Each of the ten degree possibilities available at Pittsburgh Seminary is described in detail in this section of the catalog. Degree programs are not arranged in such a way that students become locked in to one degree from the outset of studies. Interests and plans change: thus there is opportunity to transfer from one program to another within the Seminary.³⁵

In short, the curriculum was "a free elective plan. No courses are required, with the exception of Greek and Hebrew which are essential tools for theological work. Furthermore, there are no formal prerequisites, for this could be merely another way of regimenting studies."³⁶

The new curriculum did open up new courses, particularly in the Church and Ministry Division. These reflected social factors of the decade past and the changing societal contexts in which theological education was being carried out in Pittsburgh's urban setting. Courses in social ethics, sociology of religion, ecumenics, and preaching in the black church were among the new offerings.

For several years, the seminary's catalogue had described the purpose of the seminary to be "clearcut: to know our time, the gospel for the healing of our time, and the ministry for our time."³⁷ The new cur-

---

34. Pittsburgh Theological Seminary Catalogue, 1970-71, 52, 54.

35. Pittsburgh Theological Seminary Catalogue, 1972-73, 16. In the 1971-72 catalogue, the main head under Academic Programs was "The Mater of Divinity Degree" and the first subhead was "Free to Learn: the Curriculum at Pittsburgh Seminary" (16). In the next two catalogues, the main head was "Free to Learn" and the subhead was "Curriculum Freedom" (1972-73, 1973-74, page 16 in each catalogue).

36. Pittsburgh Theological Seminary Catalogue, 1971-72: 16. After indicating that there is "no 'one way' to start the study of theology," it indicates that of the varieties of approaches, "one of these approaches may be best for one student, but not for another. Only the student himself can decide" (17).

37. See page 19 in the catalogues of 1966-67, 1968-69, and 1969-70.

The Round Table (1971-1978)

riculum emphasized more expansive ways of relating the gospel to culture, the varieties of forms of ministries in contemporary society, and the validity of social science disciplines as fields of study to help those in ministry carry out their ministerial roles.

In the 1971-72 catalogue, the section on "Ministry and Theological Education" described the seminary's purpose in a more nuanced form in relation to the seminary's purposes and the complexities of changing patterns of ministries:

> Pittsburgh Theological Seminary is engaged in theological education which has as its aim the preparation of men and women for Christian ministry. This deceptively simple statement carries with it a multitude of problems and questions which are not easily resolved. For instance, there was a time when a consensus existed regarding the nature of ministry. That is, the vast majority of seminary students were preparing for the parish ministry. Presently, however, ministry is more widely understood as belonging to the whole Church, and ordained clergymen are seen as having a particular function within the broad range of the Church's ministries. Furthermore, the ordained ministry of the Church now encompasses many forms, even within the parish itself. The pattern of ministry is no longer predictable and thus preparation for ministry can no longer be uniform.[38]

This introduction to the catalogue clearly set forth the view that there is no clear consensus on the nature of ministry, that pastoral ministry in the parish is only part of the wider ministries of the whole church, and that patterns of ministry are not predictable and thus preparation for ministry must be flexible:

> Changing ministries require flexible and imaginative forms of theological education. There is no one way to prepare for ministry because there is no one form which ministry takes. Curriculum is an obvious case in point. Pittsburgh Seminary's curriculum, "Free to Learn," enables each student to devise a course of studies which is suitable for his particular plans for ministry.[39]

---

38. Pittsburgh Theological Seminary Catalogue, 1971-72, 4.
39. Pittsburgh Theological Seminary Catalogue, 1971-72, 4.

Thus the contemporary context of ministry was a primary factor to which to appeal to "make sense" out of an elective curriculum that provided both traditional theological courses and those specifically focused on current issues in church and society — with the choice left up to the student to decide in which ones to enroll.

The ongoing force of the turmoil of the 1960s on issues of race, student rebellions, civil rights, the Vietnam conflict, and the developments of forms of "secular theology" by theologians also had roles to play in the pressure to form a new curriculum. Donald Miller later recounted that "the late 60's brought the process of secularization into the seminary campus, as it did elsewhere, and the whole question of the purpose of the seminary began to change."[40] Miller's concerns about these directions were expressed before he resigned, as noted above. Emphases on individual rights and freedom of choice accompanied by calls for the church to be a more active force in society had effects on the ways American seminaries structured their curricula. Pittsburgh Seminary was not exempt from changes taking place around the country.

Reactions

The new seminary curriculum inevitably produced a wide range of reactions. Some reflected on both the internal and external forces at work in the shaping of the seminary's elective curriculum in the early 1970s. Board of Directors member Robert Vogelsang recalled that

> The free and open curriculum was a response to what we perceived as student unrest, and we attempted to let students become more and more involved in their own structuring of their own curriculum. That, in my opinion, was a mistake; but in the opinion of those who were structuring the curriculum they thought that was the way we had to go because that's what everybody else was doing. And if we weren't doing that we wouldn't get students.[41]

The students who were attending Pittsburgh Seminary by the end of the 1960s were not simply traditional students from a strong college

---

40. Cited in Brown, "Curricular Change at Pittsburgh Theological Seminary," 81.
41. Cited in Brown, "Curricular Change at Pittsburgh Theological Seminary," 82.

background, interested in the traditional theological disciplines and most often nurtured in church congregations. Students were now more diverse. Professor George Kehm, who joined the seminary faculty in 1962, saw this clearly:

> We used to get many more people who were directly out of college, young white males, who were pretty sure that they wanted to go into the ministry. There weren't that many women at the Seminary when I first got there.... There were very few Blacks. In the mid-'60s we began to try to recruit Blacks in a serious way ... the student body today is considerably different than it was in the '60s, and it didn't get that way quickly either. The first noticeable change that took place was during the civil rights protests between '63, '64, and '70. There were a lot of students who saw the Church as a change agent, who were interested in the Church because of what they thought it could do to providing a better deal in society for minorities and under-privileged groups. They weren't necessarily interested in the ministry. They were interested in theology and ethics, mostly ethics. Some of them were oriented toward religion as a way of finding meaning for their lives. When the Viet Nam [War] heated up we had a number who were here simply to avoid the draft. What this meant, though, was that there was a greater number of students on campus who were not committed Christians headed for the ministry, in contrast to what you had in the early '60s.[42]

The depth of difficulty that the proposed new curriculum precipitated in faculty and with President Miller was captured in the comments by former Dean Gordon Jackson:

> The '60s were cataclysmic. Most of our students were radicalized. We had only a minority in favor of Viet Nam; the majority ruled against it. And early on there would not even have been a minority siding with white racism against the Blacks.... So this happened at that time to be a radical center.... Our president simply could not cope with what was going on here or elsewhere. His understanding of the Seminary ... was, 'The function of the student

---

42. Cited in Brown, "Curricular Change at Pittsburgh Theological Seminary," 83.

at Pittsburgh Seminary is to be in the library doing his work and not worrying about the world out there. That's the job of others'.... And so we had a fractured community.[43]

The tensions led one observer to comment: "That this 'fractured community' was a reality is attested to by the fact that the social activist students rallied around the radical side of the faculty while the more quiescent and conservative students supported the President; this split was one of the factors leading to his resignation in 1970."[44]

The spillover and fallout from both the actions of more "radicalized" Pittsburgh Seminary students and the internal disharmony of the faculty had effects on the seminary's image among the churches and with pastors and laity in the region the seminary served, according to Jackson:

> During the 1960s, especially the late '60s, we concentrated a great deal on specialized ministry. We didn't forget the general ministry, but there was a lot of unhappiness, dis-ease about the Church, unease about the Church, if not outright antagonism toward the Church among our students. The Church had not done, at least the Church in this area, had not taken very much of a leadership role in the Viet Nam situation, the taking of a posture on behalf of the Blacks, and so forth. Our Seminary, both the student body and the faculty, played a very decisive role in both of these issues.... We had at one time thirty-five people in jail over the major marches in the South. So we had to gear our vision to what was going on in those times. We lost even more financial resources because of our commitment to radical social change.... The perception of our several "publics" out in Western Pennsylvania, Eastern Ohio and West Virginia . . . was that we were a bunch of social radicals, students and faculty alike. Since we couldn't get along with the world out there, we probably weren't getting along with each other inside. That was an inference drawn from insufficient data, but it was there.[45]

---

43. Cited in Brown, "Curricular Change at Pittsburgh Theological Seminary," 83-84.
44. Brown, "Curricular Change at Pittsburgh Theological Seminary," 84.
45. Brown, "Curricular Change at Pittsburgh Theological Seminary," 84. Brown also cites the comments of James Gittings in describing this period: "During the upheavals of

The Round Table (1971-1978)

The ongoing challenges of these perceptions in the wider public were very real for President Kadel as he dealt with the pragmatic realities of operating the seminary. Kadel commented,

> We had some incidents in the Seminary in which students had taken some actions which were really expressions of their rejection of administrative authority and power, and it got out in the hustings. Of course, it created an image. There may have been only a couple of students involved in doing some of these things, but as far as the outside community was concerned it represented everyone.... So that the image of students here was that we had a bunch of "draft dodgers," and that they were not good. It was going to ruin the Church when they really got out to be pastors. "What in the world are you doing down there? What are you up to anyway with this kind of students? Why don't you kick 'em out? Why don't you clean house? Why don't you attract other kinds of students?" That was a really big issue. We were beginning at that point in time to have in society this strong conservative reaction to the more liberal movements of the earlier decade.... The public never perceived that what happened to their young people happened before they got to the Seminary. We were inheriting the problems that the society created. We always like to find "whipping boys"; we became "whipping boys" — easy targets. You can see how when we asked for money all these things began to crop up all over the place.[46]

Divisions about the new curriculum continued in the seminary community during the early years of implementation. The students' freedom to choose from the elective offerings meant that, unlike the structured curriculum of the past, there were no core courses that all students had to take (except Greek and Hebrew) and thus there was no concentrated body of knowledge that students could be assumed to have become familiar with when they entered elective courses beyond

---

the civil-rights era Pittsburgh students and faculty members had a way of turning up on television screens in the Steel City region, as often as not in connection with demonstrations or demands for causes of the time. Their habits didn't wash well in Beaver Falls. Reaction to all of this was surprisingly late in its appearance on the seminary's admission charts and later still in its impact upon finances."

46. Cited in Brown, "Curricular Change at Pittsburgh Theological Seminary," 85-86.

the introductory level. There was no structured ordering to the sequence of courses students took, nor were there overall "goals" to the curriculum beyond the goal of enabling students to choose courses in relation to their needs and interests. Some in the seminary community believed the curriculum sacrificed academic integrity, and that a central value was lost in the shift from a two-thirds required course of study to the free electives. There were sharp disagreements about whether theology, for example, could best be learned from secularized sources and the contemporary context, compared to a concentration on the church's historic theological traditions.

On the other hand, the argument was made that the curriculum enabled a broad-based experience in theological education which forced students to be responsible for their own studies and choice of courses. In the words of Dean David T. Shannon,

> The emphasis was upon enabling persons . . . to develop cognitive skills, to be able to understand the Christian heritage, . . . to provide the necessary academic experiences that would enable students who were interested in the motivation for ministry to develop those goals and competencies. . . . There was a strong emphasis on the social milieu and the need to prepare persons to take those cognitive skills and to apply them in the social mix and to help them to catalyze the Church to become a change agent. The emphasis would be cognitive with a social thrust.[47]

Jackson summarized the pressures that led to the new curriculum:

> I think there [in 1969] we're responding to a student mind that rejected our previous required curriculum. These are students who wanted total freedom and demanded, therefore, an elective curriculum. We had to revise . . . in a mammoth way what we'd done in '59 and '60, still trying to maintain some integrity to our educational system by the way of area requirements, but that was all. And there . . . the fundamental thrust was student demands and the sense of the faculty that those demands at least were not illegitimate, and probably for the most part quite legitimate.[48]

---

47. Cited in Brown, "Curricular Change at Pittsburgh Theological Seminary," 87.
48. Cited in Brown, "Curricular Change at Pittsburgh Theological Seminary," 88.

The Round Table (1971-1978)

After several years with the new curriculum, some began to realize that with only area requirements, it was possible for students to graduate from Pittsburgh Seminary without covering some essential bases. One did not have to take a New Testament course, for example — a student could take all Old Testament courses. A later article in the *Pittsburgh Post-Gazette,* in reflecting on the period, said, "Students were given so many options in course electives that one student actually graduated without taking one course in theology."[49] The knowledge of this type of deficiency made its way into churches and surfaced in a 1973 fundraising survey conducted by Marts & Lundy, Inc.[50] In addition, students could also concentrate on taking courses from "favorite" professors or avoid taking courses from other professors that could challenge their own particular ideas. Some called this a "cafeteria-style" approach to theological education.

Further Curricular Developments

New courses that considered contemporary issues like Vietnam, racism, international politics, and black preaching were examples of a contextualized approach to theological education that used the issues of the day as a starting point for theological reflection. For a period, the seminary instituted a Community Oriented Study Program (COSP) which was designed "to provide an alternative form of theological education for a limited number of first year D.Min. and M.Div. students. The program seeks to raise inductively cultural and theological issues as students are introduced to a 'field' of ministry concurrently with the beginning of theological studies."[51] Students lived in a local community setting rather than on the seminary campus, and faculty traveled to the students to lead various courses. Otherwise, students were engaged in various types of community ministries. Thus, said the seminary catalogue, "the

---

49. Bohdan Hodiak, "Theological Seminary Seeks an Image," *Pittsburgh Post-Gazette* (June 26, 1976): 16, cited in Brown, "Curricular Change at Pittsburgh Theological Seminary," 89n.34. Brown also cites Donald Miller's comment that "under the new curriculum it was theoretically possible for a student to take a degree with no Old Testament, or no New Testament, or no theology. This seemed to me like training doctors without any course in anatomy."

50. See Brown, "Curricular Change at Pittsburgh Theological Seminary," 89 n. 34.

51. Pittsburgh Theological Seminary Catalogue, 1972-73, 24.

context for theological education is shifted from classroom to community; the situation of students become a formative factor in the way issues are addressed and insights are developed. There is a sense in which the program is a paradigm of ministry, with questions and problems arising out of the life of a real community."[52]

In a sense, too, the COSP program represented the paradigmatic shift in the curriculum as a whole. The broad breadth of the seminary curriculum now paid direct attention to the cultural and societal contexts of theological education. The COSP experience extended this reach and, in the all-elective curriculum, provided an alternative setting for the experience of theological education itself. The inductive methodology, which began with the human experience of the cultural setting, provided the approach by which theological studies were carried out. The catalogue made this plain:

> In order to gain community perspective, students engage in extensive study of the locality which has been selected on the basis of its socio-economic, racial, ecclesiastical, and cultural diversity. Issues identified in the situation, and in the process of trying to understand the situation, provide sequence and direction to psychological, historical, theological and biblical studies which the students carry on with the aid of the Seminary faculty. Lines of inquiry are developed by students and faculty out of the issues and problems which are identified in the community. Studies are focused by the situation itself rather than by an abstraction developed in a classroom.[53]

Students received a full year of academic credit (24 hours) for the COSP experience and then completed the further years of their degree program on campus.

A further significant addition to the seminary curriculum was the institution of the Doctor of Ministry (D.Min.) degree. In accord with guidelines from the American Association of Theological Schools, the seminary adopted the D.Min. program as the first professional degree in 1972. But in February 1973, the faculty approved the recommendation that the first degree for students leading to ordination be the

---

52. Pittsburgh Theological Seminary Catalogue, 1972-73, 24.
53. Pittsburgh Theological Seminary Catalogue, 1972-73, 25.

The Round Table (1971-1978)

M.Div. The D.Min., then, was an advanced professional degree. The faculty decided that the "M.Div. is a 'readiness for ministry' degree providing entry-level competence for the work of professional ministry."[54] The initial provision by which a D.Min. degree could be earned "in sequence" — by an additional year of study after the M.Div. requirements were met — was dropped. The degree became a professional degree for those already in ministry.

Further faculty initiatives for more courses in black studies were made but did not come to fruition. In August 1973, the faculty considered proposals to increase the number of black religion/theology courses and introduce more black materials into current course; to require all non-black students to "include at least one course in black theology/religion in the courses they elect to meet divisional requirements. (The purpose here is to try to insure that a mutually helpful black-white dialogue will occur in the seminary community and specifically in the academic program; presently, black students must take 'white' courses, but other students are not required to take 'black courses')"; and to request the Board of Directors to seek funding to establish a Martin Luther King Chair at the seminary.[55] These proposals were variously sent to the divisions for further study, returned to the Curriculum Committee, and sent to the Board of Directors. But no direct action was ever taken.

At its meeting of November 28, 1973, the seminary's Board of Directors adopted a report of the Task Force on Women that Pittsburgh Seminary "actively recruit women for training for ordination and for all of its degree programs" and that it do the same for positions on the faculty, the administration, and the Board of Directors.[56] On February 22, 1974, the Curriculum Committee reported to the faculty and recommended that "all faculty are encouraged to deal with the contributions of women and the treatment of women in all fields of theological study.... Such a commitment would call for the inclusion in course bibliographies of contributions made by women to the field of study as

---

54. "Minutes of the Faculty," Pittsburgh Theological Seminary (February 23, 1973), 3, cited in Brown, "Curricular Change at Pittsburgh Theological Seminary," 94.

55. "Minutes of the Faculty," Pittsburgh Theological Seminary (August 31, 1973), 3 cited in Brown, "Curricular Change at Pittsburgh Theological Seminary," 95.

56. Board of Directors Minutes, Pittsburgh Theological Seminary (November 28, 1973).

well as an effort to be cognizant of and sensitive to the women's perspective throughout the entire teaching process." The committee recommended the creation of a bibliography and expanded efforts to hire women as adjunct faculty members. It also recommended that "every attempt" be made to schedule courses "dealing with women's concerns and, when possible, other introductory courses during evening hours so that interested and qualified student spouses who work during the day may more easily take or audit such a course if there are openings in the class's enrollment."[57]

The Rea Report

The seminary's attention to the kind of institution it wanted to be and the kinds of students it wanted to serve in the context of the United Presbyterian Church and as an ecumenical theological institution in the midst of a rapidly changing culture meant that consideration needed to be given to the perception of Pittsburgh Seminary by the churches and laity it served in the tri-state region. The work of the Committee of Eleven, summarized in the document prepared by Harold Scott in Fall 1972, spoke of the seminary's fulfilling its "Now Mission" in relation to the type of institution it would be and the type of student who should be graduated from the seminary. This document gave consideration to the seminary's relationship to ecclesiastical judicatories and local churches.

Pittsburgh Seminary's internal governance, under Kadel's "round table" approach, was working with the new constitution adopted in May 1971, and in May 1973 President Kadel reported to the Board that the constitution was "working well." "From my perspective," he wrote, "life in the seminary community is showing strength.... I am more optimistic than I have been since coming to the seminary."[58] At that same meeting, the Board decided to reinstitute a winter term in January. But the following months proved to be difficult.

Perceptions about the seminary in Presbyteries and local churches began to result in reduced financial support for the school. The Board

---

57. "Minutes of the Faculty," Pittsburgh Theological Seminary (February 22, 1974): 3-4, cited in Brown, "Curricular Change at Pittsburgh Theological Seminary," 96.
58. "Board of Directors Minutes," Pittsburgh Theological Seminary (May 8, 1973).

authorized a preliminary study to see if a fundraising campaign was viable, and the study indicated the seminary's problematic image within the churches. The seminary's image would make it difficult to secure potential donors.

On November 28, 1973, the Board appointed an Advisory Committee, chaired by Mr. William Rea, a former member of the Board of Directors. The vice chairperson was Marianne L. Wolfe. The committee was charged to "study specific aspects of the Seminary operation and its relationship to its community" and enlisted over twenty church clergy and laity to take part in the study of "fact-finding and assessment" in order to "determine principally what the institution is doing, or should be doing, to make it as valuable as possible in its attempt to meet the current and future needs of the Church." The "community" of Pittsburgh Seminary was determined to be the nine-presbytery area in which the seminary was located. The committee was to advise the Board of Directors on its findings "with the understanding that the Board will give serious consideration to the findings and recommendations of the Advisory Committee."[59]

The Advisory Committee was to give guidance to the seminary's Board of Directors in seven areas: 1) institutional philosophy; 2) programmatic thrust; 3) quantity and quality of student body; 4) faculty and staff needs in future years; 5) realistic budget projections for the balance of the decade of the 1970s; 6) funding needed to meet these projections; and 7) appropriate methods of communication with churches and other constituencies. To this end, the committee held three main meetings and forty "hearings" or listening sessions throughout the nine presbytery areas. Some 418 persons attended these, plus 131 attendees from the Advisory Committee, for a total of 549 participants. Survey questionnaires were administered, with responses from 175 ministers and 209 laypersons. Of the seminary's 220 full-time students, 48 responded to questionnaires. Nineteen of twenty-one faculty members in residence also responded.

The work of the Advisory Committee was done during Fall 1974, a

---

59. Advisory Committee to Pittsburgh Theological Seminary, "Report to the Board of Directors" (March 17, 1975): 1, 2, 3. The nine presbyteries at that time were: Beaver-Butler, Eastminster, Kiskiminetas, Lake Erie, Pittsburgh, Redstone, Shenango, Upper Ohio Valley, and Washington. These were presbyteries that encompassed 848 churches with 329,703 members, and enrolled a total of 1,079 ministers.

tumultuous time for Pittsburgh Seminary. On June 24, 1974, the Executive Committee of the Board received the resignation of Mr. David Buttrick, to be effective on January 1, 1975, or not later than June 1, 1975. The Executive Committee reported to the Board at its November 1974 meeting that since that time, "there has been growing discussion from the Seminary community." This led to an October 18, 1974, resolution from the faculty:

> Resolved: That the faculty of Pittsburgh Theological Seminary humbly petition the Board of Directors of Pittsburgh Theological Seminary to reconsider their acceptance of Professor David Buttrick's resignation. The faculty notes that the resignation was extended during a period of internal strain in the school last spring and records its conviction that the welfare of the school will be better served by the continuation of Professor Buttrick's services.
>
> Professor David Buttrick's services are essential to the continued excellence of the teaching of homiletics and worship in the M.Div. and D.Min. program.[60]

At its November 1974 meeting the Academic Council resolved that it would communicate to the Board "the urgent concern on the part of the student body for a strong program in Homiletics, and of the high priority which it attaches to this area of preparation for ministry."[61] Through the student representative to the Board, Randall Frost, students also asked the Board to reconsider Buttrick's resignation. The Board, however, supported the administration, with Dr. Kadel stating that he "could not affirm the action of the faculty."

The seriousness of the times was reflected in the language of President Kadel to the Board at the November 1974 meeting, relating to his report:

> In considering this report, I urge the members of the Board of Directors to keep two things in mind: God is the Sovereign Lord of

---

60. "Board of Directors Minutes," Pittsburgh Theological Seminary (November 20, 1974), 2.

61. "Board of Directors Minutes," Pittsburgh Theological Seminary (November 20, 1974), 2.

the universe and our times are being lived out in his presence, as a part of his kingdom's work, and the ultimate victory of his people is assured; at the same time, the imminent reality is the struggle of our seminary for survival. The seminary may or may not have a viable future. But the kingdom of Christ is forever![62]

Kadel's need to articulate these affirmations came not only from the turmoil over the Buttrick resignation and the findings of the Advisory Committee, but also the projections of budgetary deficits for the next two fiscal years. A $150,000 deficit was projected for 1976-77, and a more than $200,000 deficit was projected for 1977-78. The Board was told that "increased denominational support and increased giving from individuals appear to be the only source of the very substantial sums that will be needed to keep the Seminary operating."[63] In light of the anticipated projections, varying attitudes in the seminary community were emerging. Out of various community meetings, the Board was told that

> attitudes among the Seminary family ranged across a broad spectrum, with the student representatives favoring no curtailment of the scope of present operations, with the resulting deficit to be funded by using surplus funds generated from operations in past years. At the other extreme, there was discussion of the possible necessity of severely curtailing the scope of Seminary operations, to keep the operating expenses within the income. The faculty representatives present indicated that they too preferred to keep the scope of the Seminary operation as is, even if it was at the expense of any immediate salary raises for the faculty and administration.[64]

These perspectives were considered by the Board's Education Committee, which recommended that

---

62. "Board of Directors Minutes," Pittsburgh Theological Seminary (November 20, 1974).

63. "Board of Directors Minutes," Pittsburgh Theological Seminary (November 20, 1974), 4.

64. "Board of Directors Minutes," Pittsburgh Theological Seminary (November 20, 1974), 5.

in light of the growing economic pressures upon Pittsburgh Theological Seminary, the Board declare that "Business as usual" is not a viable operational policy at this time. Therefore, the Board declare a moratorium on the application of policies normally governing the granting of faculty tenure, sabbaticals and the promotion of faculty until the Board takes further action.[65]

The Education Committee also recommended to the Board that "no unwritten contracts made by previous administrations be honored for sabbatical leaves, or any other contractual items."[66] Already these bleak economic positions had been factors in the release of several administrative and operational employees at the seminary.

On March 17, 1975, a special meeting of the Board was held to receive the report of the Advisory Committee, chaired by William Rea. The report was to have lasting effects on Pittsburgh Seminary. It attempted to assess the seminary from a variety of angles, and its recommendations set an agenda for the seminary well into the future. The committee highlighted eight areas of concern in the report and made fifteen general recommendations to address these concerns. The eight areas were presented through a series of "fact" statements with a comment from the Advisory Committee.[67]

1. *Shortage of Funds.* This was the "major problem facing the Institution. The Committee concludes that this problem is the result of more fundamental, longer duration situations which probably began with the merger of Xenia and Western Seminaries and which have produced the lack of community concern and support essential to the survival of PTS." The committee commented that "the present and near term future support levels restrict the options for change and require hard decisions on priorities" and that "a strong will and leadership at the Board level and much work and individual commitment" would be required to create future strength in budget crises.

2. *Community Relations.* The committee concluded from its analy-

---

65. "Board of Directors Minutes," Pittsburgh Theological Seminary (November 20, 1974).

66. "Board of Directors Minutes," Pittsburgh Theological Seminary (November 20, 1974).

67. The citations here are from the Advisory Committee to Pittsburgh Theological Seminary, "Report to the Board of Directors" (March 17, 1975), *passim.*

ses of its reports that the Pittsburgh Seminary community was "basically apathetic." This was based on low turnout for the committee's listening meetings (418, or one-tenth of one percent of the presbyteries' populations). Recognizing this, the committee commented that there was also "a small hard core of very concerned Presbyterians who are willing to work to change conditions relating to PTS."

3. *Service Region.* The Committee concluded that the Seminary's Board of Directors "has not clearly established the boundaries of its service area." Was the seminary trying to service the whole church in America, or the whole world, or the nine regional presbyteries surrounding it, or was it primarily interested in Pittsburgh Presbytery? The committee commented that "with limited and dwindling resources, the Seminary probably should be a much more significant factor on a regional base where it can become steeped in its own region's particular needs and render specific service" — but this did not mean the Seminary should become "provincial if it chooses to emphasize its regional position." The decision about service region the committee saw as "essential and fundamental."

4. *Parish-Seminary Relationship.* The committee concluded that "the relationship of the Seminary to the individual parishes is weak and underdeveloped." This was particularly true with churches outside of Pittsburgh Presbytery. The committee discovered a desire for "greater interest in lay education." A number of suggestions were made for strengthening these ties, including the suggestion that while on sabbaticals, "faculty members may well serve in parish churches to review the 'feel' of the parish." The problem of lay education provided "an interesting possibility for much greater cooperation between PTS and the nine presbyteries."

5. *Statement of Purpose.* The committee found "there are two very divisive aspects of the Purpose of the Seminary as stated in its Constitution and as practiced in its programs." The issue came down to the question: "Is PTS a graduate school of religion or a seminary *primarily* oriented to develop competent parish ministers?" The "community conclusions as evidenced in our Listening Sessions: PTS is primarily an academic graduate school of religion." The committee commented that during times of budget problems, when choices have to be made between upper-degree and lower-degree programs, determining the priorities reflected in its purpose was impossible to avoid. While in medical and dental schools it was standard practice to require students

to study with "experienced practitioners" in addition to "learned full time faculty," at Pittsburgh Seminary, "this does not seem to have been the procedure and . . . regardless of the budget problems the first degree students and parish alumni are very critical of their lack of contact with such experience in the classroom."

6. *Theological Stance.* A second "divisive aspect of the Purpose of The Seminary" was found in the purpose clause in the constitution. There were varying understandings of the seminary's purpose to instruct in "the doctrine, order, confessions and institutes of Worship taught in the Scriptures and summarily exhibited in the constitution of the United Presbyterian Church in the United States of America and in other disciplines and subjects related thereto." Some, the committee found, thought this meant that Pittsburgh Seminary should be an exclusively Presbyterian institution and that the seminary, in its diversities, was ignoring its own constitution. Alternatively, others believed the seminary should recognize "the whole gamut of Presbyterian theology from conservative to liberal and only will teach the more liberal." The committee commented that "there seems to be very little agreement among the faculty on these two issues." These were fundamental issues, and while "normally honest disagreements among faculty members on academic matters are a healthy thing, stimulating intellectual activity," this basic disagreement had become "emotional and shatters the unity of purpose of the institution. It creates warring factions unlikely to settle their differences intellectually." The committee identified two sources for these frictions: "the belief among some lay people, some alumni, and some students that PTS is really a graduate school of religion and not a seminary"; and second, "the merger of Western and Zenia [sic] which caused emotional schisms and is today particularly important among alumni and some older lay people causing them to exaggerate the differences and frictions they see within The Seminary." The importance of resolving these difficulties was underlined, with the committee insisting that "the very frequently repeated criticism about not enough Bible teaching relates more to theological position, to what understanding of the Bible is taught, than it does to the number of hours or credits required. Hence this criticism really becomes a major element in the concern about Purpose." Three "broad alternatives" were presented: "1) Continue its present liberal theological position; 2) Build a unique theologically conservative U.P. seminary; or 3) Develop a position covering the full spectrum

of U.P. theology. This is probably essential if PTS chooses to serve specifically the nine presbytery region."

7. *Curriculum.* Three groups of problems with the curriculum were identified at a time when the seminary's "financial situation forces contraction":

1. Those evolving from decisions on institutional purpose and theological stance. These have to do with priorities between advanced and beginning degree programs and decisions as to how much of the theological spectrum will be covered.
2. Those involving community service. This part of the curriculum had to do with extension education and to what extent it would be carried. The committee found more support for this program than for anything else PTS was presently doing.
3. The extent of required vs. elective courses — the extent of discipline and direction in the curriculum. There was much expression of desire for more required courses — an enlarged *core* curriculum — to prepare students more specifically for the parish ministry.

The committee also concluded that programs of field study and counseling were inadequate at that time.

8. *Organization.* The committee bluntly concluded that Pittsburgh Seminary was "an institution divided by dissension, suspicion and creditability gaps." This led to a failure to "enthuse or inspire the product — the student": "The structure and practice is rigid, missing the greatest opportunity small educational institutions have (and perhaps the only one) in being flexible to make decisions easily and with consensus because most individuals know and can respect each other." The committee received reports of students "who seemed lost, had no friends, and efforts are not made to bring them into The Seminary family. There were reports of cliques of students generally isolating themselves from other groups. There appears to be very little counseling available to students. Alumni feel left out and are often resentful. Faculty seem at odds with each other and with the Administration." There was confusion over the term "president" — as used both for the president of the Board of Directors and the president of the seminary. The committee's conclusion was that "the Chief Executive Officer (President of the Seminary) must be the leader of The Seminary in finding solutions to the problems which face

the Institution." Problems of policy and community relations were responsibilities of the Chief Executive Officer, while "the Board must share the leadership responsibility and must be fully involved in solving both types of problems." Thus the committee believed that "more leadership must come from the Board of Directors, possibly reconstituted, and meeting more frequently." In the midst of budget strains that "test the viability of PTS, it is essential for all groups to pull together and forget their jealousies and special citadels of power. Leadership in a new approach to problem solving must, and perhaps only can, come from the Board." The committee recognized that seminary alumni as well as surrounding presbyteries were not well represented on the Board.

The discussion of these problematic areas was followed by suggestions and recommendations from the Advisory Committee. These fell into four groups:

A. *Structure and Organization*

1. Change title of Board "President" to "Chairman" to avoid confusion with Seminary "President" and change Board to "Board of Trustees" to describe more precisely its character.
2. Consider the structure of the office of Chief Executive to obtain maximum leadership potential. Consider importance of full time occupation for Chief Executive.
3. Consider Board memberships to provide official representation by alumni groups and the nine Presbyteries.
4. Consider additional regular Board meetings.
5. Consider holding some Board meetings in "the field" with invitations to local supporters to participate and observe.

B. *Fundamental Policy*

1. Clearly identify the service area of PTS.
2. Expedite resolution of any ambiguities existing in the areas of Purpose and Theological position.
3. Decide the priorities of program — minister training, higher degrees, etc. — and establish the role of PTS.
4. Face the tenure issue which is inherent in any change of policy and program.

C. Programs and Procedures

1. Explore with other neighbor institutions and possibly with other Seminaries the opportunities for joint programs, joint faculty appointments etc.
2. Explore how practicing ministers might help in the teaching program and counseling.
3. Develop techniques for much fuller cross representation at official meetings of each Seminary group.
4. Develop Ad Hoc Committees with representation from all groups to consider major PTS problems. Invite known PTS critics to help.

D. Community Relations

1. Move quickly to build Presbytery support by organizing groups in each to help in reaching consensus on PTS problems. Liaison should be carried out by Board members, faculty, students and alumni as well as by Administrators.
2. Through a strong community relations program assure that the community thoroughly understands the PTS Purpose and Theological position.

The Report of the Advisory Committee, submitted to the Board of Directors, led to significant changes at Pittsburgh Seminary. These changes were programmatic and governmental, and they also focused on building bridges with the seminary's various constituencies. The Report served as a kind of wake-up call for the seminary, which, in the midst of a difficult financial situation, had to find ways to raise budgetary support, improve its governance, address issues of theology and diversity, and relate to its surrounding presbyteries, their churches, and pastors in ways that would lead them to value and respect the mission of the seminary.

Curriculum Revision

The impact of the Rea Report was immediate. Board members joined four committees to deal with the report's concerns: Purpose, Theological Stance, Service Area, and Organization. Within a month of the report's release, on April 11, 1975, the Long Range Planning Committee asked "the student council and the faculty to communicate to the committee what they see as long range implications of the Rea report and their comments on it." A week earlier, on April 4, 1975, the Council of Student Representatives had taken action to "send a letter to Board President Dwight C. Hanna asking for a chance to give input to these committees by meeting with them during April and agreed to draw up a questionnaire concerned with issues contained in the Rea Report, to be distributed to students next week." The faculty, at its April 1975 meeting, took action to "appoint a committee to critique the Rea Report for the Long Range Planning Committee and request opportunity to meet with the four sub-committees of the Board concerning the Rea Report."[68]

The Rea Report was the start of President Kadel's report to the Board of Directors on May 13, 1975. Kadel highlighted the significance of the items with which he would deal in his first words:

> This is doubtless the most important report I have made to the Board of Directors of Pittsburgh Theological Seminary since becoming its President. Its importance relates to the future of the seminary in the light of —
>
> 1) The changing character of theological education,
> 2) The proposed new M.Div. curriculum,
> 3) The Advisory Committee report,
> 4) Reflections on four year's experience with the present governance style, and
> 5) The reduction of the number of faculty and administration personnel.[69]

Kadel highlighted the 1972 new standards adopted by the Association of Theological Schools to emphasize for the "profession" of ministry the acquisition of skills. These were referred to as a "readiness for ministry" model. Kadel said that

---

68. These actions are cited in William H. Kadel, "Report of the President," Pittsburgh Theological Seminary (May 13, 1975), 4.

69. Kadel, "Report of the President," Pittsburgh Theological Seminary (May 13, 1975), 1.

The Round Table (1971-1978)

earlier the theological curriculum was concerned more specifically with the acquisition of certain knowledge. Today the curriculum has a more holistic focus: on the total preparation of men and women for the gospel ministry.

Methodologically the theological education of yesteryear was primarily accomplished in "the schoolhouse." Today theological educators are striving for more effective ways to prepare more effective practitioners with the additional emphases on field education, inductive learning, case studies, etc.[70]

Kadel went on to list Rea Report quotations from the nine presbyteries that, he said, "call the seminary to this task." These focused on the need for the seminary to prepare pastors for the pastoral ministry. Kadel's comment was that

The majority of our faculty are committed to these objectives. A few still hold to more classical views. The inability to live creatively with the tension caused by these divergent points of view and the inability of those holding a minority view to accept the value of this professional approach to theological education is the cause of much of the unrest within our faculty. Something must be done about this.[71]

The highlighting of the faculty disagreements here, both in terms of the content of the theological curriculum and its purposes, reflects the fact that the curriculum was again being evaluated by the faculty. A new curriculum was presented to the Board at this May meeting.

The movement to review the "elective" curriculum began with the recommendation of the Curriculum Committee to the faculty to appoint a committee to "propose revisions and/or redesign the M.Div. program with respect to goals, content and methodology within the total resources of the institution."[72] The dissatisfaction with the 1969-70 curriculum centered on the recognition that there was no "core" to the curriculum, or

---

70. Kadel, "Report of the President," Pittsburgh Theological Seminary (May 13, 1975), 1.

71. Kadel, "Report of the President," Pittsburgh Theological Seminary (May 13, 1975), 2.

72. "Minutes of the Faculty," Pittsburgh Theological Seminary (May 10, 1974), 2, cited in Brown, "Curricular Change at Pittsburgh Theological Seminary," 99.

any structure that would enable faculty to develop upper-level courses, since they could not assume a common reservoir of knowledge among students who took upper-level courses. It was not clear how the "elective" curriculum related to the goals of educating students for the professional ministry, since there was no necessary direct correlation between the students' course work and their preparations for ministry. Also, the Curriculum Committee said, there was a "lack of a sense of community centered in the academic program." A core curriculum was supposed to provide an opportunity for this sense of community to emerge.[73]

A number of committee hearings were held throughout 1974 to involve the seminary community in curriculum study. Various groups such as clergy, laity, current students, faculty, administrators, black seminarians, the Association of Women Seminarians, and others were invited to indicate what competencies they believed were required for "readiness for ministry." By April 25, 1975, a new M.Div. curriculum had been designed and recommended to the faculty. This curriculum now featured a three-term calendar and a structured core curriculum. The faculty approved the curriculum by a two-thirds vote, and on September 3-4, when it was considered again, only two faculty members voted against it.[74] It was to go into effect in September 1976.

President Kadel supported the new curriculum, and in the spring he sent the Board of Directors ten reasons why he fully endorsed the new proposal. These included that the new curriculum was emerging with "inputs" from the church; that it would enable a better preparation of students for ministry; and that it would establish a sense of community.[75] Kadel told the Board of Directors in May that "the needs of the church should be more determinative than the needs of the seminary in designing our program."[76]

---

73. These points were drawn from the "Report from the Curriculum Committee to the Faculty for Faculty Action," Pittsburgh Theological Seminary (April 25, 1975), 1, cited in Brown, "Curricular Change at Pittsburgh Theological Seminary," 99.

74. See Brown, "Curricular Change at Pittsburgh Theological Seminary," 100, which indicates that those who cast the two negative votes indicated that they could live with the majority decision.

75. Brown, "Curricular Change at Pittsburgh Theological Seminary," 100, citing Kadel's memo to the Board, "Proposed New Curriculum" (April 17, 1975).

76. Kadel, "Report of the President," Pittsburgh Theological Seminary (May 13, 1975), 3.

The Round Table (1971-1978)

Curriculum revision had been underway even as the Rea Report was coming together. Also, in 1972 the American Association of Theological Schools had established a set of "thirteen abilities" which all theological institutions were to foster in students. These "educational outcomes" for students were for the Master of Divinity program, which was designed "primarily to prepare men and women for effective ministries of church and synagogue."[77] These formed the basis for the "readiness for ministry" model which became the dominant paradigm for theological education by AATS member schools in the 1970s. All these factors came together in the shaping of a new direction for the seminary.

The Pittsburgh Seminary catalogue stated that "it is a fundamental assumption of the [new M.Div.] program that preparation for ministry in the United Presbyterian Church and other denominations cannot be separated from engagement in ministry itself." Thus, the "curriculum is designed to guide the student through a pattern of course work and experience which will lead him or her to a basic professional competency with which to begin the ordained ministry." The "educational outcomes" described in the catalogue pick up the thirteen "abilities" cited by AATS and modify a number of them for the Pittsburgh M.Div.:

- The ability to understand and make use of the basic documents of faith emphasizing scripture as well as the creeds and traditions of the church.
- The ability to communicate through preaching, writing and teaching, and to counsel and provide leadership in the program and administrative arenas, fostered by the course work in the Pastoral Studies and Professional and Personal Development sequences.
- The ability to understand in theological terms the sociological, ideological and political content of the cultures in which the church ministers.
- The ability to think theologically.
- The ability to practice ministry in an appropriate professional style.[78]

---

77. "A.A.T.S. Goals and Objectives for the Master of Divinity Program," *Bulletin*, Part 3, 1972. The complete document is provided in Brown, "Curricular Change at Pittsburgh Theological Seminary," Appendix F.

78. Catalogue, Pittsburgh Theological Seminary, 1978-80, "First Degree Programs."

President Kadel, describing the new curriculum, said that "the whole spectrum of ministerial functions requires the integration of knowledge, skills, and self-understanding. The curriculum must help make this happen, and our new program is meant to achieve this goal."[79]

Courses were now to be taught in three ten-week terms, instead of two fifteen-week terms. The new curriculum required 106 term hours, and students were required to complete a full academic year of supervised seminary-approved field education during their middler year. The courses were distributed as follows:

Junior Year

Term I

Church and Society (Local & Regional)	3
Biblical Studies I (OT)	3
Language	2
Theological Studies I	3
	(11)

Term II

Church and Society (National)	3
Biblical Studies II (NT)	3
Language	2
Historical Studies I	3
	(11)

Term III

Church and Society (Global)	3
Theological Studies II	3
Exegesis (or elective)	3
Historical Studies II	3
	(12)

Middler Year

Term I

Pastoral Studies (Education)	3
Theological Studies III	3

---

79. William H. Kadel, untitled address delivered as the opening convocation address, Pittsburgh Theological Seminary (September 5, 1975), 8, cited in Brown, "Curricular Change at Pittsburgh Theological Seminary," 103.

Biblical Studies III (NT)	3
Elective	3
	(12)

Term II

Pastoral Studies (Pastoral Care)	3
Christian Ethics	3
Biblical Studies IV (OT)	3
Elective	3
	(12)

Term III

Pastoral Studies (Homiletics)	3
Historical Studies III	3
Elective	3
Elective	3
	(12)

Senior Year

Term I

Professional & Personal Development (Credo)	3
Elective	3
Elective	3
Elective	3
	(12)

Term II

Professional & Personal Development (Faith)	3
Elective	3
Elective	3
Elective	3
	(12)

Term III

Professional & Personal Development (Ministerial Leadership)	3
Elective	3
Elective	3
Elective	3
	(12)

From the electives, students were required to take one additional course in theology and one additional course in ethics. Greek or Hebrew were required courses with students strongly encouraged to take both languages.[80]

The significant changes in the new curriculum were noted to the Board in its fall 1976 meeting. The faculty, the Board was told, "is committed to providing an educational program that enables the student to develop knowledge, skills and self understanding. We are convinced that the revised curriculum will overcome areas of weakness in the elective curriculum and provide a core of courses upon which students can build advance-level educational experiences."[81] The major changes were:

> We have gone from a two semester year to a three-year term, giving in each year three more weeks of study. Students are now able to take 36 courses instead of 26 courses under the semester plan.
> We have gone from an elective curriculum to one that is 60-65% required.
> In the first year each student is required to take courses in Church and Society which focus on the context of ministry from the local, national and inter-national perspectives.
> In the second year each student is required to take supervised field education. The studies of that year are related to their work in field education with special emphasis on Christian Education, Pastoral Care, and Homiletics.
> In the third year there is a deliberate focus on seminar groups concerned with professional and personal development. Attention is given to helping students clarify their own personal faith position, to their spiritual development, and to their ministerial leadership responsibilities.
> Finally, there is now an added requirement by Pittsburgh Seminary that every M.Div. student pass an examination in the content of the English Bible, before he or she is graduated.
> The redesigned curriculum has in no way changed the basics

---

80. See PTS catalogues subsequent to 1976. Cf. Brown, "Curricular Change at Pittsburgh Theological Seminary," 104.

81. "Board of Directors Minutes," Pittsburgh Theological Seminary (November 17, 1976), 9.

of a sound theological education grounding students in understanding the fundamentals of the Christian faith. The required courses in every major field from Biblical studies through Ethics provide the foundation upon which all other theological thinking and study is based. This still leaves time for a sufficient number of electives for students to pursue in those particular fields of study of most interest to them personally.[82]

The key concept for the curriculum was "readiness for ministry." The three-course sequence in the Junior year with a "Church and Society" course in each term provided the context for ministry. In the second year, the three-course sequence was devoted to Pastoral Studies: Education, Pastoral Care (to be taken in conjunction with Field experience), and Homiletics. In the senior year, attention was paid to helping students articulate their theological positions with courses in Professional and Personal Development: Credo, Faith Formation, and Ministerial Leadership. In sum, the Master of Divinity curriculum sought to combine classical disciplines with contemporary cultural concerns with the overall aim of preparing students for the practice of ministry — primarily in the ordained ministries of the United Presbyterian church.

Purpose and Governance

Statement of Purpose

The confluence of the many factors that were backgrounds to curriculum change also included a new statement of purpose for Pittsburgh Theological Seminary, adopted by the Board of Directors on May 13, 1975. This statement picked up concerns by the Rea Report for the seminary to understand its identity and build bridges to its constituencies in the United Presbyterian Church. While Pittsburgh Seminary continued to welcome students from a variety of denominations, including international students, the Board emphasized in the new purpose statement what the "primary" focus of the institution would be. Among the important aspects of the purpose statement were:

---

82. "Board of Directors Minutes," Pittsburgh Theological Seminary (November 17, 1976), 9.

Article II. Purpose and Scope

Accordingly, it is affirmed that this institution is a United Presbyterian Theological Seminary and that, therefore, its primary purpose is to prepare pastors for the United Presbyterian ministry. In light of this controlling purpose, it is further affirmed:

1. That the curriculum shall provide a basic course in preparation for the United Presbyterian ministry (and the consequent denominational examinations)....
2. That for the attainment of this purpose the Seminary shall provide instruction in the knowledge of the Old and New Testaments and of the doctrine, order, confessions and institutes of Worship taught in the Scriptures and summarily exhibited in the Constitution of the United Presbyterian Church in the United States of America and in other disciplines and subjects related to ministry, in order properly to prepare its students in the work of the Church.

Article III

It is further believed to be the purpose of Pittsburgh Theological Seminary:

1. To prepare the leadership of the Church so that they may demonstrate both personal piety and the keenest possible intellectual understanding of the Gospel and its implications for individual and social living.
2. To promote the peace, unity and purity of the Church among the ministers of the church.
3. To develop a Christian community at the Seminary and to lay the foundation of early and lasting friendships, productive of confidence and mutual assistance among ministers.
4. And finally, to endeavor to provide a succession of graduates at once qualified for and thoroughly committed to the work of the Gospel ministry.[83]

---

83. "Board of Directors Minutes," Pittsburgh Theological Seminary (May 13, 1975). The text is also reproduced in Brown, "Curricular Change at Pittsburgh Theological Seminary," Appendix D.

The Round Table (1971-1978)

The strong emphasis on the Presbyterian character of Pittsburgh Seminary was a response to the drastic concerns raised by the Rea Report. The seminary was signaling that it was taking seriously its relationship to the denomination and to the preparation of students for ministry who were "ready" intellectually, theologically, and spiritually. Other aspects of the purpose statement indicated the seminary's role in providing continuing education for laity, especially United Presbyterian laity, as well as its commitment to keeping the United Presbyterian Church informed theologically, through its graduates and as requested in other ways. The new purpose statement did not focus on altering society, as had been a major concern when the elective curriculum was adopted in 1969-70. Now denominational consciousness played the major role, along with an ecumenical readiness. Now the emphasis was on the student who was to be formed intellectually and spiritually and who needed to demonstrate "Readiness for Ministry," rather than on the students' "freedom" to pursue a course of study to equip them to be "enablers." More traditional understandings of ministry now came into focus. The work of the curriculum was to enable the purposes of the seminary to be carried out in service to the church.

Governance

The work of developing the curriculum took place through the various seminary committees and administrative structures. The issue of governance had been raised in the Rea Report, and in President Kadel's report to the Board of Directors on May 13, 1975, he reflected on four years' experience with the new governance style.

Kadel's comments in May 1975 should be read in light of the fact that on April 24, 1975, he had informed the Executive Committee of the Board of his intention to retire. Initially, Kadel had come one afternoon to the office of Dr. Dwight ("Pete") Hanna, the chair of the Board, while Hanna was seeing patients, to tell Hanna he wanted to resign. Hanna sent his patients home and tried to persuade Kadel to reconsider. At its May 13 meeting, the Board adopted a statement urging Kadel to withdraw his resignation and continue as president of the institution, and moved the Board communicate to Dr. Kadel its "full confidence in his administration of this institution." Kadel was persuaded to withdraw his resignation. At that meeting, a $12,146 surplus for the budget was reported, a sign that perhaps a better financial picture was emerging.

President Kadel's reflections on the four years of the community model of governance at the seminary presupposed that the model was, in Kadel's view,

> sound from both a theological and theoretical point of view. It affirms the importance of all members and each functional group within the community. It protects those who live and work in the seminary from the possible dangers of autocratic and unilateral decisions. It shares power and helpfully informs the decision making process. We have been operating under this constitution for four years and the time has come for an honest review of the process.[84]

Kadel went on to indicate that educational experts were now recognizing problems with the community model, though "no one seems to have designed a new model to date."

For Kadel, the problems of governance at Pittsburgh Seminary were "not theological or theoretical. They are practical." This is because

> The "open process" requires a high level of trust between members of the community, which is a commodity in reasonably short supply. It is a system which can be manipulated by those who seek to become centers of power for their own reasons and who would be as autocratic in the use of power as the chief administrators of the old institutional model, from whom power was "taken" by the revolution of the sixties. So that, in practice, instead of shared power, there is the danger of simply changing the power center. At the same time, accountability structures have not emerged to parallel the changed loci of responsibility.[85]

Kadel spoke specifically about the "evident problems" at Pittsburgh Seminary: "The faculty has been called upon to spend too much time in decision making at the expense of their primary teaching, advising and scholarly responsibilities." Student input in the open process "is limited because of their limited time at the seminary."

---

84. "Report of the President," Pittsburgh Theological Seminary (May 13, 1975), 5.
85. "Report of the President," Pittsburgh Theological Seminary (May 13, 1975), 5.

The Round Table (1971-1978)

Other problems Kadel cited included the "shrinking of resources (both human and financial), the difficulty of projecting the economic future, the need for flexibility in decision making and the problem of communication." His illustration was the "painful decisions in the spring of 1974" to cut positions. By fall 1974, when a first proposal for the 1975-76 fiscal budget was made, "the economic picture had not improved — if anything it had worsened." But by spring 1975, "it had considerably improved beyond any reasonable expectations." Kadel noted that while those who worked with the finances daily saw how things were emerging, "others get only periodic insights into the changing situation — and the emotional stress placed upon them is traumatic. New problems are created which require more time of persons involved in decision making and which overload an already inadequate communications system."[86]

Kadel continued, "I do not believe the administration of PTS is 'threatened' by a sense of the loss of power. I am personally very happy in the 'shared' process. I feel that the judgment of a group of our community is apt to be superior in value to the decision of any one member of the community." The frustration was, from Kadel's point of view, that the administrative was to be held to "ultimate accountability" for seeing to the "good order of the seminary and all its activities (By-Laws Article V, Section 3.a.12);" yet, on the other hand, there was the experience of the "frustrations created by the complexities of a process that 'makes haste very slowly.'"

President Kadel noted what he perceived were two problems with the Board of Directors and the present governance style. One was that while the Board adopted a "community model" for the seminary, most of the Board was experienced with the "institutional model," and Kadel was "not quite sure their sympathies are with the system they have adopted. Hence, the weaknesses of the community model create a higher level of anxiety with Board members than with faculty/student/administration types." A second difficulty, Kadel believed, was that Board members gave of their time and resources voluntarily, while for faculty, students, and administration, the seminary was the primary focus. So what was "avocational" for the Board was "vocational" for the others. Thus, said Kadel, "Board members find it difficult to invest the

---

86. "Report of the President," Pittsburgh Theological Seminary (May 13, 1975), 6.

amount of time which the community model requires for substantial involvement in the decision making process."

Kadel was not finished being candid with the Board. He mentioned that a new governance model was called for that could deal with the problems of the current governance model. He envisioned that the new paradigm would give the Board a more decisive place in establishing directions for the institution. Yet Kadel warned of problems ahead, illustrating his point with an unpleasant outcome from the recent work of the Curriculum Committee. There

> the process bogged down and the work of the past year was nearly immobilized. Student members of the committee had pretty much "gotten themselves together" but the faculty members were at serious odds. In my role as president I made a direct intervention. I asked the dean to call the faculty members of the Curriculum Committee together so that I might "strongly" urge them to come to some agreement. This action was enough to cause one faculty member to resign from the committee partly with reference to, and I quote from his memorandum to the faculty at its most recent meeting, "the President's recent mandate from the Board to govern with a strong hand; I have no quarrel with the concept of a strong president; I do question the appropriateness of the way that new stance has manifested itself in curriculum matters."[87]

Thus, cautioned Kadel, "the immediate future will not be painless, but the long range future requires some new posture of Board leadership." This led President Kadel to a difficult conclusion:

> It is with sadness I report my conviction that there are some individuals of our seminary faculty who cannot be reconciled with other members. Diversity is expected and open sharing of divergent points of view enriches any group. But when differences of opinion end up in recrimination and lack of respect, then reconciliation is impossible.
>
> The time has come for clear decisions as to who we are at Pittsburgh Theological Seminary and any and all who cannot

---

87. "Report of the President," Pittsburgh Theological Seminary (May 13, 1975), 6.

join in that community self-understanding and enterprise should be encouraged to seek vocational opportunity in other places.[88]

The admission of irreconcilable differences was difficult for a president of a theological seminary. It was a difficult ethos for the whole Pittsburgh Seminary community. The Board report of the Student Body President, Frank McGahey, had emphasized the "confusions" felt by the student body in 1974-75 with the transitions in curriculum, the Rea Report, and the resignation of David Buttrick, which "left many feeling a sense of crisis." When the financial situation started to improve, McGahey said that "the quick decisions of the fall" ["to release several of the administrative and operational people, because of the bleak economic picture"] "seem to have been too hasty." All these factors together, he said, meant that "at many occasions there was a feeling that it was time to cry out, 'What are we doing here?'"[89]

Given these cutbacks, Kadel observed that " the process of decision making must be streamlined, time spent in decision making processes must be shortened and the needs of the program must supercede [sic] individual agendas. And we must rebuild where we have been forced to 'cut back' at the earliest possible time."[90]

Transitions

The Board of Directors authorized an interim governance system which was designed by the Executive Committee in June 1975. The 1975-76 academic year was marked by the transition into this new form of seminary governance, as well as a transition into the newly designed "readiness for ministry" curriculum. As could be expected, difficulties and uncertainties followed along.

President Kadel reported these challenges in his May 4, 1976, report to the Board of Directors. The new curriculum was being tested during this year, prior to its implementation in September 1976. Kadel

---

88. "Report of the President," Pittsburgh Theological Seminary (May 13, 1975), 7.

89. Frank McGahey, "Report of the Student Body," in "Board of Directors Minutes," Pittsburgh Theological Seminary (May 13, 1975).

90. "Board of Directors Minutes," Pittsburgh Theological Seminary (May 13, 1975), 7.

said that "faculty and students are working with the new curriculum, and the experience is at times frustrating, and anxiety producing. But the 'bugs' are being worked out and a system has been designed for evaluation with the 'learnings' to be applied for the perfecting of the program."[91]

Kadel reported that the experience with the interim governance pattern had made the students feel

> powerless and faculty and students have been anxious about the new Constitution and By-Laws. Life has not been a "bed of roses" for the administration, but it is my feeling that the "rough times" have been minimal granted the realities with which we have been living. There seems to be the will to work together and that is good. And we have had enough good experiences together that the basis for a higher level of trust seems to exist. Response to more rigorous leadership made possible with the interim governance system seems to be more affirmative than negative. The future in these regards seems positive.[92]

Thus, despite the difficulties, Kadel sensed a higher level of optimism and collegiality.

At the May 4 Board meeting, a new governance system was adopted, with a new constitution and bylaws. The title of the head of the Board was changed to "Chairman," indicating clearly that the president of the seminary was the chief executive officer. Students and faculty members in committees of the Board and administration were now given "consultative" status, unless voting power was specifically granted. While the work of the Board continued to be done in committees with broad powers to act within their limits, the basic decisions were reserved for the whole Board or its Executive Committee.

The 1976-77 academic year saw the proposal for a major fundraising campaign. In March 1977, at a special meeting, the Board pledged full participation in a "Turning to the Future" capital funds campaign. The program, to raise ten million dollars, was put in the hands of the Ketchum company.

On campus, the Student Association and the faculty took stands

---

91. "Report of the President," Pittsburgh Theological Seminary (May 4, 1976), 1.
92. "Report of the President," Pittsburgh Theological Seminary (May 4, 1976), 1.

The Round Table (1971-1978)

against discrimination in admissions on the basis of personal sexual morality. At the November 1976 Board meeting, however, the Board passed a resolution in support of the president in refusing admission to avowed homosexuals. Out of these actions, a task force to study homosexuality was established.[93]

This issue and others led to some tensions in Board-faculty relations. President Kadel reported in May 1977 that

> assuming some resolution to the seminary's financial dilemma, the next most important item on the seminary's agenda is continued work to improve the relationship between members of the Board and members of the faculty. Honesty requires that I report a basic cleavage between these two "groups" of very important people. I may be wrong and I earnestly pray that I am. But I sense a level of distrust and suspicion which is two directional. Faculty members fear the power of the Board will be used arbitrarily and that the Board perceives them as "hired help"; Board members cannot understand why faculty do not attend chapel regularly, setting an example for students, why they are not one in spirit, and there is even a readiness to believe that some are not sound in the faith. From my perspective, we have good (no one is perfect) people in both of these groups. And the way to better relations is through person-to-person knowing, and sharing with, one another. We have begun a program of one-on-one visits. My thanks to those who are participating in this venture. But more will need to be done over a longer period of time. The continued health of PTS will rest in large measure, this is my judgment, on the success of this undertaking. I pray God for his help in this matter.[94]

Outside evaluations of the seminary continued. In May 1977, the report of the Middles States accrediting visit was made. The seminary's new Doctor of Ministry program received full accreditation, and a reaffirmation of the accreditation of the other seminary educational program was passed. Yet difficulties in morale were not helped by the re-

---

93. "Board of Directors Minutes," Pittsburgh Theological Seminary (November 17, 1976).

94. "Report of the President," Pittsburgh Theological Seminary (May 24, 1977), 7.

port of "The Futures Committee" that the campaign was not performing well, and that it doubted that even $2 million could be raised. The president reported that "while the hostility and anger directed at PTS during the last two decades has subsided, the confidence of many 'potential large gift' contributors so needful in a campaign like this has not returned and rebuilding it will take a long time.[95] This led to the termination of Ketchum's work and the campaign the following year. The money that was raised, however, added to endowment funds and did fund some of the property maintenance work, which was badly needed.

By Fall 1977, the Board was able to lift the moratorium on tenure. During this period, an Investment Committee was established as a subcommittee of the Board's Finance Committee to help manage the seminary's endowment fund. To this point, income from the endowment had been used for operations. But budgeting in advance was a problem, since the income to be earned in the next year was unknown. A new policy was put in place to provide for a fixed percentage of the total value of the endowment, as determined by a formula, to be transferred into the seminary's operating fund for yearly expenses. This allowed the financial needs of the operational budget to be set with certainty, while also permitting the fund for long-term growth to be managed as an investment. This would increase the total value of the fund.[96]

Also, some of the bequests made to Pittsburgh-Xenia and Western Seminaries continued to mature, some in substantial amounts. Church and individual giving began to improve as the seminary sought to make better connections with presbyteries and individual congregations. As these elements began to bear results, President Kadel was able to say to the Board on November 16, 1977:

> By and large the morale of the seminary community is good. There will always be a few exceptions to such a generalization — and there are now. But comparatively speaking from the Spring of 1971 to the Fall of 1977 is like climbing from the hot desert around the Dead Sea at high noon on a summer day to the refreshing coolness of that evening on the top of Mt. Scopus in Je-

---

95. "Board of Directors Minutes," Pittsburgh Theological Seminary (May 16, 1977).
96. Herchenroether, "Pittsburgh Theological Seminary 1959-1999," 25.

The Round Table (1971-1978)

rusalem: the view is so much better, the atmosphere so much more comfortable, and one senses himself a little bit closer to God. May it be so![97]

Evaluation of the Rea Report

The changes the seminary was making after the "wake-up call" of the Rea Report in 1975 were carried out in a number of ways. In early 1978, the Executive Committee of the Board had appointed a committee of three Board members, chaired by Marianne L. Wolfe, to evaluate the Board and administration response to the recommendations of the Rea Report. This committee studied Board documents that reflected actions taken as a response to the report, and it interviewed persons connected with the report or implementation of its findings. The small committee made its report to the Board in two parts, on May 23 and November 15, 1978. The Evaluation Committee found the following in relation to the concerns of the Rea Committee[98]:

1. *Shortage of Funds.* The capital campaign was successful for its purpose of raising funds and was accompanied by a public-relations campaign to address funding problems. Tuition increases were enacted, and greater attention was paid to student financial aid. In the 1978-79 year, tuition would be raised 23 percent.
2. *Community Reactions* and 4. *Parish-Seminary Relationships.* In 1978, Pittsburgh Seminary hired a full-time director of Continuing and Lay Education. A lay education program, in cooperation with Pittsburgh Presbytery, was enacted. Additionally, the field education program for M.Div. students was strengthened and a full-time Director of Field Education was to be hired for the 1978-79 year. Twenty-two of twenty-four faculty participated in some

---

97. "Report of the President," Pittsburgh Theological Seminary (November 16, 1977), 6.

98. Quotes and references are to "Evaluation of the Rea Report" (May 23, 1978), and "Report to the Board of Directors of Pittsburgh Theological Seminary, November 15, 1978, by The Committee to Evaluate Progress on the Rea Report Recommendations," Part II.

form of local church leadership. The committee wrote that "both the lay and ministerial communities are realizing that the seminary has a direct relationship to their areas of need as it develops essential support programs and services." The Seminary's Doctor of Ministry program was another source of strengthening ties with pastors and churches.

3. *Service Region.* The Rea Report indicated that the seminary's natural service area was the nine presbyteries in the surrounding Pittsburgh region. The Board, on November 19, 1975, said that "in recruiting for the M.Div. Program, this should continue to be nation-wide and world-wide, as far as possible, to draw students from a variety of areas, representing the spectrum of theological positions within the U.P. church and recruiting U.P. minorities and women." In addition, in light of the high concentration of United Presbyterians in the geographical area surrounding Pittsburgh, a "greater effort" should be made to encourage students from this area to attend Pittsburgh Seminary. The Board also determined that directors should be recruited nationwide and that directors and students should represent the spectrum of theological views held within the United Presbyterian Church. The alumni association was asked to elect annually one alumnus/a for a three-year term on the Board. In 1977, a "President's Round Table" advisory group was established to broaden participation of clergy and laity in the seminary's life. On March 1, 1977, eighteen people met to share perceptions and advice for the president.[99]

5. *Statement of Purpose.* The Board's amendment of the constitution in 1976 made it clear that the seminary's purpose was to prepare pastors for the United Presbyterian Church and provide continuing education for clergy and laity, especially Presbyterians. Joint degree programs with local universities provided opportunities for students who sought specialized ministries outside the parish.

6. *Theological stance.* The clarification of the constitution in

---

99. Pittsburgh Seminary "Panorama" (April 1977).

The Round Table (1971-1978)

1976 to indicate that Pittsburgh Seminary was a seminary of the United Presbyterian Church meant that its theological stance was defined in relation to the denomination's *Book of Confessions.* On November 19, 1975, the Board said that "diversity of theological views within the framework of these confessions is inevitable. That there is considerable diversity of theological views within the Seminary is evident. . . . It is of critical importance that those holding different theological viewpoints . . . respect one another, accept criticism of one another's views in a Christian spirit . . . and be tolerant of those views. . . . The Seminary should be a visible Christian witness that in Christ there is unity in diversity." The Board further said that "at least 75% of all persons recommended for employment as faculty should be from the UPCUSA or be members of churches associated with the World Alliance of Reformed Churches for the next five years until at least 2/3's portion of the faculty is of that reformed group."

7. *Curriculum.* At the time the Evaluation Committee reported, it was not possible to assess the values of the newly instituted curriculum. But the Evaluation Committee stated that "there can be no doubt that Rea report recommendations were addressed."

8. *Organization.* The changes in the constitution and bylaws, adopted on May 4, 1976, addressed the Rea Report's concern about confusion of titles and the lines of authority. The president of the seminary was the institution's chief executive officer. The role of students in the decision-making process was modified as well, "maintaining student input, but taking away much voting power."[100]

The evaluation of the work done toward implementing the findings of the Rea Report indicated that Pittsburgh Seminary was seeking ways of addressing the crucial needs that the report had uncovered. After

---

100. It was noted orally by Mr. Rea that "local pastors and other Presbyterians thought the Faculty was running the Seminary, a perception due to a large extent to the perceived difference between the authority and the responsibility of the President of the Seminary." See Herchenroether, "Pittsburgh Theological Seminary 1959-1999," 22.

three years, and the many difficulties of moving into a new curriculum and facing other internal problems, the assessment of the Evaluation Committee came out as a positive portrayal of the strides that had been taken.

End of a Presidential Era

The final transition of this period was the retirement of William Kadel, announced in early 1978, to take effect on December 31, 1978. On November 14, 1978, a Kadel retirement banquet was held at the seminary. Meanwhile the Board, on May 23, 1978, established procedures for seeking and calling a new president. The Presidential Search Committee included Board, faculty, and student members. While the hope was that a new president could be called soon after Kadel's retirement, it was clear by the time of the November 1978 Board meeting that this would not be possible. W. Paul Ludwig, chair of the Board and a prominent retired Pittsburgh Presbyterian minister, was named interim president. He was to work with President Kadel through December. Kadel was named President Emeritus.

Kadel began his last report to the Board this way:

> The Oxford Illustrated Dictionary indicates that a legend dating way back states that a swan is supposed to sing *melodiously* just before its death. In modern vernacular a person's swan song is the last production of that person — especially one of artistic accomplishment. Since I am not in the artistic field, neither can I sing melodiously, and this report is not a production, and by God's grace, there are many things I have in mind doing before crossing the great river, this is not my swan song. It is simply my final report to the Board of Directors as President of Pittsburgh Theological Seminary.[101]

In his report, Kadel highlighted items of special interest, including the work of the women's center and shelter housed in the basement of Fisher Hall. Kadel noted that "from January 1 to September 30, 1978

---

101. "Report of the President," Pittsburgh Theological Seminary (November 15, 1978), 1.

The Round Table (1971-1978)

4,456 nights of shelter were provided, 1,937 for women and 2,519 for children. 10,346 phone calls were received on the 24 hour hotline."

Funding for two named chairs had been established. One was the Scharfe Chair in Homiletics, in honor of Dr. Howard C. Scharfe. The first holder of the chair would be Dr. Richard J. Oman, who was named to the chair on October 2, 1978 and would begin teaching in Term II. The other, the William F. Orr Chair in New Testament, would be established on November 29, 1978, with Dr. Douglas R. A. Hare to be installed as its first occupant.

Kadel's comments indicated his perceptions of the broad current of movements in the seminary during his administration:

> These have been interesting years, to say the least. We have moved from confrontation to cooperation, as a lifestyle, from unclarity to confidence about the theological task, from radical fragmentation to less radical fragmentation (as a community), from anger and hostility to acceptance and support from our constituency, from a position of uncertainty to one of relative security about the continuation of PTS as a viable seminary of the UPCUSA.[102]

Kadel went on to list seven hopes he had for the future of Pittsburgh Seminary. His final point was:

> *I express the hope that my successor will find as much satisfaction in the ministry he/she will be able to offer to the church through the office of President of PTS as I have.* In saying this, I am not forgetting the problems and hurts of living in such days as we have experienced in past years. It has been a matter, as George Matheson said many years ago, of "tracing the rainbow through the rain" and of feeling "the promise is not vain." My deep thanks to the Board members for their confidence in and support of my administration! My unbounding gratitude to God for his faithfulness to me. But for his grace, I could leave here an angry person! Because of my perception of his constant presence, I leave this responsibility with gratitude to my colleagues of the faculty, ad-

---

102. "Report of the President," Pittsburgh Theological Seminary (November 15, 1978), 3.

ministration, staff, and student body for their devotion to our common cause and with a good feeling about the future of Pittsburgh Theological Seminary.[103]

Faculty

The Kadel years at Pittsburgh Seminary saw the coming of a number of faculty members. John Wiley Nelson taught theology at the seminary from 1971 through 1979. From 1971 until 1975, the distinguished Barth scholar Arthur C. Cochrane taught theology and later returned to Dubuque, Iowa, to teach at Wartburg Seminary, having taught at the University of Dubuque Theological Seminary before coming to Pittsburgh. John S. Walker taught Black Studies for the 1971-72 year and Samuel K. Roberts taught the Sociology of Religion from 1973 to 1976, the first professor to teach that subject. Roberts was succeeded by Gonzalo Castillo-Cardenas, who began teaching in 1973 and taught in the Church and Ministry Division until his retirement in 2004. M. Harjie Likens taught Church and Ministry from 1973 to 1998. From 1977 to 1990, Marjorie Suchocki taught Theology. Also joining the faculty in 1977 was Ulrich W. Mauser in New Testament, who later served as dean from 1981 until 1990. Charles B. Partee was called to teach Church History, until his retirement in 2009.

Among those who served as administrators in these years were William Phillippe, Frank T. Hainer, Joseph D. Small III, and Richard J. Rapp. Rapp directed the Doctor of Ministry and Continuing Education programs. After his death, his work in Continuing Education was assumed by his wife, Jeannette, who also coordinated special events. George Tutweiler began to serve as the Seminary's organist and lecturer in Church Music and Methodist Studies after the retirement of Howard L. Ralston, who had served both Pittsburgh-Xenia and Western Seminaries from 1960 until 1972.

Others who retired during this period were long-serving faculty members Sidney O. Hills (1954-75), John M. Bald (1957-77), and William A. Nicolson (1960-75)

---

103. "Report of the President," Pittsburgh Theological Seminary (November 15, 1978), 7.

The Round Table (1971-1978)

During the Kadel years, other seminary faculty members departed. Markus Barth left to teach at Basel in 1972, the same year that Lynn Boyd Hinds resigned. David Buttrick left for St. Meinrad Seminary in 1975. Harold E. Scott, who had joined the Pittsburgh-Xenia faculty in 1959, became the General Presbyter of Pittsburgh Presbytery in 1978. Robert Paul left to teach at Austin Seminary in 1977, and Ford Lewis Battles left in 1978 for Calvin Seminary.

Students Speak

The reverberations of the turmoil of the 1960s coupled with the open, participatory style of leadership from President Kadel gave students at Pittsburgh Seminary a prominent role to play during most of the decade of the 1970s. As the seminary struggled to continue to join together two educational and ecclesiastical traditions from the Presbyterian church merger (1958) and the consolidation of the two seminaries (1959), stresses within the faculty and administration permeated student life as well. The change to the elective curriculum gave students a sense of finding their own paths in theological education, but without good guidance, it seemed, for many during the early Kadel years. The introduction of the new curriculum, which had more structure and direction, was marked initially by a period of transition in which many students still felt adrift until the new rhythms of a three-term academic year began to take hold in the seminary community.

One student who attended the seminary at the end of the 1960s and beginning of the 1970s said, "We went through many changes in the administration. Don Miller left after my first year, and all hell broke out among the faculty (in-fighting). I experienced several deans and found my curriculum changing each semester — that drove me a little nuts. The requirements for graduation were in flux with students able to choose most of their courses — the 'core' requirements were too thin. You could graduate without taking one Bible course."

In general, the seminary was perceived by many students as being "strong into concerns about the Vietnam War and societal issues including civil rights and concerns for the poor and less fortunate." This led one student from this period to comment that "because of the war concerns, it seemed to me that the classes and extra-curricular activi-

**Repairing the Rooster on the
Hicks Family Memorial Chapel**

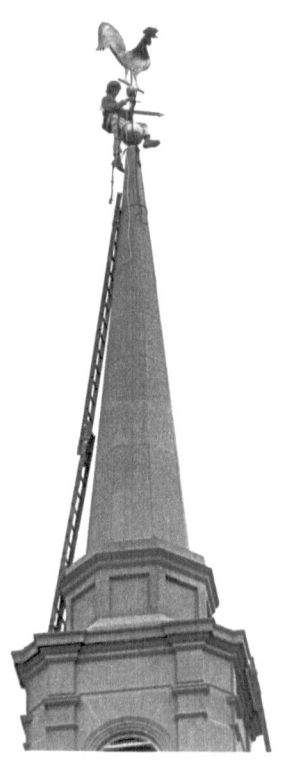

ties at this time were directed more at solving the secular and political concerns than preparing students for typical pastoral positions in churches. It seemed to me then (and still does) that there was far more discussion between faculty and students, and between students themselves, dealing with societal ills than theological issues." Another student commented, though, that among his best memories from his student years were "the controversy around the Berrigan brothers and the play the Catonsville Nine, participation in the march in Pittsburgh for African-American participation in the labors unions, and participation in the anti-war protest in Washington DC."

Political tensions were often felt to fragment and polarize the student body. These were added to theological disagreements that were always part of the student experience. One student felt that "people did not know how to disagree with each other."

In addition to the paintings on the chapel wall, other destructive instances occurred during these years. The security of the campus, especially in relation to those from outside the seminary community who used seminary facilities, was always a concern. There were instances of vandalism and car break-ins from parking lots. The shooting of the rooster on Hicks Chapel — a very visible symbol for the seminary community — was remembered this way by a first-year student: "One day while walking near the chapel, I looked up to contemplate the rooster, symbol of the Reformation, which stood atop the steeple. After studying the faded, gold tones of the crowing bird, I noticed what looked like bullet holes running through it. A classmate confirmed my observations. He knew the young man who, having become exasperated with rules, regulations, requirements and 'hide-bound church tradition,' took out his .22 caliber rifle and riddled the rooster."

Another instance along this line from the early 1970s: "We had a 'portrait of the Black Christ' hung on one of the walls in the seminary, and one night someone slashed the picture with a knife, leaving about four or five slash marks across the face of the Black Jesus. But, as a student body, we decided to leave the picture hanging as it was, and not repair it, thereby 'making a social statement'!"

Perceptions of the seminary by its constitutive communities, an element that was a major focus of the Rea Report, were evidenced in many ways. One student recalled a conversation with a group of students at a Presbyterian-related college in which discussion turned to Pittsburgh Seminary. He wrote that "when they learned that I was a senior at PTS, one of the students made the comment: 'Oh, that's where they don't believe in the divinity of Christ!' Well, to say the least, the comment 'stunned me,' and I responded by asking: 'Where in the world did you get that garbage?' Well, our discussion went on for quite a lengthy time, and I soon convinced them that our seminary did, in fact, believe and teach the 'divinity of Jesus Christ'! That incident just taught me how easy it is for people to accept and believe mis-truths, misunderstandings, and complete lies!"

The flux in the curriculum and the strengths of the faculty at various points led many students to answer the question of whether the seminary prepared them adequately for their ministries by responding, "Yes and No." One student said, "I believed the seminary prepared me biblically and theologically. Practically, with the day to day 'STUFF' of ministry — it could have done more." Another said, "I wish my seminary training had included more classroom discussions on ministry with persons with mental illness and disabilities. Also, more family dynamics, and practical discussions of conflict management with congregations. There was so much focus on the traditional academic requirements — Bible, language, theology, history, that ministry skills took a disadvantageous back seat." The same student found that her year at Shadyside Hospital in the emergency room "prepared me for ministry in more ways than did the classroom." From another student: "Preparation for *practical* ministry was severely lacking: how to do weddings, funerals, budgets, lead Session and other meetings, what pre-marital counseling should cover, etc. etc." Typical among responses was the student who said, "In the basic areas of theology, Bible, preaching and worship I was adequately prepared. I feel that I was able to teach and preach with a very good grasp of our historic faith and apply it to the lives of the churches I served. In the practical areas of local ministry, administration, leadership and practical counseling my preparation was less than adequate. This, however, was not a complete drawback, as it forced me to concentrate on these areas in continuing education and provided a reason to further my education." Then, upon more reflection: "There is another side benefit of my education and training at PTS, I was encouraged to be a life long learner. The skills in study, reflection and development that were begun at PTS have continued through the years and gave me the ability to make up for any weaknesses from my seminary experience." Relatedly, another student wrote:

> Yes, in many ways I found myself prepared to enter into the ministry. If nothing else than having whet my appetite, it laid the groundwork for me to continue my growth in the pastoral ministry. Were there holes? Certainly. Many of us had come straight from college to the seminary and from the seminary to the church. We weren't prepared to be administrators. We didn't understand business. We weren't into management. We weren't taught to be effective leaders. Much of this was assumed, but much could have been addressed and wasn't. But I still believe that seminaries are meant to prepare pastors to be effective communicators of the gospel and that more than anything else

should be their mission. That it was true at Pittsburgh when I attended is clear.

Student life at the seminary was affected by the varieties of tensions within the faculty, administration, and the continuing need for greater funding. The increase in the number of married students during this period also contributed to a "gap" between married and single students while often "attempts at holding campus wide social events did not work well at all." One student recalled that the weaknesses of the seminary during her time there were "community worship and spiritual growth, lack of involvement with surrounding community, a dangerous location. The Finances of the institution often took precedence over people. The facilities provided little for dorm students who were forced to provide their own evening meals. Every little item we were able to get, was hard-fought to get."

Bright spots during this period were the development of a seminary recycling program and the seminary choir under the leadership of LindaJo McKim in the mid-1970s and also the development of child care and the day care facility. In the early 1970s, one student transferred to Pittsburgh Seminary from the Pacific School of Religion (PSR) in Berkeley, California. She wrote of Pittsburgh that "as for childcare, the seminary was far, far ahead ... an on campus day care facility, with occasional visits by Fred Rogers! At PSR, I had organized the first childcare co-op which eventually became a full day care facility, but when I arrived at PTS, childcare was not an issue. Thank you very much."

The emergence of women candidates for ministry was a significant shift in this period. Pittsburgh Seminary was also the context for the judicial case in the United Presbyterian Church in the USA in which Walter Wynn Kenyon (PTS '73) indicated in his trials before Pittsburgh Presbytery that he could not, in good conscience and on biblical grounds, participate in the ordination of women as elders or ministers of the Word and Sacraments. After court judicial cases, the denomination determined that participation in the ordination of women was a requirement for ordination in the denomination. Kenyon and other students from this time, who were highly influenced by Dr. John H. Gerstner, professor of Church History (who had joined the Pittsburgh-Xenia faculty in 1950 and taught at the seminary until 1980), thus were not ordained in the UPCUSA. A number of them were ordained in the

Presbyterian Church in America, which had been founded in 1973, and held that women should not be ordained as elders or ministers of the Word.

The polarities within the UPCUSA on this issue were reflected in the student body of the seminary, with one woman student reporting that "there was a group of male students who met daily to pray for the heathen souls of the three women students in the Middler class and the other women students — which all totaled then may have been eight or nine." Another woman recalled, "there was a small group on campus, students surrounding one professor, who did not accept me as a woman preparing for ministry." Upon her graduation in 1972, one woman student recalled that she was "offered a seminary tie from the seminary as a graduation gift." The emergence of the Women Seminarians group during this time began to give "strength and support."

The relation of the seminary community and facilities to the surrounding neighborhood continued to be an issue during this period. One student said that "unfortunately the East Liberty area was in economic and social decline during my student years in the early 70s. As a newly married couple, both my wife and I were security conscious owing to the nature of the local neighborhood." The seminary was across the street from Peabody High School, and there were times in the early 1970s when Peabody students would come on the seminary campus and use, particularly, the Hungry-I-Thou — the place where seminary students assembled for food and conversation. One seminary student recalled watching "three kids overdose on drugs before their school started at Peabody one morning."

An issue much discussed was the request to house a battered women's shelter in the basement of Fisher Hall. One student recalled a vote in the dormitory on the issue: "at the beginning of the meeting most were taking a NIMBY (not in my backyard) view. Only a few of us saw the obvious Good Samaritan connection. One student, and I'm sorry it wasn't me, finally stood up and made that point which swayed the vote. They were allowed in and I thought it was one of the best things the seminary did while I was there."

Most students from this period felt — in varying proportions — that the faculty was a good group of scholars and teachers. One student said that when he began at Pittsburgh Seminary in the mid-1970s, "there was still an air of something important and exciting in the air.

The Round Table (1971-1978)

The smell of pipe smoke everywhere was evidence of hard-working brains, thinking great thoughts about the church and the world. The strength of the library did not dawn on me at first. But the more time I spent there the more impressed I was." A number of "favorite professors" are typically listed by students who felt that overall the faculty was strong.

Of course, in hindsight, limitations appear. As one student from the mid-1970s put it,

> The faculty had some "stars" and was probably better than average for its day. The school had also lost some top faculty (Markus Barth, etc.) to other schools. At the time, I had the feeling that the faculty was in transition rather than stable. The curriculum was solid and standard for the day. What seems quite odd now is the lack of women on the faculty and also the lack of theological books written by women. Also, there was no "global Christianity" back then and the church history that was taught was European and American only. In Bible we were taught higher criticism, but none of the newer approaches that have so enriched our understanding of the scriptures.... So while the curriculum was good, it was seriously flawed from today's perspective!

Participation in theological education and a seminary community brings with it a host of challenges. The period of the 1970s at Pittsburgh Theological Seminary certainly presented these in abundance. Yet many of the students, despite the difficulties, have fond memories of the institution as well as the significant experience of entering into a new world of life and study. One student captured this drama this way:

> I arrived on campus in the Fall of 1977 with my wife, our daughter aged 7, and our sons aged 5 and 2. At that time I had been out of a college classroom for eight years. What a culture shock! A whole new language was spoken there... a language that I barely could understand. I went there with a very solid sense of God's having called me there so I figured "I best get at it." My first month I spent going to bed late at night, getting up early in the morning, and basically living in the library and classrooms. My wife pulled me aside and exclaimed, "We can't go on like this for three years. Our children need a father and I need a husband." I

determined then I would not be an "A" student but am proud that I was able to sustain a solid "B" average. In May of 1978 my wife produced steaks for barbecue. Our children, recognizing the unusual nature of this event, asked, "What's the celebration?" Their mother responded, "Daddy got through the first year of seminary!"

These achievements, both academic and personal, marked the paths of many Pittsburgh Seminary students. This student concluded, "By and large, and in spite of a few bumps in the road, the experience at PTS was most positive, for me and my family. Even though there was an abundance of anger on campus during the three years I was there it seemed to be focused within groups of people. My attentions were focused on individuals rather than groups, and I just loved my time there."

CHAPTER 6

Transition and the Search for Excellence

(1979-2006)

The interim presidency of W. Paul Ludwig lasted for a little more than a year. Ludwig worked with President Kadel during the month of December 1978, in the midst of which Dean David Shannon suddenly resigned for personal reasons. Douglas Hare was asked by the Executive Committee of the Board to accept a temporary appointment as dean.

The Presidential Search Committee found it difficult to obtain applications for the presidency of the seminary. Some perceived this was because of Pittsburgh Seminary's reputation as being a place where bad relations among the president, faculty, and Board existed. Student participation in the search process was prominent, with insistence that candidates be brought before the whole campus, presumably discouraging some applicants who did not want to be embarrassed in their present positions if they did not secure the presidency.

In early 1979, Ludwig informed the chair of the Board that he could no longer continue in the position of interim president and left Pittsburgh for Florida. For a few months, an administrative committee consisting of the dean, the director of development, and the business manager fulfilled presidential duties. About a dozen retired Presbyterian clergy were contacted about serving as an interim president, and all declined. A disagreement among the Administrative Committee occurred, causing a further weakening in the already difficult situation.

After the May 16, 1979, meeting in which the Board was briefed on the difficulties filling the presidency, Dr. Robert Cleveland Holland, pastor of the Shadyside Presbyterian Church in Pittsburgh, conveyed the name of Dr. Ronald V. Wells as a possible candidate to be interim president. Dr. Wells had retired, having served as president of Colgate-Rochester Seminary. He was a Baptist but had served as executive director of the Major Mission Fund of the United Presbyterian Church. After correspondence and a campus visit, Dr. Wells agreed to become interim president of Pittsburgh Theological Seminary. He was appointed by the Executive Committee of the Board on June 20, 1979, and began his work soon after.

During the next year, Dr. Wells kept the seminary functioning, including development efforts, thus helping to stabilize the financial picture for the seminary. There were improvements in faculty salaries, which had fallen beneath the median levels among similar seminaries. At the May 14, 1980, Board meeting, Dr. Wells agreed to continue as interim president until June 30, 1981, if necessary.

The New President: Carnegie Samuel Calian

On October 2, 1980, a special meeting of the Board of Directors was called to receive a nomination for president. The candidate was Dr. Carnegie Samuel Calian, a United Presbyterian minister who had served for a number of years as professor of theology at the University of Dubuque Theological Seminary. Dr. Calian had met with faculty, students, and administrators, all of whom were impressed with his energetic approach and vision for Pittsburgh Theological Seminary. Dr. Calian deferred his coming until the end of the fall semester in Dubuque and arrived on the Pittsburgh Seminary campus on February 1, 1981.

Carnegie Samuel ("Sam") Calian was born in the Bronx, New York, and raised in Los Angeles. He was baptized in the Orthodox tradition of the Armenian Apostolic Church. He was a graduate of Occidental College, Princeton Theological Seminary, and received his Doctor of Theology degree from the University of Basel. He was ordained in 1958. In an interview with the *Pittsburgh Press,* Calian remarked that his proudest accomplishment was marrying his wife, Doris, in 1959. When asked what three words describe him best, he said: "Energetic, caring, and inquisitive." His "secret vice" was "a passion for chocolate Klondikes" and his answer to the question of what people may be surprised to know

Transition and the Search for Excellence (1979-2006)

President Carnegie Samuel Calian and Doris Calian

about him was that "my name has nothing to do with Andrew Carnegie."[1] His first name, "Carnegie," is "an anglicized version of his Armenian given name, Carnig."[2]

Dr. Calian had published a number of books and articles by the time he became president of Pittsburgh Seminary. Among these were *Icon and Pulpit: The Protestant-Orthodox Encounter* (Westminster Press, 1968); *Grace, Guts and Goods: How to Stay Christian in an Affluent Society* (Thomas Nelson, 1971); *The Gospel According to the Wall Street Journal* (John Knox Press, 1975); *Today's Pastor in Tomorrow's World* (Hawthorn Books, 1977); and *For All Your Seasons: Biblical Direction Through Life's Passages* (John Knox Press, 1979).

Within the first several months, Calian's presence on campus was

---

1. *Pittsburgh Press,* September 1981.

2. David Smith, "Pittsburgh Theological Seminary: 200 Years Old and Still Going Strong with Sharp Eye to Future, *The Sewickley Herald* (March 16, 1994): 33.

greeted with hope. The president of the Student Association, Beverly W. James, wrote on April 22, 1981, that

> the arrival of Dr. Calian, and his already demonstrated willingness to listen to student concerns and opinions, is another positive part of the year 1980-81. It is difficult, of course, to speak for the amorphous student "body," but if I could take the "temperature" of my seminary colleagues, I would describe the present state as positive, anticipating, willing to affirm and to listen, and energetic. There is, of course, mixed in, a cautious realism about what may actually be possible. But, there is a definite resurgence of hope.[3]

State of the Seminary

The Board of Directors met on May 13, 1981, just a couple of months after President Calian began to serve. They received his Board report, in which he acknowledged the "whirlwind of activity and information gathering" in which he had been involved, having to attend to the "many facets of theological education and several publics all needing attention *at the same time.*" While he felt "overwhelmed at times," Calian was also "exhilarated and excited concerning all the plans and possibilities for the future."[4]

President Calian's initial assessment of the "State of the seminary" to the Board addressed a "Politics of Resurrection" which he said he hoped would be a "process of renewal" for the next several years. First, he said, this concept "implies that the seminary community has suffered sufficiently in recent years from a bad press; due largely to a breakdown of communication, suspicion, and poor mouthing." Calian said, "I think it has gone far enough; personally I do not care to hear any more negative talk about the seminary's past." He acknowledged the work of Ronald Wells's interim presidency to "improve the avenues of communication, to allow the various groups within the seminary to express their hurts and expectations, and to enable us to realize that we

---

3. Beverly W. James, Student Association Report, April 22, 1981.
4. "President's Report to the Board of Directors," Board of Directors Minutes, Pittsburgh Theological Seminary (May 13, 1981): 1.

Transition and the Search for Excellence (1979-2006)

are entering a new chapter in the life of Pittsburgh Theological Seminary." Calian's further comments on this point conveyed the administrative style he intended to take in leading the seminary forward:

> Further dialogue and discovery within our midst is necessary, if trust building is to continue. Many layers of suspicion have been removed, but there are still some remaining. While the presidential office has great power constitutionally and can act in a unilateral manner, my own style of leadership has placed emphasis instead upon a sense of openness, firmness, and the honest recognition that committee process also has its limitations. By limited, I mean that excessive committees overlapping in functions can contribute to a state of paralysis, preventing efficient and flexible administrative handling of day to day decisions. Ownership through the committee process is essential to the life of the seminary and is in keeping with our Reformed polity; however decisiveness is necessary if we are to regain ground lost in recent years. Greater trust toward the administration, not more power of authority, must be extended by the seminary community to allow us to move ahead with a minimum of "red tape."[5]

A second point Calian made was that "the politics of resurrection requires the Board to act swiftly to appropriate funds for the immediate improvement internally and externally of the seminary facilities." This set his agenda for the upgrading of seminary facilities and the future improvements to the seminary campus. As Calian put it, "attention must be paid not only cosmetically, but to the mechanical and structural aspects of our facilities. In addition we need to provide some immediate recreation facilities such as tennis courts and a grass area for football, soccer, etc. In the long run we will need an enclosed recreation and conference center for both continuing education purposes and for improving the quality of life for the entire Seminary community." Calian wanted the improvements to begin so that changes would be made by the fall term in September.

The third point was that "the politics [of] resurrection requires that we communicate more clearly and effectively our mission and image to

---

5. "President's Report to the Board of Directors," Board of Directors Minutes, Pittsburgh Theological Seminary (May 13, 1981): 1.

the outside world as well as among ourselves." Calian said that the seminary is "essentially an academic faith community responsive to the needs of the church and society, preparing men and women for the practice of ministry." The seminary also exists to further "Christian leadership among the laity and advanced training for the clergy," citing the increased momentum of the Doctor of Ministry program. Related to this overall goal, Calian announced that design and communications specialists who were dedicated Christians had "graciously donated their time and service to help us. These suggestions will culminate in a series of publications and brochures implementing our renewal in continuity with the significant history of the school's past achievements."[6]

These three points helped plot a trajectory for Calian's early efforts: administrative reorganization, physical improvements, and positive communications with constituencies. To carry these out, Calian continued in his report to indicate initiatives to fix the disarray that had come to the Business Office in the past several years, to increase efforts in Development and Giving — challenging the Board of Directors to "set the pace for the seminary community and larger public with the kind of giving and commitment that will enable this Seminary to reach a higher plateau of commitment," and then announcing that the faculty was "engaged in redefining its workload and preparing for various shifts in assignments for our program needs."[7] This was followed by a list of personnel assignments and recommendations, the first being the appointment of Professor Ulrich Mauser as dean of the seminary for a two-year term (1981-83), replacing Dr. Douglas Hare, who had served in the office and who would receive a sabbatical leave. Calian concluded his report with a statement of purpose: "It is the intention of this administration to usher Pittsburgh Theological Seminary into a new decade of service and commitment to the Lordship of Jesus Christ. It is this administration's expectation that every Board member will actively assist us through your financial gifts, commitment of time and talent, and above all your prayers, in making the politics of resurrection a reality in our midst."[8]

---

6. "President's Report to the Board of Directors," Board of Directors Minutes, Pittsburgh Theological Seminary (May 13, 1981): 2.

7. "President's Report to the Board of Directors," Board of Directors Minutes, Pittsburgh Theological Seminary (May 13, 1981): 2-3.

8. "President's Report to the Board of Directors," Board of Directors Minutes, Pittsburgh Theological Seminary (May 13, 1981): 5.

Transition and the Search for Excellence (1979-2006)

Presidential Initiatives

President Calian began quickly to act on a number of fronts. Former President Kadel's round table was removed from the president's office, a symbol of a new approach to decision-making at the seminary. Daily chapel services, which had been discontinued because of lack of interest, were restored. A "Spring Cleaning Day" was held on May 6, involving faculty, students, staff, and directors, followed by a picnic supper supplied by a local church. "While many projects were tackled on that particular day," Calian said, "in many ways the most important part of the day was working together and discovering each other."[9]

The formal inauguration of Dr. Carnegie Samuel Calian as president of Pittsburgh Theological Seminary was held on September 18, 1981. At the Board of Directors meeting on November 11, some eight months into Calian's presidency, the Property Committee reported a number of activities to refurbish buildings on campus.[10] Improvements to the physical plant were beginning!

Calian discussed five expectations he had for Board members. His theme was stewardship based on thankfulness. He expected Board of Directors members:

1. Will be praying for the seminary.
2. Will give a commitment of their time.
3. Will share their talent.
4. Will be enthusiastic and excited about the seminary.
5. Will commit their financial support which increases annually.

He told the Board that "in my estimation, increasing the enrollment and increasing the endowment are our two fundamental targets."[11]

Calian held an all-employees meeting on October 9 and organized an Advisory Administrative Council to deal with matters of communication and community. It was reported to the Board that there were now

---

9. "President's Report to the Board of Directors," Board of Directors Minutes, Pittsburgh Theological Seminary (May 13, 1981): 4.

10. Board of Directors Minutes, Pittsburgh Theological Seminary (November 11, 1981).

11. Board of Directors Minutes, Pittsburgh Theological Seminary (November 11, 1981).

315 students in all programs for a "Full-time equivalency" (FTE) of 195. This was a 13 percent increase in the FTE and an overall increase in enrollment of 10.7 percent. The hope was to reach the goal of 400 students by 1985.[12] Meanwhile, efforts to get the Business Office functioning efficiently were continuing. Calian said that "this whole process is taking far more time than I anticipated, but then I wasn't fully aware of the poor condition of our past records. Believe me, I would not like to see this happen ever again! It is detrimental not only to the life of the school, but is certainly a handicap for a new administration." But overall, in less than a year, the president reported that "the climate on campus with the students is wholesome and vital. There is a positive mood on the campus. This is essential. *Our goal is to be a caring community in which academic studies of the highest quality can be carried out.* This sense of caring must be expressed not only in words, but also in deeds. It is great to know that student contact with professors does not end in the classroom, but extends into the homes of faculty and staff as well."[13]

A Distinguished Pastor in Residence program was begun. President Calian said that the goal was "not only to have pastoral presence in our midst, but to serve as models of ministry for our students." The first to hold this position were Dr. Edwin and Dr. Marion Fairman. Both Fairmans were former missionaries. Ed was a pastor and mission executive, while Marion was a professor of English. Both were greatly engaged in mission efforts in the United Presbyterian Church. Others who served in the early years of this program were Michael Elligan in urban and minority ministries, and F. Morgan Roberts for preaching and a staff model of ministry.

To coordinate the Continuing Education program, the seminary hired Mrs. Jeannette Rapp, who replaced her husband, Dr. Richard A. Rapp in that position. Dick Rapp had served from his appointment on June 1, 1978, until his death in December 1979. Another significant appointment was Rev. John E. White, a graduate of the seminary, as director of admissions. He began work on August 1, 1981.

---

12. Board of Directors Minutes, Pittsburgh Theological Seminary (November 11, 1981). The "full-time equivalency" marker is the number of students who would be considered "full-time students" by Association of Theological Schools' standards if every student carried a full academic load.

13. Board of Directors Minutes, Pittsburgh Theological Seminary (November 11, 1981).

Transition and the Search for Excellence (1979-2006)

In academic matters, Dean Mauser reported to the Board that "the academic program at Pittsburgh Theological Seminary has received a tremendous boost through the arrival of Dr. C. S. Calian as President of the institution. His vigor and imagination have already led to significant expansions of existing programs and to the inauguration of innovative ventures in theological education."[14] In part, Mauser was alluding to new joint programs with the University of Pittsburgh and new degree programs featuring an M.A. and STM degree for international Christian studies.

The Role of the President

The flurry of activity associated with President Calian's first year in office was noticed throughout the seminary community, the church community, and even more broadly. He clearly saw himself as an activist president who tended to the needs of the seminary over a very wide range of concerns.

After a year and a few months in office, Calian discussed "The Role of the President" in his report to the Board of Directors on May 5, 1982:

> My primary purpose, as I understand it, is to help us articulate the vision for which we stand as an institution. The articulation of that vision must undergo constant dialogue with all members of our seminary community including graduates, members of the Board, denominational officials, and educational authorities. The seminary exists to serve the church intellectually, spiritually, prophetically, and practically in equipping men and women for ministry through the church to the world. How does the seminary do this best? *By educating us to think more deeply about our faith commitment, helping us to develop practical skills for communicating ministry and challenging us to a never ending process of renewal and rebirth.*[15]

---

14. Board of Directors Minutes, Pittsburgh Theological Seminary (November 11, 1981).

15. "President's Report to the Board of Directors," Board of Directors Minutes, Pittsburgh Theological Seminary (May 5, 1982): 3.

Throughout his presidency, Calian would refer to the "vision" of Pittsburgh Seminary, which pulls the institution through the present and into the future. The vision would have many contours and many facets. But it is the galvanizing purpose that gives meaning and significance to the work of Pittsburgh Theological Seminary: "Ever a vision!"

The role of the president, according to Calian, was to help articulate the vision in a dialogical fashion with a broad constituency. The presidential role was key to providing direction as well as opportunities for the seminary to consider its vision and calling and to be thoroughly engaged with the church and the world as it carried out its task of theological education. This requires a vigorous presidency, and Calian went on to indicate the kind of "vigorous program of discipline and time management" that would enable him to carry out his role as president and "faithful catalyst." Since Calian's leadership did prove to be so vigorous and important for Pittsburgh Seminary in the twenty-five years of his presidency, his early comments on his views about "the role of the president" are worth seeing in full:

> After one year in my present responsibilities, it has become increasingly clear to me that if I am to be a faithful catalyst, it is necessary for me to follow a vigorous program of discipline and time management that will enable me to do the following: 1) To give direction on policy matters and to have the time for reflection and perspective. 2) To teach at least one required course each academic year, as well as serve in an ex-officio capacity on all faculty committees, in order to have an intellectual relationship with my students and colleagues. It would be sad indeed to be a stranger in one's own house. 3) To promote the mission and purpose of the seminary among the churches, schools, business and professional organizations regionally and nationally. Attached to my report is a partial list of places where I have spoken since my presidency in promoting and re-educating perceptions regarding the seminary. My chief concern in-house and to the larger public has been to increase the level of appreciation for the excellent achievement of our seminary. 4) To encourage the spiritual development of the seminary community not only through our daily chapel services but in more intimate one-on-one contacts which take place regularly in our seminary life. We

Transition and the Search for Excellence (1979-2006)

still have a great deal of development to do in bringing about the quality of spiritual formation along with our strong commitment for intellectual growth. 5) To assist in the process of resolving conflicts caused at times by the diversity of our seminary family. Conflict is a necessary and important means of enabling dialogue to proceed at deeper levels. It would be a sad day indeed if we were free of all conflicts. This statement may surprise you; why do I say this? Conflict becomes often a means of stimulating growth and clarifying goals — a healthy school will have several conflicts and dialogues at any given time, helping us thereby to reflect on ourselves and our outreach to others. 6) To affirm the positive in all aspects of the seminary community's life. It is my and others' perception that there has been a great deal of negativeness in the history of our seminary. I have found it therefore important to accentuate the examples of responsible stewardship and positive qualities that exist here. 7) Finally, to administer in such a manner that communicates respect for the constituents who make up the seminary community and defines the limits of governance for each group.[16]

These elements became part of Calian's presidential direction and style through the next quarter-century. He took a very hands-on approach to policy issues, maintained a regular classroom teaching commitment, and was tireless in his activities to promote the seminary in the church and wider community, particularly the business community. Calian sought ways to enhance the spiritual life of the seminary and was often involved in the conflicts within the seminary community, in various capacities. His outlook for the seminary remained optimistic even in the midst of difficulties. He sought to respect the seminary's constituents, even when disagreements occurred among them. Calian reported to the Board in this May meeting that "The positive news in student enrollment is due in large measure to the greater sense of caring by our entire seminary community. . . . *Caring, competence, and commitment are notable characteristics of our seminary style at Pittsburgh Seminary.*"[17]

---

16. "President's Report to the Board of Directors," Board of Directors Minutes, Pittsburgh Theological Seminary (May 5, 1982): 3.

17. "President's Report to the Board of Directors," Board of Directors Minutes, Pittsburgh Theological Seminary (May 5, 1982).

President Calian reported on the number of his visitations from February 1981 until April 1982:

Churches-36
Presbyteries & related-10
Colleges-5
Alumni Groups-8

The first year had been busy but satisfying. Robert Cleveland Holland reported for the Executive Committee of the Board from the report of its Presidential Evaluation Committee for 1981 with the verdict that "The committee reflected its great satisfaction with Pittsburgh Theological Seminary's image through the dedicated work of Dr. Calian."[18]

A Widening Vision

In November 1982, President Calian announced the results for the accrediting visit for Pittsburgh Seminary by the Association of Theological Schools and the Middle States Association. The visiting team asked the seminary to develop by June 1, 1983, a five-year forecast of the finances of the seminary, an evaluation procedure for all persons related to the seminary community, and a clarification of functional objectives, particularly of the M.A. program.[19]

The accrediting team brought up both strengths of Pittsburgh Seminary as well as issues of concern. As Calian summarized these, the team noted the strengths of 1) a new spirit with the appointment of the new president; 2) an enthusiastic and active Board of Directors; 3) a fine faculty; 4) a good student body; 5) an outstanding library and library facility; 6) an excellent physical plant; 7) a good basic degree program; 8) a strong and excellent Doctor of Ministry program. The concerns were 1) the need for long-range strategic planning including financial planning; 2) the need for clarification of the policy regarding the Chief Academic Officer; 3) the need to complete appointments to fill faculty vacancies and to develop a more realistic definition of faculty load; 4) the need for building

---

18. Board of Directors Minutes, Pittsburgh Theological Seminary (May 5, 1982).

19. Board of Directors Minutes, Pittsburgh Theological Seminary (November 17, 1982).

Transition and the Search for Excellence (1979-2006)

up the endowment and the implementation of sound policies in the Business Office; 5) the need for evaluative procedures; 6) the need for functional objectives in the various masters-level programs.

On balance, the report by the accrediting agencies was positive, and the seminary received its ten-year accreditation of its basic degree programs.[20] The enduring strengths identified in the report were ones that continued through the Calian presidency and still may be said to be true today. The concerns included evaluative processes, which are always needed and must be reevaluated for any educational institution, and which were to continue as a challenge for Pittsburgh Seminary. Undoubtedly, however, the concern to bolster the seminary's endowment was one that was more than met in the two decades to follow.

The accrediting team's concerns for sound policies for the Business Office would be met with the appointment of Douglas N. Clasper as the business manager. He began on June 23, 1982, and was to continue his service beyond 2006 and the end of the Calian presidency. Clasper's management of financial interests and control over business elements became an important part of Pittsburgh Seminary's history for the next quarter century.

The Search for Excellence

At the November 17, 1982, Board meeting, President Calian expressed the widening focus of Pittsburgh Seminary under his administration by highlighting the following six distinguishing characteristics. He wanted the seminary to be

1. The outstanding school of the region.
2. Reformed, ecumenical, and urban.
3. Competent, caring and offering teaching of the highest order.
4. An inclusive school in every respect — physically, theologically, and socially.
5. The center of outreach to the marketplace and the business and professional communities.

---

20. Board of Directors Minutes, Pittsburgh Theological Seminary (November 17, 1982).

6. An innovative and creative theological and biblical resource center to the church and to society.

The elements Calian emphasized here were to become repeated refrains through the years. An emphasis on "excellence" was beginning to emerge. The vision was for Pittsburgh Seminary to become the "best" it could be — and to be recognized as such. The focus of the vision for Pittsburgh Seminary was both widening and sharpening as Calian attempted to give leadership that would both strengthen the seminary's inner life and also give it visibility as a premier theological institution embodying excellent characteristics.

At this Board meeting too, the term of Dean Ulrich Mauser was extended for an additional year, to May 31, 1984, and the decision was made to give definite names to rooms in the seminary, which to that point had only been known through a general designation, such as the President's Dining Room. The retirements of longtime faculty members Gordon Jackson and James Arthur Walter were announced as scheduled for May 31, 1983.

The matter of the position of Pittsburgh Theological Seminary among other theological seminaries in the nation and within the United Presbyterian Church took on more significance in 1983 when two Presbyterian bodies separated since the Civil War were reunited. The United Presbyterian Church in the United States in America and the Presbyterian Church in the United States merged in 1983. The "northern church" (UPUSA) and the "southern church" (PCUS) came together in a ceremony in Atlanta, bringing the two largest Presbyterian bodies in the country into one denomination, the Presbyterian Church (USA). At the time of merger, the question was inevitably raised as to whether the new denomination needed all the seminaries that were parts of the former churches. The PC(USA) would now have eleven theological institutions.[21] All the denominational seminaries felt the need to raise the visibility of their contributions to theological education. Pittsburgh Seminary would need to push ahead to insure its place as an

---

21. The theological seminaries were Austin, Columbia, the University of Dubuque Theological Seminary, Johnson C. Smith, Louisville, McCormick, Pittsburgh, Princeton, San Francisco, Union (Richmond) and the Presbyterian School of Christian Education. Later, Union Seminary and the Presbyterian School of Christian Education joined to become Union-PSCE.

"excellent" theological school in the pantheon of Presbyterian theological institutions.

A Strategic Vision

The push for excellence at Pittsburgh Seminary was consistent with the times and denominational posturing, but it was driven by President Calian's initiatives in a number of directions. Calian told the Board of Directors on May 4, 1983, that "the two primary tasks facing us as a Board are as follows: *a constructive approach to long range planning and increasing significantly our financial support.*"[22] As a way into long-range planning, Calian talked about developing a "strategic vision" for the seminary, of which he said, "it becomes increasingly clear that we must *all share a common strategic vision for the future* if we are to make significant progress as a pilgrim community. Our common vision must be mindful of everyone — students, faculty, staff, administration, alumni, friends, Board, and churches we serve."[23]

Calian laid out four elements for the strategic vision. First, "The seminary's strength resides in the quality of its faculty." Second, "As an academic Christian community, students must join faculty in striving for excellence in our intellectual pursuits whether it be term papers, discussions, projects, articles, books, or research." Third, "This seminary's unique character is reflected in the diversity of persons and interests attracted to our community." Fourth, "The seminary must constantly nurture and serve the needs of its constituency."[24]

The pursuit of excellence emphasized in these points led President Calian to touch on items such as obtaining the best-qualified faculty persons, faculty morale being bolstered by "pleasant surroundings, adequate compensation, and teamwork among all the employees of the seminary community," the linkage of all parts of the community, accountability, attracting the "highest caliber of students," nurturing and

---

22. "President's Report to the Board of Directors," Board of Directors Minutes, Pittsburgh Theological Seminary (May 4, 1983).

23. "President's Report to the Board of Directors," Board of Directors Minutes, Pittsburgh Theological Seminary (May 4, 1983).

24. "President's Report to the Board of Directors," Board of Directors Minutes, Pittsburgh Theological Seminary (May 4, 1983).

supporting the seminary's "rich pluralism," the reaffirmation of the institution's commitment to "equal opportunity employment and affirmative action for women and minorities," and the recognition that Pittsburgh Seminary's "primary constituency are the churches and the pastors and individuals within these congregations. Since this "primary constituency" also supplies the seminary's financial means, "to serve the needs of our contributors ought to be the central focus of our efforts." With an eye toward this constituency, Calian went on to say:

> Our prophetic and pastoral functions within the seminary must always be governed and disciplined by this educational ministry. Our reputation stands or falls not only on our competence, but our ability to reach out with caring effective communication. We must be recognized and appreciated as *the* seminary of the region, blessed as we are with our stimulating cultural, educational, and urban environments. We must at the same time guard our academic freedom and protect our responsibility for the pursuit of truth in the name of Christ.[25]

Calian's efforts to connect the seminary and the churches more closely came in many forms, one of which was his urging for the faculty "to increase research with the church in mind. We must pursue our studies with a more conscious effort to enrich the life of the church and her witness in the world. The apparent gap between pure research and application must be bridged in theological education. Our goal is creative synthesis whenever possible."[26] In this, Calian was picking up a thread that had been part of the Pittsburgh Seminary history since consolidation: the basic character of the seminary as a school for the church, with faculty members pursuing theological research in service to the church and as theologians of the church, rather than seeing themselves as purely scholars in an academic environment. Pittsburgh Seminary's joint Ph.D. program with the University of Pittsburgh in religion continued. But the primary focus of the faculty's commitments was to be enrichment of the church's life and witness in the world.

---

25. "President's Report to the Board of Directors," Board of Directors Minutes, Pittsburgh Theological Seminary (May 4, 1983).

26. "President's Report to the Board of Directors," Board of Directors Minutes, Pittsburgh Theological Seminary (May 4, 1983).

Transition and the Search for Excellence (1979-2006)

The overall effect of Calian's plea for a strategic vision was captured in his closing remarks: "the question facing us today is not whether Pittsburgh Seminary will survive in a reunited church, but rather the question is what kind of future will we choose to have in a united church. We have an obligation to our forebears to lift the seminary to a new level of spiritual awakening."[27]

The president's report at this Board meeting was supplemented by a written address to the Board by President Calian on the question "Where are we going as a seminary?"

Calian began by saying that while this was a good and pertinent question, he said, "I must confess it is a little different than the question that was put to me when I was being interviewed for the presidency of the seminary in September of 1980. The question at that time was 'What will make the seminary go?' As you can see there has been a shift in the line of questioning. We know now that we *are moving* and have the luxury of asking *where* are we going."[28]

Drawing on a then-popular TV series, Calian commented:

> Some days that question is clearer to me than on other days. As I was sharing with the faculty recently, I find the seminary at times to be a cross between "Hill Street Blues" and the Pittsburgh Symphony. When we harmonize together it is beautiful. At other times I am very sympathetic with the precinct captain in the "Hill Street Blues" who is trying to [p]reside over what seems, at times, to be a human zoo. Whatever the case, there is plenty of promise, excitement, and stimulation on campus. There is a pulsating life here that is both exhilarating and frustrating; we are indeed a pilgrim community on the move.[29]

The very first point of Calian's presentation went right to the heart of the search for excellence: "In the *first place* we are headed in the direction of our forebears, namely, to become one of the finest theological

---

27. "President's Report to the Board of Directors," Board of Directors Minutes, Pittsburgh Theological Seminary (May 4, 1983).

28. C. S. Calian, "Where are We Going as a Seminary?" Board of Directors Minutes, Pittsburgh Theological Seminary (May 4, 1983): Paper A: 1.

29. Calian, "Where are We Going as a Seminary?" Board of Directors Minutes, Pittsburgh Theological Seminary (May 4, 1983): Paper A: 1.

seminaries in the country. We are not there yet and hopefully will never be so content to say that we have arrived. We are building on the high standards of academic competence associated with Pittsburgh Seminary." This encapsulated the emphases Calian had been making in his widening vision for Pittsburgh Seminary as an institution of the church to make the seminary "one of the finest" theological seminaries.

Second, said Calian, "in faithfulness to our past, we want to reassert our reformed roots, proud of our Presbyterian heritage that is biblical and ecumenical in its orientation and relevant to a marketplace that is changing daily."

Third, Calian was aiming in the direction of "making the seminary the most exciting intellectual center of Christian witness in this region," emphasizing that the seminary should be willing to be "experimental and even controversial at times as we address issues within contemporary society." Controversy was all right, since "a healthy campus like a healthy church must discuss and even disagree on issues of importance, not allowing ourselves to become polarized over any single issue." Calian reminded his audience that "ours is an educational mission; we are not called upon to displace the prophetic and pastoral witness of local churches." It is the local church which is "the grassroots center that must translate the conscience-raising and intellectual stimulation at the seminary into practical terms within the reach of every Christian community."

Fourth, "we must all consciously strive to enhance the image and the importance of the seminary among our constituents," for "without their financial and moral support we aren't really going anywhere." Calian claimed that everyone should be ready to answer the question, "What has the seminary done lately that deserves my support?" The seminary, he maintained, is actually "the most vital link the grassroots church has between its past and its future. The seminary is a constant reminder to the church that the lessons of history are important in shaping the church's future and its ethical priorities."

Fifth, Calian addressed the issue of "whether our seminary should have some more narrowly defined character of uniqueness or distinction." On questions of the seminary's optimal size for the student body, faculty, and financial resources, he deferred to the future work of the Long Range Planning committee. But for now, "we must give our energies to strengthening the posture of Pittsburgh Seminary within the life of a reunited church, which means continuing to improve our financial base, enhance the quality and quantity of our student body, and do a careful job of scrutinizing and shaping our academic resources."

In conclusion, Calian called on the Board to "consciously declare our dependence on God, the leading of the Holy Spirit, and a renewing of our personal commitment to the Lordship of Jesus Christ if we are to build more than a house of clay. As the seminary seeks continual renewal, the impact will be felt positively among the churches regionally, nationally, and internationally."[30]

The strategic vision outlined here was one that described a seminary in continuity with its past and "reformed roots" which was on the move to becoming "one of the finest theological seminaries in the country." This drive toward excellence would establish Pittsburgh Seminary as "the most exciting intellectual center of Christian witness" in the region, which would link intellectual theological thought with the practicalities of the "grassroots" church members. Calian desired "strengthening the posture of Pittsburgh Seminary within the life of a reunited church" which, in turn, called for action in improving finances, the quality and quantity of students, and the careful shaping of academic resources. It was an ambitious vision.

Adjusting the Focus

In addition to the Board report by the president and the strategic vision paper presented to the Board, a Presidential Evaluation Committee for 1982 made a report at the May 4, 1983, Board meeting. The committee had met on April 21 to "evaluate the president's performance and problems during the previous years." This was the second of what was to be an annual presidential evaluation meeting.

The Board minutes convey the essence of the report. They are relevant not only to indicate the kinds of expectations the Board of Directors had for the office of the president, but also as a record of the ways in which the Calian presidency was being perceived in the seminary community, by the Board of Directors, and by Sam Calian himself. The committee mentioned some concerns indicated by the president:

---

30. Calian, "Where are We Going as a Seminary?" Board of Directors Minutes, Pittsburgh Theological Seminary (May 4, 1983): Paper A: 1-4.

Feeling on the defensive when attempting to interpret the seminary to the broad community. He constantly feels the money squeeze and wishes that the endowment were larger. He feels that he spends a great deal of time trying to keep people happy and that he involves himself with too much trivia. Sam questions whether one can be both a scholar and an administrator and whether he is deriving the satisfaction from his job that he feels he should. Also, he expressed a desire to attend a course at the Harvard Business School involving two six-week terms in successive years. To this request, it was the feeling of the gathered group that money should be found for this purpose.[31]

This self-evaluation was supplemented by the report of the committee, which stated its feeling that

Sam, indeed, has made a large impression on the Pittsburgh Theological Seminary in his two years of service and that his performance has been extraordinary. The other thoughts expressed were that Sam should be able to delegate more authority on the actual running of the school and to raising money. It was also felt that more effective long-range planning would be helpful in fund raising. It was agreed that Sam is a fountain of ideas but that some of the overall plans for the seminary need to be better elucidated, either through him or the long-range planning committee. Some thought that Sam was working too hard and that now that he has had wide exposure throughout the community he should cut his working hours and concentrate on such problems as faculty development. This would give him more time for those duties usually performed by most presidents.[32]

Meanwhile, student focus for the 1982-83 school year was on the theme "Community Means We are One!" One of their goals for the year related to the hiring of a "qualified full-time black faculty member," recognizing the work being done in this regard by the search committees, the administration, and the Board. Another goal was "to bring together the student body into a community type setting... A better rela-

---

31. Board of Directors Minutes, Pittsburgh Theological Seminary (May 4, 1983): 2.
32. Board of Directors Minutes, Pittsburgh Theological Seminary (May 4, 1983): 2.

Transition and the Search for Excellence (1979-2006)

tionship throughout the entire student body is needed so that we can be more sensitive to the needs of others."[33]

Another form of focus at the May 1983 Board meeting was the decision that the deanship be filled from within the faculty on a rotating three-year basis, renewable for a second three-year term. With this format, Dean Ulrich Mauser would be appointed for a second term (June 1984-May 1987). The continuity in the dean's office with the work done by Dr. Mauser was a stabilizing factor for the seminary and enabled the academic program to function well even as the seminary was striving to reach so many other goals.

Further Growth

The 1983-84 academic year featured a unique focus: an emphasis on peace studies throughout the entire curriculum. Since 1980, there had been a Peace Fellowship at Pittsburgh Seminary — students, faculty, and staff devoted to keeping the needs of peacemaking in front of the seminary community. Through funding from the PC(USA) and its Peacemaking Committee, a series of special programs were held throughout the year with courses devoted to a peace focus. Among the activities during this year were faculty Forums; conferences, seminars, and continuing education events on peacemaking; individual course evaluation and restructuring to add appropriate dimensions to the curriculum; a team-taught course in the third term; and faculty and student projects on peacemaking. Four lectures devoted to the topics were given at the Pittsburgh Biblical Colloquium on October 12-13, 1984, and were published in the seminary-sponsored journal *Horizons in Biblical Theology* (Winter 1984).

Student enrollment continued to grow. The seminary had experienced increased enrollment every year since 1980-81. For 1983-84, enrollment stood at 434 total (256 full-time equivalent). In 1982-1983, the full-time equivalent total was 220. Total enrollment figures for the recent years were reported as:

---

33. Student Association Report, Board of Directors Minutes, Pittsburgh Theological Seminary (May 4, 1983).

1983-84	434
1982-83	370
1981-82	315
1980-81	282

In October 1983, the Student Association report to the Board indicated that "for the first time in the last three years, we have more students interested in serving on committees than we have committees. There is definitely a decrease in apathy and a deeper commitment to positive action."[34]

By the time of the fall Board meeting on November 9, 1983, the president was also feeling better about his work and the position of the seminary. Dr. Calian said to the Board: "For the first time since my arrival at Pittsburgh Seminary, I can sincerely say that I am beginning to enjoy my job. Perhaps that is my way of saying that I am beginning to sense significant momentum and progress from the seed work of the past two and a half years."[35]

At this meeting President Calian focused on the seminary's primary purpose as he saw it: "to educate qualified and committed men and women for ministry; to provide inservice educational degree programs for clergy; and to engage the church, clergy and laity in continuing education and growth experiences to further their discipleship. In short, we are in the business of Christian Education for the church's nurture and leadership in the world."[36] Here, as always, Calian's emphasis was on the preparation of clergy for ministries in churches and the nurture of churches to assume a position of "leadership" in the world.

At the May 9, 1984, Board meeting, President Calian outlined what he considered six areas of tension facing Presbyterian theological education. These were drawn on the general map of the denomination, but of course had specific, local importance for Pittsburgh Seminary. The six areas of tension were:

> 1. Tension between seminary's desire for autonomy and Church's wish for accountability. How can the seminary be free *for* the church?

34. Thomas A. Lamb, "Student Association Report," October 1983.
35. Board of Directors Minutes, Pittsburgh Theological Seminary (November 9, 1983).
36. Board of Directors Minutes, Pittsburgh Theological Seminary (November 9, 1983).

2. Tension between regional orientation and the need for a national perspective for recruitment and funding. Can we be both regional and national?
3. Tension between being a graduate and professional school of the Church and being a graduate school of academia. Is academic excellence and Church commitment compatible?
4. Tension between theological research and practical service to the church. What are real expectations of the Church regarding theological education?
5. Tension between Reformed Presbyterian ethos and the increasing evangelical (para church) climate at the grassroots. Why should the Church support Presbyterian seminaries?
6. Tension between a theological curriculum of basic subjects and contemporary issues. To what extent should course offerings reflect current trends and expectations for ordination?[37]

Long-Range Planning

At the May 1984 Board meeting a long-range plan for the seminary was presented. The plan was a ten-year plan that sought "not to describe the predictable, but rather the preferable." The goal was to "hold the seminary accountable for shaping its own future." The plan was described as "systematic," with directions for the school's mission identified and the goals and outcomes listed. Each part was to be viewed as part of a whole, "each part working toward its particular end, while at the same time benefiting from and being benefited by the remaining parts."[38]

The theological statement which began the document indicated the seminary's nature and task:

---

[37]. "Underlying Tensions Facing Presbyterian Theological Education Today," Board of Directors Minutes, Pittsburgh Theological Seminary (May 9, 1984): Exhibit A.

[38]. Board of Directors Minutes, Pittsburgh Theological Seminary (May 9, 1984): "Proposed Long Range Plan," Fifth Draft.

Pittsburgh Theological Seminary is a graduate professional institution of the Presbyterian Church (U.S.A.). Located in the heartland of Presbyterianism, and part of a thriving city, we seek to prepare men and women for dynamic pastoral ministry and Christian lay leadership in all phases of the Church's outreach.

Dedicated to excellence in theological education, the twenty-member faculty strives to prepare graduates who will demonstrate both personal piety and the keenest possible intellectual understanding of the Gospel and its implication for individual and social living. Serious attention is given to the study of biblical languages, and to the teaching of theological, historical, ethical, and practical disciplines for the successful and meaningful practice of ministry.

The Seminary is rooted in the Reformed history of faithfulness to Scripture and commitment to the Gospel of Jesus Christ. In keeping with our tradition, we continue our mission to be a caring and ecumenical community, to nurture personal faith and corporate worship, to promote global consciousness and service, and to encourage students and faculty to relate their studies to the numerous styles of ministry.[39]

The six mission directions identified in the plan related to four areas of the seminary's activity: The Seminary's Community (Students and faculty/Administration; mission directions 1 and 2); The Seminary's Program (mission directions 3 and 4); The Seminary's Facilities (mission direction 5); and The Seminary's Financial Support and Funding (mission direction No. 6). The Executive Committee of the Board of Directors was the group charged "to see that the plans set forth here are worked upon, and [in] God's time, bear fruit."

The six Mission Directions were then set forth with a number of goals listed under each one; a date given by which the goal was to be met; and an accountability column indicating the office or specific person who was charged with meeting the goal.

Mission Direction 1. "Pittsburgh Theological Seminary needs to broaden its base of recruitment to include new fields and forms of recruiting, in order to insure high student quality, optimum growth in en-

---

39. Board of Directors Minutes, Pittsburgh Theological Seminary (May 9, 1984): "Proposed Long Range Plan," Fifth Draft.

rollment (400 full-time equivalent), and participation in all of its educational offerings." Nine goals were listed. These included continuing to improve procedures for "intentional recruitment of women and minority students for all phases of the seminary curriculum"; seeking ways to recruit persons considering a "career change"; and also maintaining communication with "Committees on Candidates of appropriate governing bodies."

Mission Direction 2. "Pittsburgh Theological Seminary needs to develop ways and means to complete the funding of partially endowed professorial chairs, to fund additional professorial chairs and to add administrative personnel. Consideration will be given to gaps presently existing in curriculum offerings, the desirable faculty-student ratio (approximately 1:14) and administrative tasks either now unattended or being done by faculty members under temporary part-time arrangement." Here ten goals were listed. Among these were the goal to attain at least 75 percent endowments for nine chairs, and a priority list for nine new professorial chairs. A full complement of twenty-eight full-time faculty members was called for along with other positions, including a director of the Doctor of Ministry Program and a director of Planned Giving.

Mission Direction 3. "Pittsburgh Theological Seminary, affirming the Master of Divinity as the basic theological Degree of the seminary, needs to engage in a planned comprehensive program of education and Seminary life which integrates materials from different academic disciplines, addresses issues facing the church and society, and looks constructively and relevantly to the future." Five goals were identified. In addition to relating the teaching and service program of the seminary to the church and community, two of the goals here were to "develop a means by which the seminary's educational offerings and communal life helps prepare students for the *breadth* and practice of ministry"; and "to engage in on-going identification of the issues of church and society and the relationship of the two which should be incorporated in the education and life of the seminary drawing in part upon Presbyterian Church actions and priorities (e.g. authority of Scripture, peacemaking, politics and the Reformed tradition)."

Mission Direction 4. "Pittsburgh Theological Seminary needs further to define and to expand degree programs and the continuing education programs which contribute to a relevant ministry for laity and clergy in a contemporary church in a rapidly changing world." Eight goals were identified. These included expanded continuing education programs, joint and dual degree programs, dialogues with business and corporate leaders on human values in both degree and continuing education programs, as well as opportunities for urban ministry emphases on issues such as poverty, race, ethnicity, and urban politics, and the "interrelatedness of the 'worlds' (first, second, and third) in which students and scholarly study are exchanged with Christian churches around the world in order to enhance global consciousness of the church."

Mission Direction 5. "Pittsburgh Theological Seminary needs to renovate and augment the existing physical plant and grounds in creative ways which enhance the educational, spiritual, and social life of the total Seminary community and provide for the total program set forth in these Mission Directives." Ten goals were identified. These included virtually every aspect of the seminary's grounds and buildings. Needs across the whole of the campus were to be targeted with refurbishing, upgrading, and renovations. Included too was a feasibility study for acquiring existing lots on the seminary block.

Mission Directive 6. "Pittsburgh Theological Seminary needs to be aggressive in proposing changes for the way in which the Church funds its theological education and in securing adequate resources for developing our own programs." Four goals were identified. An ambitious goal here was to "design strategy to bring about change in the General Assembly funding policies for theological education and pursue that strategy within the councils of the church." This was to seek for a "greater fund-raising autonomy to the seminary within its service area" and a "strategy which will strengthen the denomination's responsibility for theological education." Additionally, the directive here also sought to increase the seminary's financial resources by expanding the number of donors by 10 to 20 percent and increase the level of donor support by 10 to 20 percent annually. The final listed goal was to increase Pittsburgh Seminary's endowment to "at least $50 million by the 200th Anniversary of the seminary," which would be in 1994.

Implementing the Plan

New faculty joined the seminary in this period including Andrew Purves in Pastoral Care (1983), Ronald H. Cram in Education (1983), John E.

Transition and the Search for Excellence (1979-2006)

Wilson Jr. in Church History (1984), and Susan Nelson in Theology (1984).

In fall 1984, the Board was told that enrollment at Pittsburgh Seminary stood at 436 students (322 men and 114 women; 402 white students, 23 black students, and 11 of other races). President Calian said, "Today, our seminary is stronger and our spirits higher than ever. Of course, we 'haven't arrived' as yet and probably never will, but we can say that our theological education at Pittsburgh Theological Seminary is advancing, and we all ought to rejoice and praise God for the grace bestowed upon us."

This optimism, grounded in theological affirmation, was offered in the face of the economic realities that would need to be surmounted if the goals of the long-range plan were to be met. One of the greatest of these challenges was to endow faculty chairs. The plan called for endowments for nine chairs at a 75 percent level or beyond, as well as a prioritized list for nine new professorial chairs. Calian indicated that "our goal in academic support is to fully endow all our faculty chairs. This is a major item to concern the entire Board since to date we do not have a single fully endowed chair. The life blood of the school is faculty, and we must work toward funding this endowed support." Through the years that followed, the progress made toward endowments for faculty chairs was one of the seminary's most notable achievements. The endowed support enabled other funds to be used for an array of purposes without being tied to the seminary's largest single financial outlay for faculty salaries.

As efforts began to be made to enact the seminary's long-range plan, President Calian was proceeding to lead and then to ask a defining question: "What quality of excellence do we wish to achieve at Pittsburgh Seminary?" In the mid-1980s, one of the major questions for American theological education was what constituted a "good" theological school and what elements could make an institution an "excellent" theological seminary. Later, President Calian contributed to the literature on this topic through his book *The Ideal Seminary: Pursuing Excellence in Theological Education.*[40]

As the mid-1980s progressed, Pittsburgh Seminary began to make

---

40. Carnegie Samuel Calian, *The Ideal Seminary: Pursuing Excellence in Theological Education* (Louisville: Westminster John Knox Press, 2001).

progress on implementing many of the directives set forth in the long-range plan. Dr. John E. Mehl was hired as director of the D.Min. program on February 15, 1985, to give focus and direction to this program which was becoming increasingly important for the seminary's overall mission and influence both regionally and nationally. A 15 percent tuition increase and a 10 percent housing increase was approved by the Board of Directors for two academic years — 1985-86 and 1986-87 — on May 8, 1985. Plans were announced to install an elevator shaft in the Long Administration Building to make that building more accessible. Programmatically, a three-year pilot project on theological education and aging was established. The goal was to bring the needs of aging Presbyterian church members to the attention of theological studies and the theological curriculum as well as to the churches of the presbytery.

At the May 1985 Board meeting, the announcement was made that an anonymous donor had pledged $750,000 to endow the Robert Cleveland Holland Chair in Old Testament. Its first occupant was Professor Donald E. Gowan. In February 1985, the seminary adopted guidelines for special endowments, setting the amount needed to endow a faculty chair at between $750,000 and $1 million, and stating that no appointment to a chair should be made until the chair was fully funded. The minimum amount for a chair endowment was subsequently raised to $1.5 million. The gift for the Holland Chair was the first of many gifts that would help the seminary meet its goal for the endowment of faculty chairs.[41]

The fall enrollment for 1985 was announced to the Board on November 13, 1985 as 425 students, with a full-time equivalency (the number of students if each student were taking what the accrediting agency considered a "full-time" load of courses) was 244.83. There were 313 men and 112 women; 398 students were white, 22 were black, and 5 were of other races. A total of 160 students were enrolled in the D.Min. program.

In 1980, revenues for the seminary had totaled $2.3 million, but by 1985-86, the figure had increased to $3.3 million. Endowment income was now at approximately $1 million per year. With so much money coming in, the Board felt comfortable adjusting the rate of endowment utilization from 8 percent to 7 percent. Whereas the market value of the endowment had been less than $13 million in 1981, it had jumped to

---

41. Board of Directors Minutes, Pittsburgh Theological Seminary (May 8, 1985).

Transition and the Search for Excellence (1979-2006)

"We are Famil-ee"

$23.5 million by 1985. That year the Board was also told that an anonymous foundation would provide $1 million to endow the Director of the Library/Professor of Bibliography Chair.

A sense of optimism for the institution was conveyed by the report from the Student Association President, Lisa Dormire Foster:

> There is a new spirit of optimism that seems to be blowing through the student body here at P.T.S.! Just as the seminary as a whole seems to be pointing in a direction of positive growth and change, the Student Association reflects this positive attitude about Pittsburgh Seminary. We are proud of where we've come from and look forward to where we're going![42]

The theme for the 1985 student orientation was taken from the popular song by Sister Sledge, "We Are Family!"

---

42. "Report of the Student Association to the Board of Directors," Board of Directors Minutes, Pittsburgh Theological Seminary (November 13, 1985).

The Student Association report also took note of an increasingly prominent factor in seminary life: "We are facing up to the reality of the larger number of commuter students who make up our student population and making an attempt to gear at least part of our student programming towards these people with their special needs and concerns."[43] This recognition targeted what was to become a very prominent factor in American theological education in the 1980s and beyond: the changing demographic of seminary students from full-time resident students to commuters who attended part-time. The implications of this transformation for nearly every facet of a seminary's life have been far-reaching through the entire seminary program. The degree to which part-time and/or commuter students were present at Pittsburgh is apparent in the ratio cited above: the "head count" of students (425) to the full-time equivalent amount (244.83). As commuter students were becoming recognized as a distinct and prominent campus group, Pittsburgh Seminary began to offer evening courses and eventually to make it possible for students to obtain the M.Div. degree through the evening program. The development of this means of delivery for theological education emerged over time. But Pittsburgh Seminary along with other seminaries recognized the need to adapt their programs in this way in order to meet student needs and to maintain their student enrollments in the midst of the changing patterns of seminary attendance.

A Politics of Hospitality and Scholarship

The May 1986 Board of Directors meeting featured the announcement of several major initiatives.

President Calian presented a proposal for a Center for Business, Religion, and the Professions. This proposal eventually grew into The Center for Business, Religion and Public Life, which seeks to create dialogue between business, religious, and professional communities; assist corporate, professional, religious, and education persons, as well as their organizations, to identify, analyze, and address the social issues

---

43. "Report of the Student Association to the Board of Directors," Board of Directors Minutes, Pittsburgh Theological Seminary (November 13, 1985).

Transition and the Search for Excellence (1979-2006)

affecting our culture and our region; and explore creative options for complex social issues to enhance the quality of life in our communities.[44] This center was an expression of Calian's own longstanding interest in the interaction of business and religion.

The Board was told that there was now a third fully funded faculty chair: the Howard C. Scharfe Chair in Homiletics. The seminary was now one-seventh of the way to endowing all faculty chairs, with three of the twenty-one full-time faculty holding endowed chairs.

To support this dream further along with the other elements of the long-range plan, a major fund drive was now announced. The goal for the drive was set at $10.75 million. It was to have three phases:

Bicentennial Campaign (1987-89) — 3 years
Phase II of Bicentennial Campaign (1990-94) — 4 years
The Seminary's Third Century Campaign (1995-2000) — 5 years[45]

In the mid-1980s the Presbyterian Church (USA) wanted all Presbyterian institutions to refrain from direct financial campaigns so as not to conflict with an anticipated campaign to be begun by the church. But the denominational campaign failed to move quickly, so the way was clear for Pittsburgh Seminary's major fund drive to begin in 1987.

The main elements for the campaign were faculty chairs, property items, and the permanent endowment. The annual fund drive was to continue through the campaign in order to maintain momentum and also to keep support coming for the seminary's operating budget. By the end of the campaign, the Bicentennial Fund was oversubscribed at $13,150,131.[46]

At the beginning of the campaign, and in support of its goals, President Calian hearkened to the image of Pittsburgh Seminary he proposed when he had become president five years before. Then he said that Pittsburgh Seminary needed to engage in a "Politics of Resurrection." The five years from 1981-86 had seen that resurrection. In spring 1986, with both finances and enrollment on an upward statistical trend, Calian could sum up this period by telling the Board that "more important than

---

44. Pittsburgh Theological Seminary, Catalog 2006-2007, 36.
45. Board of Directors Minutes, Pittsburgh Theological Seminary (May 7, 1986).
46. Henry C. Herchentoether, "Pittsburgh Theological Seminary 1959-1999," 32.

statistics, has been a rising feeling of self-esteem among faculty, staff, administration and students. This spirit and attitude is resurrection at its best." But "as we look to the next five years, we must move on toward a *politics of hospitality and scholarship.*"[47] This represented a logical next step to Calian: to build on the growing strength of the seminary by presenting a vision of Pittsburgh Seminary as a welcoming place for theological students, for pastors from regional churches, and for those in the community in search of theological dialogue and education — all funded by a first-rate faculty committed to excellence for academic scholarship and the preparation of persons for church ministries. Pittsburgh Seminary would be a place of welcome and excellence as it served as a theological resource for church and society.

Continuing Challenges

When the Board met on November 12, 1986, the enrollment for the 1986-87 school year stood at 395 students (at a full-time equivalent of 239), of which there were 288 men and 107 women. Some 367 students were white, 20 were black, and 8 were of other races. Building on the "We Are Family" theme of the previous year, the Student Association theme for 1986-87 was "Stories of the Family." Students were now urged to share their personal stories with each other. As Student Association President Sharon L. Williams put it, "We, as ministers, have a tendency to play the 'perfect person' and hide our faults. By sharing ourselves, by learning to communicate honestly, we can do much to enhance our relationships."

But the seminary faced a challenge during the 1986-87 school year. The Board was told in May 1987 that there was a decrease of 27.4 percent in the number of applicants for the M.Div. and M.A. degrees from the year before. In searching for reasons for the drop-off, John E. White, Director of Admissions, pointed out that "first and foremost is the fact that in the academic year 1986-87 and 1987-88 Pittsburgh Theological Seminary has had and will continue to have the highest tuition among the ten seminaries of the Presbyterian Church (U.S.A.)." The Student Association report to the Board the next year pointedly spoke about the

47. Board of Directors Minutes, Pittsburgh Theological Seminary (May 7, 1986).

cost of on-campus housing; it noted that "the rental rates for campus apartments will be comparable with other area apartments when the new rates go into effect in June."[48]

White highlighted another problem as well: "It continues to be damaging that the seminary does not have one black faculty member. This may discourage black candidates as well as other students who want to attend a seminary that is representative of both the church and the world."[49] While securing a black faculty member had been recognized as a vital need, the fact was that no such person had yet been called to the seminary faculty. Again the Student Association report the following May pointed out that "the concern that we have a black in a position of authority is not just a minority concern for itself but that of a majority concern for our diversity." The situation was exacerbated in 1988 when John White, the single African American administrator, resigned.[50]

The good news during this period was that the Board itself contributed over one million dollars to the capital campaign. This was five times the amount raised from the Board in the previous campaign of 1977. The fund drive was announced as "The Pittsburgh Seminary 199th Year Campaign." It was to run from December 1987 until January 1993. By May 1988, the chairs of the capital campaign had been announced. They were Dwight C. Hanna, Robert H. Meneilly '47, and Harold E. Scott '46. The honorary chair was Pittsburgh industrialist G. Albert Shoemaker.[51]

Programmatically, plans for an Institute of Metro-Urban Ministry were announced. This was to be a joint venture by Pittsburgh Presbytery and Pittsburgh Presbytery to provide a specialized focus on issues and problems of cities and their ministries. This program evolved into The Metro-Urban Institute, which continues to have long-lasting effects as it combines the theory and practice of collaborative community ministry into a program of urban theological education.

Total enrollment for the 1987-88 school year stood at 343: 158 in the M.Div program; 15 in the M.A. program; 1 in the Master of Sacred

---

48. Board of Directors Minutes, Pittsburgh Theological Seminary (May 10, 1988). The concern had also been voiced in the Student Association Report to the Board on May 7, 1986.
49. Board of Directors Minutes, Pittsburgh Theological Seminary (May 13, 1987).
50. Board of Directors Minutes, Pittsburgh Theological Seminary (May 10, 1988).
51. Board of Directors Minutes, Pittsburgh Theological Seminary (May 10, 1988).

Theology Program; 20 special students; 42 in the Ph.D. program; and 107 in the D.Min. program. In part the decline was attributed to "more stringent application of criteria for admission; the clearing of the Doctor of Ministry lists by enforcement of completion deadlines and encouragement of withdrawal of those who had little potential of finishing."[52] The year also marked the establishment of a prayer room in the seminary, initiated by students who worked with the administration. Also, on November 20, 1987, Pittsburgh Seminary was reaccredited by the Middle States Association.[53]

Pressure Points

Challenges for the seminary persisted on a number of fronts. These were termed by President Calian as "pressure points" when he spoke of them in October 1988 and then reported on them to the Board of Directors at its November 1988 meeting. These were, said Calian, "the concerns that are pressing in upon us. As the seminary makes progress, it is at the same time a precarious balancing act responding to the needs inherent in these concerns."[54]

President Calian grouped these pressure points under the headings of People, Program, and Property, in keeping with the seminary's long-range plan.

People Pressures
1. Increase student enrollment without diminishing quality.
2. Raise salaries and performance levels for faculty, staff, and administrators.
3. To have a Black faculty presence as soon as possible.
4. Escalating health costs for everyone in the seminary's employment.

---

52. Board of Directors Minutes, Pittsburgh Theological Seminary (November 10, 1987).

53. Board of Directors Minutes, Pittsburgh Theological Seminary (November 10, 1987 and May 10, 1988).

54. "President's Report: Revised Pressure Points of Concern Presently on My Desk," Board of Directors Minutes, Pittsburgh Theological Seminary (November 9, 1988): 1.

5. Increase Barbour Library staff to enhance services and automation.
6. Sensitivity to minimize increases in fees and tuition. Most of our students are hard pressed economically. We must be compassionate, competitive, and still pay our bills.
7. The aging of Seminary faculty. The current median age is 55.6.
8. Maintain warm, supportive community among residents, commuters, faculty, and all employees.

Program Pressures

1. General Assembly financial support (currently less than 6% of budget) will diminish.
2. The 199th Year Campaign needs a dramatic boost; the campaign is centered on increasing endowment to bolster program support.
3. Completion of the McClure Chair in World Mission and Evangelism as soon as possible.
4. Development of a Metro-Urban ministry with support.
5. Development and promotion of joint degree programs (e.g. theology and library science, theology and social work, etc.).
6. Automation of Barbour Library.
7. Ph.D. doctoral mentorship for minority candidates.
8. The establishment of a faculty chair in Theology and the Sciences (including Medical Ethics).
9. Development of a *Campus Center* in the Hungry-I to enhance community life.
10. Development of a video cassette film for Seminary promotion (for enrollment and development).

Property Pressures

1. Delayed maintenance on campus isn't over and never will be. For example, we need a new roof for the library, etc.
2. Resurfacing campus parking area.
3. Updating kitchen equipment in many student apartments.
4. Remodeling remaining classrooms.

These "pressure points" helped form an agenda for the seminary administration to follow for the next years in addressing needs in these broad categories. Some of the items could be met and resolved, while others persisted.

Within the next months, a description for the Director of the Metro-Urban Ministry Program was drafted and sent to the Board. At its May 1989 meeting, the Board was also told that there was an increase in the number of applicants for admission for the 1989-90 school year.[55] When the enrollment figures were presented on November 8, 1989, they showed a total enrollment of 301 (147 in the M.Div. program; 1 in the M.A.; 1 in the S.T.M.; 11 special students; and 115 in the D.Min. program). Of these, 196 were men and 105 were women; 270 were white, 23 were black, and 8 were of other races). The admissions report also indicated that the previous year, for the first time, women were the majority of the entering class. In the current year, there were 39 men and 37 women.[56]

The Board was also told at this meeting that pledges had been received to complete the endowments of five more faculty chairs. By 1994, there should be nine endowed faculty positions. A part of this initiative was a challenge gift of $1 million received from G. Albert and Mercedes Shoemaker to endow a faculty chair. The first occupant of the chair was long-time New Testament professor Robert L. Kelley Jr., who became the G. Albert Shoemaker Professor of Bible and Archaeology.[57]

It was announced as well that the position of Dean would be open as of June 1, 1990, since Ulrich Mauser was returning to teaching. At the next Board meeting, on May 9, 1990, Mauser resigned, effective July 31, 1990, to take a position on the faculty of Princeton Theological Seminary. He had been dean since 1981. Mauser's work as dean had been effective over a long period of time. As a result of this and other developments among the faculty, Donald Gowan, who represented the faculty to the Board, commented that "at present there is a spirit of trust and consideration that did not exist some years ago."[58]

---

55. Board of Directors Minutes, Pittsburgh Theological Seminary (May 10, 1989).

56. Board of Directors Minutes, Pittsburgh Theological Seminary (May 10, 1989) and Admissions Report, Board of Directors Minutes, Pittsburgh Theological Seminary (November 8, 1989).

57. Board of Directors Minutes, Pittsburgh Theological Seminary (November 8, 1989).

58. Board of Directors Minutes, Pittsburgh Theological Seminary (May 9, 1990).

Transition and the Search for Excellence (1979-2006)

Keith F. Nickle was named vice president for Academic Affairs and dean of the faculty and professor of New Testament, to begin his work on November 1, 1990. In another staff development, Mary Lee Talbot was named as director of Continuing Education and Special Events, replacing Jeanette Rapp, who resigned on December 31, 1989, and under whose leadership the continuing education program had grown considerably.

Ronald H. Peters was named director of the Metro-Urban Ministry Institute. A $135,000 grant from the Luce Foundation to be paid over three years enabled the institute to begin its work. Peters was named as an assistant professor until his doctoral studies were completed; he became the seminary's only African American faculty member.[59]

The official announcement of the beginning of the Metro-Urban Institute (MUI) was made in March 1991. Its purpose was to provide a program to develop religious leaders in the increasingly metropolitan environment of Pittsburgh and beyond. The goal was to combine the theory and practice of collaborative community ministries into an urban theological education program that "prepares students for excellence in any context of ministry, but with particular attention to public realities affecting the urban environment." The MUI "encourages interdisciplinary and interfaith approaches to solving social problems and reconciling human beings to God and to one another." The context in which the MUI does its work is one in which theoretical and practical dimensions of theological education are combined. The MUI seeks to "encourage compassionate ministries of justice, service, and advocacy, while promoting systemic change to improve the quality of life especially among those impacted by societal issues and difficulties." The MUI has developed, over time, an ecumenical network of churches and community groups which collaborate to conduct various ministries focused on "the welfare of the city" (Jeremiah 29:7). Together these groups also provide resources for the MUI's educational program, combining course work, seminars, field education, and internship possibilities. Special events relating to the urban environment are also held.[60] The MUI provides

---

59. Board of Directors Minutes, Pittsburgh Theological Seminary (November 7, 1990).

60. The Metro Urban Institute has evolved into these present-day functions since its beginnings in 1991. See Pittsburgh Theological Seminary, Catalog 2006-2007, 29.

President Calian Receiving a Portrait of Dr. Martin Luther King Jr.

programs offered at all degree levels, for students with no formal college education to those pursuing doctoral studies. It enables Pittsburgh Theological Seminary to be an important place for studies in urban ministry.

In the early 1990s, Pittsburgh Seminary began to provide for the needs of part-time and commuter students by offering evening classes on a regular and systematic basis. [61] Now it would be possible to obtain the M.Div. degree in the evening program in a period of six years of part-time study. Another important initiative from Calian's "pressure points" was the automation of Barbour Library. This work was under the direction of Stephen D. Crocco, who had begun as the director of the Barbour Library on June 1, 1987. Longtime librarian Mary Ellen Scott retired on May 1, 1991, but continued to work as a volunteer for the library on a long-term basis.

The May 1992 Board meeting featured announcement of the inten-

---

61. Board of Directors Minutes, Pittsburgh Theological Seminary (November 7, 1990).

tion of H. Parker Sharp, a Pittsburgh Seminary director emeritus, to establish the H. Parker Sharp Chair in Theology and Ethics with a $1 million gift. The Ada and Peter Rossin Chair in Church History was established as well, and Charles Partee was named as the occupant. Partee had joined the faculty in 1978 to teach Church History and had also been serving in the W. Don McClure Chair of World Missions and Evangelism. He was relieved of this latter duty to teach in the Rossin Chair. On May 12, 1992, Professor Ronald H. Stone was inaugurated to the John Witherspoon Chair in Christian Ethics. Stone had taught at Pittsburgh Seminary since 1969. The Board was told that the seminary's endowment stood at $61 million in 1992 — an increase of almost $50 million in ten years.

Accreditation Visit

A visiting team from the Association of Theological Schools made an accreditation visit to Pittsburgh Theological Seminary on October 4-7, 1992. In preparation, as usual, the seminary had been involved in a self-study process for a number of months.

The report from the visiting team was thorough. The group explored all the dimensions of the seminary's self-study report, finding that the self-study was "broadly participatory" and produced useful results. However, the team found it deficient in several ways: in numeric data, particularly for multiyear comparisons, and in its lack of "a certain toughness of analysis."[62]

The visiting team recognized a number of strengths of Pittsburgh Seminary:

- Energetic and effective presidential leadership
- Financial aid and attention to special needs of students
- Small faculty/student ratio
- Generous leave of absence policy for faculty scholarship
- Financial stability
- Well maintained and commodious facilities
- Library collections and continuing support for collections

62. "Report of the Visiting Team, October 4-7, 1992," 1.

- Loyal and knowledgeable Board of Directors
- The field education component of the M.Div.

At the same time, the visiting team targeted some weaknesses and concerns:

- Ambiguity about mission statement of institutional purpose
- Lack of effective faculty replacement plan
- Lack of educational program priorities and budget priorities
- Insufficient attention to the collegiality with faculty in setting educational and budgetary priorities
- Lack of effective internal mechanisms to support program initiatives with adequate financial and personnel resources.

Standards

The report of the visiting team focused on the accrediting standards and the team's perceptions of the ways in which these were being met or not met by Pittsburgh Seminary.

1. *Purpose.* The first of these items was an element that had surfaced before in the history of Pittsburgh Seminary: "There is ambiguity within Pittsburgh Theological Seminary about its purpose." This statement is reminiscent of discussions from the early days of the consolidation of Pittsburgh-Xenia and Western Seminaries about the seminary's purpose and echoed at a later date in the Rea Report. The team saw this ambiguity as reflected directly in three ways:

> The *Catalog* identifies the preparation of "men and women for pastoral ministry and Christian lay leadership in all phases of the Church's outreach" as the school's purpose, whereas the *Self-Study* states that "the primary purpose of the seminary is to provide sound theological education for persons preparing to enter the ordained ministry of the Presbyterian Church (USA) and of other denominations."[63]

63. "Report of the Visiting Team, October 4-7, 1992," 1-2.

Transition and the Search for Excellence (1979-2006)

The team noted that while these two statements are "not mutually inconsistent, they reflect an ambiguity in the central vision of the institution." Further, the ambiguity was reflected in the

> extensive range of degree programs offered by PTS. In addition to the conventional M.Div. program driven by the needs of ordained pastoral ministry, the school offers six joint M.Div. programs in Law, Library Science, Business Administration, Social Work, Health Administration, and Public Policy and Management; an M.A. and a D.Min; and a joint Ph.D. in seven fields. (The joint degree programs are offered with the University of Pittsburgh, Carnegie-Mellon University and/or Duquesne University.) As the team was visiting the school it was announcing a certificate program in Urban Ministry for undergraduates.[64]

It was noted that discussion with Board and faculty members also surfaced this ambiguity, most particularly in discussions about long-range planning. The team asked if the seminary's

> commitment to international students, questions about the school's reformed ethos in contrast to an ecumenical ethos, and the apparent reluctance on the part of at least some of the community to engage in strenuous thinking about some gender issues and alternative life-style issues are not a reflection — at least in part — of some confusion about the school's purpose.[65]

The team hoped that initiatives underway to review the seminary's mission statement in light of long-range planning would help to clarify this issue and urged this work to be completed promptly and "with full faculty involvement."

2. *Students.* The team's report indicated

> a concern, and we expect it to grow, about the level and range of services which are provided to evening and D.Min. students. In moving toward alternative schedules, PTS is following well known patterns in other institutions, but it is not apparent that

---

64. "Report of the Visiting Team, October 4-7, 1992," 2.
65. "Report of the Visiting Team, October 4-7, 1992," 2.

the school is offering these students the same quality of service as more traditional day time students receive.[66]

The team recognized that the "spirituality and community life" of the institution had been enlarged through groups which participated in daily chapel and through the community social times which follow chapel. But it also indicated the need for more professional counseling for students, including those in the evening program and also for D.Min. students.

3. *Faculty.* The section on faculty in the visiting team's report commended the seventeen full-time and nine adjunct faculty members for their deep commitment to their vocation of scholarship and good teaching. They recognized the faculty's "demonstrated ability to combine instruction, scholarly production and dedicated service to church and society." The team also recognized that "many of these persons have lived through some 'tough times' in the life of the school, yet they have remained loyal, and deeply committed."[67]

The team indicated good policies were in place for sabbaticals and their use for scholarly endeavors. But it was concerned that "this is an aging faculty with a majority reaching the normal retirement age of 65 before 2000." What was needed was a "careful faculty development plan" which would include faculty members declaring a year in which they expect to retire so that the administration and the Board could plan a program of faculty replacement.

In addition, concerns were expressed about faculty load and "the tendency of the faculty to over-administer" related to the number of programs in which the seminary was involved, from the certification program to providing guidance for Ph.D. students. "It is not clear to us," the team said, "that the faculty can service this range of programs while remaining productive scholars."[68] The team recognized that faculty spent "considerable time in committees dealing with administrative functions." The team suggested that while the faculty rightfully was involved with setting educational policy, "the administration of these policies belongs to the Dean" — who was accountable to the faculty for educational policy administration.

---

66. "Report of the Visiting Team, October 4-7, 1992," 3.
67. "Report of the Visiting Team, October 4-7, 1992," 3.
68. "Report of the Visiting Team, October 4-7, 1992," 4.

Transition and the Search for Excellence (1979-2006)

A final comment about the faculty related to faculty morale, which must "continue to be [of] concern to the administration." The team reported finding evidence of faculty morale issues "around faculty perceptions of certain administration priorities." This was coupled with "an apparent lack of collegiality between faculty and administration, or again at least the perception that such collegiality is less than would be expected in a small institution." Yet, all in all, "the standards pertaining to faculty . . . are clearly and consistently met and some with distinction."[69]

4. *Governance and Administration.* The visiting team found that governance standards were being met at the seminary. The Board of Directors was said to be "loyal and knowledgeable" and understanding their "proper role in the life of the school." The seminary had a "diligent, working Board."

Several concerns surfaced, however, in the area of internal administration. After affirming the importance of the recommendations of the seminary's self-study in the area of governance and administration, the team voiced several concerns:

- Ambiguity in the delegation of responsibility and authority, and the lack of clear lines of administrative reporting commonly followed in profit and not-for-profit institutions.
- Apparent absence of opportunity for middle- or second-tier administrators to have effective input to administrative decision making. One result of this is considerable confusion about institutional priorities, program directions, and resource allocation.
- The budgetary process seems to be the point at which governance and administrative procedures at PTS are most open to question. . . . The budget is constructed without significant involvement on the part of faculty and even middle and upper level administrators. As a result program initiatives are being launched without adequate consideration to resource allocation. Furthermore, the school is in danger of protecting its future economic security —

---

69. "Report of the Visiting Team, October 4-7, 1992," 4.

which it certainly is doing — by neglecting present needs be they personnel, program or equipment. Whatever the merits and/or results of the current financial policy may be, the processes by which budgetary priorities are set do not provide for open discussion. This factor, as much as anything, is creating a sense of stress within the institution. The school should be encouraged to implement effective mechanisms to reduce the uncertainty caused by the current structure.[70]

The team's recommendation was that

in light of the *Self-Study's* call for better "communication and integration of governing functions" (p. 98), the senior administration review its management style to determine if sufficient room is being allowed for faculty and academic administrators to share in decision making and the setting of priorities. Both the *Self-Study* and the results of our visit indicate that PTS is [a] highly controlled institution and there is at least the risk that this control will lead to institutional demoralization and underachievement.[71]

The team expressed its hope that the delegation of the seminary's academic life to the office of the dean, and the recently appointed Dean Keith F. Nickle, would meet many of the concerns raised in the self-study. The team hoped and expected that "this structure will be strengthened by enlarging its role in setting educational policy and budget priorities."

5. *Finance.* "PTS has achieved extraordinary financial stability," despite the previous ten years and some modest planned deficits, the report proclaimed. The market value of the seminary's endowment had moved from $12 million in 1982 to more than $63 million in 1992. While $22 million of this increase was due to market value growth, $29 million was added in new endowment. With adjustments in the amount of "draw" from the endowment in relation to the seminary's overall operating budget, Pittsburgh Seminary was able to decrease its

---

70. "Report of the Visiting Team, October 4-7, 1992," 5.
71. "Report of the Visiting Team, October 4-7, 1992," 5.

dependence on tuition revenue. The value of this was that "the seminary's concern with full-time enrollment becomes less a matter of balancing the budget and more a matter of attracting highly qualified students." The team declared that all financial standards are met, but even more that "the school, and especially its president must be commended for the truly notable accomplishments in achieving financial stability in less than a decade."[72]

6. *Library.* Another area in which Pittsburgh Seminary was commended was for the Barbour Library. The team indicated that "the collection is outstanding and one of the school's richest intellectual and research assets." The building itself and its new climate control system protected the collections. The library's automation project, "while in some eyes overdue, will provide a new range of service and outreach for the school." The "standing order list is among the strongest of any North American theological library and, indeed, without access to the PTS library, it is doubtful the University of Pittsburgh could offer the level of doctoral work it is now providing."[73]

While noting that "the intellectual and profession[al] credentials of the staff" are "highly commendable," the team indicated that the staffing level was "inadequate." The challenges of keeping up to date with cataloguing and the needs to respond to the evening program by extending coverage and support meant, according to the team and the *Self-Study* report, that additional salaried staff must be provided.

7. *Buildings.* The physical plant of the seminary, the team's report noted, had not been neglected on the seminary's way toward financial stability. The buildings, it found, were "attractive, durable, and in excellent condition" with "little or no evidence of deferred maintenance." Classrooms had been thoroughly renovated, short-term apartments had been added, and some faculty offices had been modernized. The library HVAC was upgraded and practically the whole campus had been retrofitted for handicapped access. The seminary's work had met and even exceeded all the standards in this area.

8. *Evaluation.* An important area on which accreditation visits focus is an institution's means of evaluating "outcomes" or the "results" of its educational program. This was a major issue for Pittsburgh Semi-

---

72. "Report of the Visiting Team, October 4-7, 1992," 6.
73. "Report of the Visiting Team, October 4-7, 1992," 6.

nary. For assessments to be effective, institutions need a "clear sense of identity and mission with more specific descriptions of goals and objectives."[74]

Evaluations are to take place throughout the seminary. Students are evaluated through the grades they receive in courses. Faculty are evaluated in the course evaluations that students complete at the end of a course. Pittsburgh faculty members were evaluated by peers in three-year cycles, and through the promotion and tenure processes, faculty were evaluated by peers and administration. However, no formal review process was in place for the evaluation of senior administrators, though the team report noted the Board of Directors was close to establishing this process.

The team found also that there was "no systematic program evaluation." In part, this was attributed to the report's earlier indication of the "lack of clarity about the institution's mission and its educational goals." The view of the team was that "once these are clarified, a more rigorous assessment of outcomes also will be possible." To this end, the team recommended that "a structured system for assessing outcomes be made part of the long-range planning cycle currently under discussion by the Directors."[75]

A continuing need, the report noted, was the evaluation of the role of the seminary's Business Office in the life of the institution. The team was clear that this office had "done its principal work effectively, yet a perception persists, chiefly on the part of faculty, that the Business Office treats them as somehow likely to be irresponsible in *their* management of the school's resources." The hope was that "ongoing evaluation of all functions in the school should help alleviate this type of misunderstanding."[76]

9. *Globalization.* Pittsburgh Seminary was commended for its attention to issues of globalization. Positive factors were that faculty members were encouraged to apply for research grants, courses were offered as both required and elective, guest lecturers and professors were invited to campus, and international students were afforded many opportunities. The team encouraged the seminary, however, "to give atten-

---

74. "Report of the Visiting Team, October 4-7, 1992," 7.
75. "Report of the Visiting Team, October 4-7, 1992," 7.
76. "Report of the Visiting Team, October 4-7, 1992," 8.

Transition and the Search for Excellence (1979-2006)

tion to the needs of globalization in theological education in its plans for future faculty."[77]

10. *Minority and Women's Concerns.* The visiting team found that the accreditation standard in this area was met, but also noted "a range of opinion about its bearing on life at the school":

> On the one hand we heard in some quarters that the school's posture of inclusiveness is eroding its purpose and quality and in other quarters we heard that women feel a high degree of personal comfort in the institution. In general, women and other minorities feel accepted in the PTS community both as employees and students. The team did hear concern expressed about the acceptance of persons preferring alternate lifestyles.
>
> Some students and faculty interviewed by the team thought there could be more discussion in classrooms about these issues as they are facing the church. Also, some students are looking for greater presence of women's concerns and materials in courses.[78]

This section of the report closed by noting that "although PTS has a written statement about inclusive language, it does not appear to be in general use."[79] Concerns about inclusive language had been of longstanding debate at Pittsburgh Seminary since the 1970s.

11. and 12. *Off Campus Programs* and *Placement.* Pittsburgh Seminary had no off-campus programs to be evaluated. Placement at the seminary for senior students was found to be "well organized and extensive." The placement program "accords closely with the operations of the Presbyterian church, but students in other denominations are provided comparable assistance."[80]

The rest of the visiting team's report centered on the various degree programs. The team noted that the M.Div. curriculum had been in place for nearly seventeen years and "there is evidence that a major revision may be required soon." While the field education component of the degree program had been substantially strengthened since the last accreditation visit, there was concern that "supervisory training is not

---

77. "Report of the Visiting Team, October 4-7, 1992," 8.
78. "Report of the Visiting Team, October 4-7, 1992," 8.
79. "Report of the Visiting Team, October 4-7, 1992," 8.
80. "Report of the Visiting Team, October 4-7, 1992," 8.

fully adequate, especially as it pertains to student pastors." There was a concern that "placement design also needs more scrutiny to assure that students in parish placements obtain wide exposure to the full dimension of pastoral ministry."[81]

The most significant change in the degree since the last accrediting visit, however, was with the introduction of the evening program and an urban ministry track. The evening program spread the M.Div. degree program over six years of part-time study. The urban ministry track provided for some free elective courses to be taken in this specialization. The challenge in the evening program, recognized by the faculty, was to avoid reliance on adjunct teaching faculty while also recognizing the concern that "the faculty may not have the energy to provide the required schedule of evening classes." Also, evening students did not have access to the full range of seminary services such as the library, bookstore, and other services. The team found that "it is not clear that the school has addressed the issues of personal and spiritual formation for these students as required by the standards."[82]

The seminary offered six joint M.Div. programs with local Pittsburgh schools, but the team noted their small enrollments and wished to "encourage the review of these programs with the anticipation that several of them will be closed immediately." The degree program targeted in this respect was the S.T.M. While some faculty defended the program because it provided a good preparatory base for doctoral study, "the school seems intent on structuring the program for the needs of international students." The report noted that the S.T.M. had been discontinued for two years and then reactivated in 1988 with a solid enrollment. But presently the enrollment had dropped to three students, which the team found to be an "insufficient base for a vigorous peer community."[83]

The D.Min. program with its three tracks — parish focus, Reformed focus, and pastoral care focus — presented several concerns:

> there is need for an ongoing means for reviewing the goals and objectives of the program; the selection and function of the "lo-

---

81. "Report of the Visiting Team, October 4-7, 1992," 9.
82. "Report of the Visiting Team, October 4-7, 1992," 9.
83. "Report of the Visiting Team, October 4-7, 1992," 10.

Transition and the Search for Excellence (1979-2006)

cal committees" developed by each student in his/her place of service needs clarification; the use of adjunct faculty must be evaluated periodically; stronger student advising, perhaps requiring more involvement of the program Director, is needed especially in the areas of elective selection.[84]

The team did not review the Ph.D. program, since it was not a degree granted by the seminary but was conducted in conjunction with the University of Pittsburgh, which granted the degree. It was noted that this program was important to the faculty, though "the partnership with the university appears to be one-sided. The program could not flourish without PTS's library, but seminary faculty feel they do not have an active hand in shaping the program. The team encourages the Dean to work towards a review of these issues."[85] The three non-degree programs offered — continuing education; the Center for Business, Religion and the Professions; and the Institute on Metro-Urban Ministry — were also mentioned. The team noted the "lack of any overarching coordination between these three programs."[86]

In light of the strengths and weaknesses, the visiting team had "Suggestions for Consideration":

- Clarification of internal channels of administration, delegation of responsibility and authority;
- Strengthen office and function of academic vice-president and dean;
- Involve faculty effectively in setting academic priorities, and academic policy, while reducing faculty involvement in administrative matters,
- Accelerate long range planning and involve faculty early in this process,
- Establish evaluation mechanisms for educational program, particularly the M.Div. program.

The team recommended reaffirmation of accreditation for the M.Div., M.A., S.T.M., and D.Min. degrees for ten years. It included two

---

84. "Report of the Visiting Team, October 4-7, 1992," 10.
85. "Report of the Visiting Team, October 4-7, 1992," 11.
86. "Report of the Visiting Team, October 4-7, 1992," 11.

notations: that there was an "insufficient number of students in one or more of this school's degree programs" (S.T.M.), and that "the library staff is inadequate." It was also recommended that the seminary be required to "submit a report in two years on the enrollment and staffing of the Metro-Urban and evening M.Div. programs."

This reaffirmation of accreditation was an important achievement for Pittsburgh Seminary. It signaled that the seminary as an institution and its overall program were moving in good directions. The suggestions in the visiting team's report, the notations, and the areas of weakness were ones that the seminary would need to address through the next decade.

The Vision Continues

The Pittsburgh Seminary Board of Directors received word of the seminary's reaccreditation at its November 1992 meeting. At that meeting it was also told of a $360,000 gift from the David and Lois Shakarian Foundation to renovate the Hungry-I-Thou to become the "Lois Shakarian James Center," with the facility becoming known as "The Shak." This facility continues to be a welcoming place for students and faculty to gather.

Enrollment for the 1992-93 academic year was announced as 310, with 144 in the M.Div. program, 125 in the D.Min. program, 15 in the M.A., 8 in the S.T.M., and 17 special students, with one intern. Overall there were 206 men and 104 women; 276 students were white, 23 black, and 11 of other races. The denominational breakdown was 148 Presbyterians, 55 United Methodists, 18 Lutherans, 13 United Church of Christ, 12 American Baptist, 6 Baptist, 8 Episcopal, 6 Roman Catholic, 4 Disciples of Christ students, and 40 members of other denominations. The spread of denominations here indicates at this point how broadly ecumenical Pittsburgh Seminary was becoming. While Presbyterians outnumbered the second-most represented denomination, the United Methodists, substantially, the United Methodist presence was of great importance to the seminary. Since the United Methodist Church indicates which seminaries are approved for its candidates, it has always been important for Pittsburgh Seminary to have a Methodist presence in the faculty and in the institution and to

Transition and the Search for Excellence (1979-2006)

provide the courses necessary for United Methodist students to fulfill their ordination requirements.

The Alternative Evening Program had 34 students participating, 13 of whom were entering students in fall 1992. The Student Association report to the Board at this meeting stated that "the seminary, including the Student Association, must strive to find ways to build community for the evening students."[87] Important too was the need to have the same high-quality classes available for this program as for the traditional program.

At the May 1993 Board meeting, Richard J. Oman was named acting vice president for Academic Affairs and acting dean of the faculty, effective June 1, 1993 (the "acting" title was removed at the next Board meeting). Keith F. Nickle had served two years in that position but wished to focus on classroom teaching and later resigned from the seminary as of July 15, 1994, to serve as a pastor.

The 199th Year Capital Campaign was announced at $13,150,231, surpassing the original goal of $10.750 million which was revised to $12.750 million and then to $13.1 million. On December 7, 1990, the seminary lost longtime Board member and benefactor Albert Shoemaker. Byron H. Jackson was named to the Louise and Perry Dick Chair in Church Education. The retirements of two longtime faculty members approached: Douglas R. A. Hare, who joined the faculty in 1964, was to retire on May 31, 1993, and Hans Eberhard von Waldow, who had been a faculty member since 1966, was to retire on the same date.[88]

The Board meeting of November 1993 was marked by the sad note of the death of the beloved Dr. William F. Orr at age eighty-six. Dr. Orr had taught at the seminary for thirty-seven years, beginning his career at Western Seminary in 1936 by teaching theology. He later switched to New Testament in 1957. He was famed for his participation in summer conferences for young people and later for his lectures on marriage and sexuality. Dr. Orr's personality, concern for students, and liveliness endeared him to generations of students, a sentiment captured in the title to a collection of essays in his honor published by a group of his former

---

87. Board of Directors Minutes, Pittsburgh Theological Seminary (November 11, 1992).

88. Board of Directors Minutes, Pittsburgh Theological Seminary (May 12, 1993).

students in 1990: *He Came Here and Loved Us: A Festschrift in Honor of William F. Orr.*[89]

The "Search for Excellence" in theological education was a theme that continued to figure into Pittsburgh Seminary's directions and commitments. Dr. Calian suggested to the Board at its November 1993 meeting that "clergy excellence" should be enhanced through the seminary's degree programs and continuing education events. The degrees should provide "a high level of competent leadership for the congregations" and the continuing education program "should not only stimulate but fill needed areas missing in a pastor's education."[90] Calian continued:

> those of us here at Pittsburgh Seminary have a major task before us in the coming years, namely, to reach a common understanding of excellence for this Seminary. What will it take for us to be an outstanding school for theological reflection, learning, and research? We are presently engaged in the politics of excellence. In the months ahead we must challenge one another in our search for excellence. After all the rhetoric, we frankly do not all share the same standards for excellence; open and honest dialogue must continue among us as we seek to reach consensus as we enter our Third Century in faithfulness to the reforming Spirit of our heritage.[91]

As the seminary continued to struggle with and dialogue about the nature of an "excellent" seminary and "excellent" pastoral leadership, it was seeking input from its various constituencies, including students. The Executive Committee of the Board adopted a Sexual Harassment Policy on September 13, 1993, which had been developed by Pittsburgh Seminary students, faculty, and administrators.

At its November Board meeting, the Board received the concerns of the Student Association. One element of importance in this report was

---

89. Robert C. Currey, Thomas J. Kelso, and Charlene Stoner Maue, eds., *He Came Here and Loved Us: A Festschrift in Honor of William F. Orr* (Watsontown, Pa.: The William F. Orr Festschrift Foundation, Inc., 1990). Cf. Howard Eshbaugh and James Arthur Walther, "Western Seminary," in *Ever a Frontier*, 150-52.

90. Board of Directors Minutes, Pittsburgh Theological Seminary (November 10, 1993).

91. Board of Directors Minutes, Pittsburgh Theological Seminary (November 10, 1993).

Transition and the Search for Excellence (1979-2006)

the need for the seminary to provide computers for student use. Subsequently, a computer lab was developed. A larger list of concerns of the Student Association had been on the agenda for a proposed dialogue between the student body and the faculty and administration on September 28, 1993. Since these concerns were wide-ranging and represent student input into the "search for excellence," their content is important to reproduce:

1. Student evaluations of all PTS courses should be published and open for student inspection.
2. The faculty should freshly commit themselves first and foremost to teaching PTS students; and secondly to scholarly publishing; and thirdly, to community involvement.
3. Course descriptions in the Catalog should be precisely reflected in course content.
4. PTS needs to ensure adherence to the seminary's Mission Statement.
5. Written student work submitted to instructors for evaluation should be returned to students in a timely manner with constructive, substantive and critical written comments by the Instructor.
6. A confidential psychological assessment needs to be part of the Admission policy.
7. The Instructors' grading policy should match PTS' official grading system.
8. If student presentations are to be a part of a class then they should constitute no more than 50% of class time.
9. A semester system should be implemented.
10. There should be a re-evaluation and publication of the process for awards, special scholarships and grants.
11. Professors should have posted office hours and should faithfully maintain these hours.

The voice of the students was further raised with proposals for a Town Meeting which was to be held on October 28, 1993. Proposals for consideration in this meeting:

1. A more aggressive financial aid policy should be investigated in order to make the seminary more affordable.

2. More funds need to be directed toward human resources.
3. In order to serve the PTS community better, facility hours should be expanded.
4. The PTS Bookstore should expand to a full service bookstore to include supplies, clothing, etc.
5. Security measures at PTS need to be improved.[92]

The concerns and proposals expressed here were ones the seminary community continued to work on through the following years. In some cases, changes were made and improvements were forthcoming; in other cases — such as the proposal to switch to the semester system — the seminary made no changes.

The Bicentennial (1994)

The bicentennial year of Pittsburgh Theological Seminary opened on January 9, 1994. The celebrations of two hundred years of theological education under the broad umbrella of "Pittsburgh Theological Seminary" were highlighted. This focus was on the seminary's claim to be both the "oldest and the youngest" of the seminaries in the American Presbyterian family and what is now the Presbyterian Church (USA). It is the "oldest" with roots stretching back to 1794; it is the "youngest" in that the current seminary was formed through the consolidation of Western and Pittsburgh-Xenia seminaries in 1959. A highlight of the bicentennial year was the history of the seminary edited by James Arthur Walther, emeritus professor of New Testament Literature and Exegesis, *Ever a Frontier: The Bicentennial History of the Pittsburgh Theological Seminary,* which featured historical essays from a number of writers as well as studies of special aspects of Pittsburgh Seminary's work, including pieces on the library, world mission, and archaeology.[93]

An article in a local newspaper in March 1994, titled "Pittsburgh Theological Seminary: 200 Years Old and Still Going Strong with Sharp Eye to Future," featured a number of facets of the seminary's history

---

92. "Concerns of the Student Association" with Board of Directors Minutes, Pittsburgh Theological Seminary (November 10, 1993).
93. See *Ever a Frontier.*

Transition and the Search for Excellence (1979-2006)

Pittsburgh Theological Seminary Logo

and present mission.[94] The piece pointed out that "where, a few decades ago, the average age of students at PTS was 22, it is now 35" with "women and minorities well represented, as well as commuting students." The roots of this change, it was noted,

> lie in the magnetism PTS has for adults perhaps hearing the call later in life, after embarking on a first career out of college, and the broader, more high-profile role in which PTS is engaging in the educational community, in the business world and in tackling urban social problems with a two-millenia-old formula ever more critical to man's survival.[95]

The seminary's new programs, such as the Center of Business-Religion-Professionals which "seeks to relate value questions in the society to people's life situations" and the Metro-Urban Institute, were also cited, with President Calian being quoted as saying that the seminary wants "to assist people not to run from the city's problems but to see how do we engage them and how the church can be supportive in giving moral direction."[96]

Calian also addressed the student average age question, saying he would like to see it reduced to "around 30." While "people are rethinking their life and are telling themselves they are not trapped by a seemingly empty vocation or career" and are "seeking a greater fulfillment,"

---

94. David Smith, "Pittsburgh Theological Seminary: 200 Years Old and Still Going Strong with Sharp Eye to Future," *The Sewickley Herald* (March 16, 1994): 32-33.
95. Smith, "Pittsburgh Theological Seminary," 33.
96. Smith, "Pittsburgh Theological Seminary," 34.

he indicated he felt there was a need "to recruit first career people," though it was not as easy as it had been to do so.[97]

The article said that with Pittsburgh's Seminary's "gifted faculty, one of the finest libraries in the nation and the James L. Kelso Bible Lands Museum, alive with archeological fragments of the past in and around the Holy Land," PTS "may well be the best-kept secret in Pittsburgh." The piece quoted Professor Robert Kelley, associated with the seminary at that point for thirty-eight years, as saying, "What really makes this place special are the three P's — plant, program and people."[98]

The piece concluded with evocations of images of the seminary's setting, past, and hope for the future:

> In a world that often seems on the edge of full-throttle breakdown, it would be understandable to imagine a theological seminary as a fading ember, a stodgy vestige of another era.
>
> But as another spring peppers the trees with life reborn along Highland Avenue, a heart continues to beat louder at PTS.
>
> From humble beginnings in the wilderness, it is a heart of many colors, many faces; a heart of many visions that inexorably link the past with the present through human hands joined in spirit.
>
> It is, after two centuries, a spirit thriving, flowering ever more brilliantly from a simple seed planted in the wilderness.[99]

Further Visions

Further visions for the future were set forth in an oral report to the Board of Directors presented by President Calian on May 11, 1994. This was an emerging process in planning called "Strategy 300." The plan was to be the first step in a constant process of planning and evaluation for the seminary's future, a "reality check to guide us into the future." This was set in the context of recognizing that "those who have their hope in Christ" are "ultimately subject to Divine intervention and guid-

---

97. Smith, "Pittsburgh Theological Seminary," 34.
98. Smith, "Pittsburgh Theological Seminary," 33.
99. Smith, "Pittsburgh Theological Seminary," 34.

ance anytime in our journey of faith. Our plans at best are penultimate; finality in the planning process belongs to God alone."[100]

President Calian highlighted issues confronting the schools of the Association of Theological Schools for the coming decade as identified by James Waits: 1) The Education of Theological faculty; 2) The Future of Accrediting Standards; 3) The Impact and Potential of Technology; 4) Underrepresentation in Theological Schools; and 5) Resources. To these, President Calian added five more issues: 6) The Composition of Students; 7) Pluralism and Globalization; 8) The Church; 9) Public Role of Religion; and 10) The Ownership Question. Calian identified three potential models that might serve Pittsburgh Seminary in the years ahead: 1) Continuing and Fine Turning the Present Curriculum and Programs; 2) Revisioning our Curriculum; 3) A Reduced and More Selective Student Body and an Expanded Continuing Education Program.

In all these, the emphasis was toward what the seminary could and should be for the future. The seminary's curriculum, which had not been fully changed for seventeen years, was a central concern. What might a new curriculum look like with a closer integration of theory and praxis and tying theological education to field experience? A revised curriculum might also lead to a new three-term schedule, the 4-1-4, with "at least one month in every school year dedicated to field experiences to widen the student's horizon to the raw realities of life." In the third and most extensive model, the underlying assumptions of the first two models gave way to the view that the seminary should have "*a dual purpose for existence* — dividing our resources equally between degree programs and continuing education events for clergy and laity." This model would open the seminary to the churches even more, and call for two student bodies, "co-existing together — seminarians preparing to be clergy as well as lay seminarians, both of whom will receive financial assistance."[101]

"Strategy 300" raised issues that continued to be part of Pittsburgh Seminary's ongoing discussions through the mid and late 1990s. In various forms, these issues became part of the seminary's long-range planning and discussions over curriculum and the ways in which the semi-

---

100. Carnegie Samuel Calian, "Strategy 300 — An Emerging Process in Planning," Board of Directors Minutes, Pittsburgh Theological Seminary (May 11, 1994), 1.
101. Calian, "Strategy 300," 1-7.

nary could serve the wider church. President Calian went on to develop some of his own views further in his book *The Ideal Seminary: Pursuing Excellence in Theological Education* (2002).[102]

Examination of the big questions of theological education continued in Calian's presentation to the Board at the November 1994 Board meeting when he addressed the question of the day for the Association of Theological Schools: "What is a good theological school?" He identified fourteen "benchmarks" from recent ATS literature and led the Board in a discussion of their own views on this question.[103]

The seminary's road toward financial stability was marked by the endowment being announced at the November Board meeting as standing at $76,728,478 (May 1994), up from $11,899,582 at the same time in 1980. The Doctor of Ministry program added a new focus to its program: the focus on Eastern Christian Context, to be carried out in conjunction with the Antiochian House of Studies in Bolivar, Pennsylvania. This venture would bring together Pittsburgh Seminary faculty with Eastern Orthodox Church scholars.

---

102. Calian, *The Ideal Seminary*.

103. Discussions about the nature of theological education in the 1990s were influenced by Edward Farley's *Theologia: The Fragmentation and Unity of Theological Education* (Philadelphia: Fortress Press, 1994) and earlier, David Kelsey's *To Understand God Truly: What's Theological about a Theological School* (Louisville: Westminster John Knox Press, 1992). The fourteen benchmarks identified by President Calian were: 1) The curriculum includes critical reflection with the integration of academic and experiential elements; 2) The school's mission expresses dual emphasis on theological and spiritual formation; scholarship and piety belong together; 3) Education engenders leadership that builds up the institution as well as being prophetic in society. Being loyal and critical at the same time are both important aspects for leadership; 4) The faculty supports academic as well as spiritual formation; 5) The faculty mentors as well as provides academic expertise; 6) The faculty are learners as well as teachers. The students are teachers as well as learners; 7) Resources are efficiently used to achieve mission; 8) There is flexibility within the school's mission; 9) There is adjustment and adapting to the post-Gutenberg (computer) era; 10) The school markets the ethos of tradition and also embraces the wider community of faith; 11) The school is strong financially and makes good use of limited resources; 12) The school's program strives for intentional coherence; 13) The program is global in outlook — to cover: evangelization, ecumenical cooperation, interfaith dialogue, peace and justice issues, relating to global and local needs; 14) The school is asking itself the question: Will the current practice of theological education in confessional schools (i.e. denominational seminaries) go the way of dinosaurs? See "Board Highlights" (November 1994).

Transition and the Search for Excellence (1979-2006)

By the next spring, the endowment had reached $78 million. It was announced that Ronald Cole-Turner of Memphis Theological Seminary would join the faculty in the endowed H. Parker Sharp Chair of Theology and Ethics and that Martha Bowman Robbins would become the first occupant of the Joan Marshall Chair in Pastoral Studies. This was the first endowed chair to be named after a woman, and Robbins became the first woman to occupy an endowed chair at Pittsburgh Theological Seminary. The Board also received a long-range plan that incorporated a number of elements from recent discussions throughout the seminary community.

The process of automating Barbour Library had been underway for some time. Librarian Dr. Stephen D. Crocco announced that spring that the library's new online "Calvin" system for accessing library information was becoming operative. This greatly enhanced the usability of the library's fine theological collection, which stood at 239,947 volumes, with 14,936 new items acquired during the previous year.

A gift from Mercedes and Albert Shoemaker was announced at the November 1995 Board meeting. This took the form of the "Shoemaker Round Table Discussion," a program to bring together a core group of seminary faculty members with twenty-five prominent clergy and laity for the purposes of discussion. The first roundtable was scheduled for October 1996, when the topic would center on "Future Scenarios for the Church."

Meanwhile the endowment of Pittsburgh Seminary continued to rise. The Board was told in November 1996 that the market value of the endowment had reached $99,608,561. Ten years earlier, on June 1, 1986, it had been at $31,003,968.

The summer of 1997 marked the beginning of what would become a significant ongoing program of Pittsburgh Seminary, the Summer Youth Institute (SYI). This initiative had its origins in 1994, when the seminary's Director of Admissions, Mary Serovy, wrote a proposal which sought funding for a program that would strengthen the "feeder systems" of the church, encouraging young people of high-school age to consider Christian ministry as a vocation. The routes to the ministry through the years had included a number of programs and approaches in churches that had been weakened. The grant was to provide an immersion experience for young people between their junior and senior years of high school to come to Pittsburgh Seminary for a week of theological and personal reflection to introduce them to the possibilities of ministry as a way to live out their Christian callings. This approach would reach them at a crucial period in their lives. The "scholars" would attend lectures by seminary faculty and engage in a number of activities to form community and also to enable reflection about Christian vocation and their choices for the future. The first Summer Youth Institute was held on the seminary campus on July 12-18, 1997, and was attended by thirty-one high school students.

From this beginning, the SYI has continued to grow, helped by funding from the Lilly Endowment, which gave a grant of $25,150 in December 1998, and later over $1.5 million. Support also comes from churches, institutions, and individuals who believe in the purpose of the SYI:

> to provide young people a Christian community where they can be challenged to move beyond their comfort zone in order to grow in faith, engage in academic theological study, explore ministry as a vocation, and learn about Pittsburgh Theological Seminary. SYI fosters intelligent, theologically informed leadership, provides skill training, encourages faith formation, and launches young people into service in the church and the world.[104]

In the ten years that followed, 315 young people participated in the SYI, representing 104 presbyteries, 38 states, and Puerto Rico. During the decade, 21 percent of the 131 alums who graduated from college attended seminary. Pittsburgh Seminary received seven of these twenty-eight students (the greatest number of SYI alums at any seminary), and by the time of "SYI X: A Celebration of Ten Years of the Summer Institute" in the summer of 2007, three of the SYI alums had graduated from Pittsburgh Seminary. The director of the SYI has been Rev. Mary Eleanor Johns, a Pittsburgh Seminary graduate. She began as an associate director of the program in 2000, became its director, and continues to visit over 75 percent of the SYI alums. By so doing she affirms to the young people that "they are an important part of the church." The visits "provide them with ongoing dialogue about their vocation as children of God serving the church and the world."[105]

---

104. Pittsburgh Theological Seminary, Catalog 2006-2007, 39.
105. Rev. Mary Eleanor Johns, "Report of the Summer Youth Institute to the Board of Directors, Pittsburgh Theological Seminary" (May 2007): 2.

Transition and the Search for Excellence (1979-2006)

PTS Students Beside PTS Banner

Another program that was to impact the seminary in the coming years was the inauguration of the Robert Meneilly Chair of Leadership and Ministry. This program enables the participation of a distinguished pastoral leader to be on campus, teach, and provide resources for students that directly relate to pastoral ministry. The first occupant of the chair was Dr. Richard A. Ray, a longtime pastor and former editor for John Knox Press. Ray served for two terms in this position, and his ministries were throughout much appreciated by students and seminary community.

In student life, the admission of one student made a significant impact on the community. Debbie Bower was an entering student in 1996 who did not have usable eyesight. Administrators began to provide for her special needs. One helped get academic material in accessible formats, even procuring plastic refrigerator magnets of the Hebrew alphabet so she could learn letter shapes by feeling them, as well as arranging for the time of a Hebrew tutor. Fellow students in the required Church

History class took turns taping readings for her as well as other class materials. PTS work-study students scanned other texts so that her talking computer could read files to her. The library located materials and secured an institutional membership with Recordings for the Blind and Dyslexic for access to already-recorded texts. Bower said that "through God's blessings, my resourcefulness, and the invaluable support of PTS" she achieved a 4.0 in her first year in seminary and graduated in 2000.[106]

As Pittsburgh Seminary approached the end of the 1990s, President Calian addressed "Eight Salient Trends" in theological education at the Board's November 1998 meeting:

1. Increased diversification within seminary communities of faculty, staff, students and trustees.
2. Emphasis on recruiting quality seminarians for leadership in the church.
3. Developing and implementing adequate systems of feedback — outcome assessments.
4. Place of tenure in theological education: the benefits and liabilities.
5. Expanding globalization on campus, mission concerns and interfaith dialogue.
6. Greater emphasis on trustee and presidential accountability and leadership within the context of shared governance.
7. Serving the people of God — increased lay theological education along with traditional theological education for seminarians.
8. The growing emphasis on technology in theological education and its impact on the learning process.

This listing of trends by President Calian was both descriptive and prescriptive. They emerged from Calian's experience of nearly twenty years as the seminary's president, and they pointed toward directions the seminary would pursue in the next years as Pittsburgh Seminary approached the new century.

At the November Board meeting, the Board was also given a "pop

---

106. Debbie Bower, personal correspondence.

Transition and the Search for Excellence (1979-2006)

quiz." The answers were facts about the seminary. These included: number of students: 306; full-time faculty: 23; full-time administrators: 11; employees: 76; volumes in the library: 322,000; continuing education attendance: 2015; adjunct professors: 13; number of seminary personal computers: 101; fully endowed chairs: 19; number of buildings: nine, on thirteen acres; endowment as of May 31, 1998: 130 million.[107]

On June 1, 1999, John E. Wilson Jr., Church History professor on the faculty, was named vice president of Academic Affairs and dean of the faculty, to serve until 2005.[108] Wilson's leadership was to prove important in helping the seminary navigate a number of issues and in its interface with accrediting agencies. His work as dean also drew wide support from among the faculty.

The seminary's educational program continued to expand. At the November 1999 Board meeting, Board members learned about the partnering of the seminary's D. Min. program in its "Reformed Focus" track with the University of Aberdeen, Scotland. This new joint venture, which entailed exchanges of students and faculty, brought the number of D.Min. students to 125.

At the same time, the seminary's enrollment stood at 318, including 152 in the M.Div. program. There were 120 women and 198 men. The largest student denominational group was the Presbyterian Church (USA) with 130 students, followed by 59 students from the United Methodist Church. 40 students were enrolled in the evening program, with four having graduated in May 1999. Seventeen percent of the entering class signed up for the evening program.[109]

By the next May — the first Board meeting of the new century — the seminary elected Nancy Lapp as curator emerita of the seminary's Kelso Bible Lands Museum. Nancy Lapp served faithfully for thirty years, after the death of her husband, Paul. Returning to the seminary was John White as dean of students. White had been an effective director of Admissions and Student Relations at his alma mater from 1980-88 and lately had served on the Board of Directors.[110]

---

107. Board of Directors Minutes, Pittsburgh Theological Seminary (November 11, 1998).

108. Board of Directors Minutes, Pittsburgh Theological Seminary (May 12, 1999).

109. Board of Directors Minutes, Pittsburgh Theological Seminary (November 10, 1999).

110. Board of Directors Minutes, Pittsburgh Theological Seminary (May 10, 2000).

The U.S. economy and the stock market had negative effects on Pittsburgh Seminary's endowment. At the May 2001 Board meeting, the Finance Committee reported a decrease in the endowment from $136 million on December 31, 2000, to $131 million in April 2001.[111] The bad trend continued: by November 2001 the endowment had decreased by another six million dollars, and the three-month period ending on September 30, 2001, had been one of the twenty worst quarters in the history of the stock market.[112] Yet through this period, the seminary continued to advance in program and facilities.

The most visible sign of facility development was the decision at the May 2001 Board meeting to demolish Fisher Hall instead of renovating it and to construct a new dormitory. The estimated cost was $6 million (with a 5 percent contingency). The Board was told that "the construction of a new building will be more economical than renovations to Fisher Hall." The new dormitory would be built almost exactly parallel to Fisher and a few feet in front of it. Fisher Hall had served the seminary as a residence facility for forty years.

With the new century underway, President Calian spoke of "Nine Challenges for Seminary Education Today." Once again, these took the "temperature" of theological education in America, particularly at Pittsburgh Seminary, and looked into the opening years of the new century and the challenges being posed to contemporary theological education:

1. Educating for leadership and change in our churches and institutions.
2. Maintaining academic freedom while being faithful to confessional traditions.
3. Who owns the seminary? Clarifying issues of governance, accountability, responsibility, and communication.
4. What is our message? Witnessing to incarnate forgiveness within a more cohesive curriculum.
5. Making the world our classroom, discovering new ways to minister in a global, multi-cultural and technological society.

---

111. Board of Directors Minutes, Pittsburgh Theological Seminary (May 9, 2001).

112. Board of Directors Minutes, Pittsburgh Theological Seminary (November 14, 2001). The Board Minutes mistakenly indicate the 122 million figure for November 9, 2002, instead of 2001.

Transition and the Search for Excellence (1979-2006)

6. Shifting from a predominantly "clergy paradigm" to a "people of God" paradigm; expanding the horizons of theological education.
7. Enlisting and retaining qualified seminarians.
8. Becoming a more intentional community of faith through worship, study, and fellowship.
9. Developing financial stability: money follows ministry and increases visibility.[113]

As usual, Calian's listings here were wide-ranging in scope. They were indicative of the challenges to U.S. seminaries on a whole spectrum of fronts. Meanwhile, the seminary's programs kept growing. The Lilly Endowment announced it would provide the Summer Youth Institute with a $300,000 grant to keep the program operative for 2003-05. Dr. James E. Davison became the director of Continuing Education on October 1, 2001, replacing Mary Lee Talbot. Charles Hambrick-Stowe, who had replaced Dr. John E. Mehl as director of the D.Min. program, announced a new Urban Church focus for the program, to be carried out in partnership with the seminary's Metro-Urban Institute. This meant the Doctor of Ministry program now had five areas or tracks: Parish, Pastoral Care, Reformed, Eastern Christian, and Urban. Mehl had been named director emeritus of the Doctor of Ministry Program in May 2001 and had led the program since February 1985. During that time the Pastoral Care focus had been reinstituted; the Reformed Focus had been linked with the University of Aberdeen, Scotland; the Ministry in the Eastern Christian Context Focus had begun; and the Parish focus had been modified to emphasize rural and small-town settings.[114]

In October 2002, Pittsburgh Seminary received an accreditation visit from the Association of Theological Schools and the Middle States Association of Colleges and Schools. This visit assessed the life and work of the seminary, using in particular the extensive self-study document completed by the seminary in June 2002. This document examined many areas of the seminary, made recommendations, and was commended by the accrediting team as a "full and serious engagement

---

113. Board of Directors Minutes, Pittsburgh Theological Seminary (May 9, 2001).

114. Board of Directors Minutes, Pittsburgh Theological Seminary (May 9, 2001 and November 14, 2001).

in the self-study process."[115] The self-study noted a measure of the changes that had taken place at the seminary since the last accreditation visit in 1992 when it indicated that "Over 50% of our faculty have retired and been replaced by new personnel since 1992."[116]

On February 14, 2003, ATS notified the seminary that it was reaffirming Pittsburgh Seminary's accreditation for a period of ten years (until Fall 2012). On March 10, 2003, the Middle States Commission did the same. ATS commended a number of "distinctive strengths" of the seminary including its fiscal vitality; the maintenance, improvement, and addition of new facilities; library resources; the Metro-Urban Institute; and the high caliber of faculty teaching and scholarship. The commission issued no official "notations" but did target areas of needed growth during the next accreditation period and required a report by April 1, 2004 on several issues: analysis of seminary governance, the disposition of curriculum review, and the implementation of institutional assessment to revise a mission-driven, long-range plan of the institution.

A highlight of the Board of Directors meeting in May 2003 was the dedication of the seminary's new residence hall to replace Fisher Hall. This facility was begun in fall 2001 and was opened in January 2003. The hall houses single students (male and female) during the academic year and serves as housing for campus guests and continuing education participants. Later, the hall was named Calian Hall, in honor of Sam Calian and his wife, Doris, in recognition of their twenty-five years of service to the seminary.

A program of growing prominence within the seminary in these years was the World Mission Initiative (WMI). This program seeks to develop mission vision among students and laypersons, nurture missionary vocations, and cultivate missional congregations throughout the church. To this end, WMI organizes cross-cultural mission trips and initiates internships to give students a view of the global church. Participation in these events is urged for students as part of their seminary education. The initiative builds networks with various groups to com-

---

115. The Association of Theological Schools in the United States and Canada and the Middle States Association of Colleges and Schools, "Report of a Comprehensive Visit to Pittsburgh Theological Seminary" (October 13-16, 2002), 4.

116. Pittsburgh Theological Seminary, "Self-Study" (April 22, 2002), 1.

Transition and the Search for Excellence (1979-2006)

Calian Hall

municate the gospel and seeks to connect local congregations with people, resources, and opportunities to live out the Great Commission. Donald Dawson became director of the program in 2001.

A further connection of Pittsburgh Seminary with a particular local church was announced at the Board meeting of November 2003 with the pastor/professor partnership between the seminary and Shadyside Presbyterian Church. Dr. M. Craig Barnes, who had been serving the seminary as the Meneilly Professor of Leadership and Ministry, was also called to become the pastor of the Shadyside church. Thus Barnes began to fulfill a single ministry with two components, as professor and pastor. The seminary has seen this arrangement as part of its mission to serve local churches, while the Shadyside Church expands its wider ministry in teaching through the work of its pastor. In interpreting this arrangement in the installation sermon for Dr. Barnes in the Shadyside Church, President Calian said, "Pittsburgh Seminary's classroom and Shadyside's pulpit have been joined together for the mutual benefit not only of our students but for the edification of this congregation in our common ministry to the glory of God."[117]

The seminary's ongoing work to respond to the requests by the Association of Theological Schools for analysis of the seminary's governance, disposition of a curriculum review, and the implementation of institutional assessment was presented to the Board on May 12, 2004. This work had involved a number of committees and persons for a period of many months. The follow-up visit of ATS and the Middle States Association was scheduled for October 26-27, 2004. When the Board received the report on May 11, 2005, it was pleased to learn that the seminary "has made demonstrable progress in terms of the issues raised in the ATS accreditation report. With a committed faculty of scholars and administrators, supportive Board of Trustees, and strong physical and financial resources it is well poised to meet the challenges and transitions before it and continue its wonderful tradition."[118]

The work of developing a new M.Div. curriculum to replace the one that had been in place since the 1970s had been long and arduous. Spurred by the prescription to do so in relation to the visits of ATS and the Middle States teams, a number of options had been discussed. Prominent among these were a return to a two-semester academic calendar and the instituting of a January term between the two semesters. In the end, the decision was made to continue the three-term structure but to adjust required courses.

At the May 2005 Board meeting, the Board approved these changes to the M.Div. curriculum:

> All incoming students, beginning with the 2006/07 academic year, must take both introductory Bible courses (two in Old Testament, two in New Testament). Students are no longer required to take 1) Church and Society Global, 2) one elective each in Theology and Ethics (beyond the required introductory courses), and 3) Biblical Theology. (Current students, however,

---

117. Carnegie Samuel Calian, "Toward the Ideal Church," February 15, 2004, in *Pittsburgh Theological Seminary Panorama* 44:1 (Lent/Easter 2004): 9.

118. The Association of Theological Schools in the United States and Canada and for the Middle States Association of Colleges and Schools, "Report of a Focused Visit to Pittsburgh Theological Seminary," October 26-27, 2004.

Transition and the Search for Excellence (1979-2006)

shall be given a choice of the existing curriculum or the prospective curriculum.)[119]

Particular concern about the loss of the Church and Society (Global) course had been expressed by some faculty, since for decades this course had helped introduce students to church and society issues beyond their own communities and nation.

A change in faculty governance should also be noted. The Board approved the replacement of the Faculty Review Committee, the group that had examined faculty work in relation to issues of tenure and promotion, with the body of all tenured faculty, who became the overseeing group to make recommendations on these issues to the president of the seminary. The expected effect of this change was to insure that this work was carried out by those who had already had experience in these processes.

A highlight of the Board meeting of November 9, 2005, was an announcement of international interest. Professor Ron E. Tappy, G. Albert Shoemaker Professor of Bible and Archaelogy and Director of the Kelso Bible Lands Museum, had been leading archaeological expeditions and digging in the lowlands of Juday (Abrabic: *Zeitah*) since 1999. Approximately twenty-five Pittsburgh Seminary students had excavated with him there through the years. On July 15, 2005, they made a dramatic discovery at Tel Zayit. It was "an inscription that bears the oldest known securely datable example of an abecedary, that is, the letters of the alphabet written out from beginning to end in their traditional sequence." According to Tappy, the finding represented "an extremely important landmark in the history of alphabetic writing. All successive alphabets in the ancient world (including non-Semitic ones, such as Greek) derived from the alphabet seen in the Tel Zayit inscription." This story broke in the *New York Times* on November 9, 2005, the same day as the seminary's Board meeting. Dr. Tappy explained the significance of this find to the Board, and the history of Pittsburgh Seminary's long involvement with archaeological research continued.[120]

---

119. Board of Directors Minutes, Pittsburgh Theological Seminary (May 11, 2005): 4. The four required Bible courses are: Historical Books; Prophets and Psalms; Gospels, Acts, and Johannine Epistles; New Testament Letters.

120. Ron E. Tappy, "This Summer: The 2006 Season of Excavations at Tel Zayit, Israel" *Pittsburgh Theological Seminary Panorama*, 45:3 (Spring 2006): 8-9. The excavation's website is www.zeitah.net

Toward Transition

In the background for over a year by this time was Calian's announcement of his intention to retire on January 31, 2006, after serving twenty-five years as president of Pittsburgh Seminary. In May 2004, Board President Robert T. Harper formed a Transition Committee to prepare the way for the change in leadership at Pittsburgh Seminary. This committee made its first report at the Board meeting of November 10, 2004. The next steps were the formation of a Presidential Search Committee, chaired by longtime Board member Thomas Nelson. The vice chair was Board member John Isherwood. An academic consultant service was employed to begin to assemble and vet potential candidates for the position. By February 2005, a Presidential Search profile was completed. This laid out a vision for Pittsburgh Seminary's continued growth and the qualities for leadership necessary in the next president.

The elements in the "Vision for New Leadership," identified for the seminary's next President, included

- Development of an Enabling Strategic Plan
- Application of Seasoned Administrative Skills
- Sustaining the Human Resource
- Building a Positive Institutional Culture
- Fund Development
- Enhancing the seminary's Public Profile and Global Reputation

The plan was to have a new president-elect who could work with and learn from President Calian for a period of time before assuming the presidency. This would ensure that the passing of the torch of presidential leadership would proceed smoothly.

President Calian's Quarter-century of Service

In reflecting on his presidency in July 2004, President Calian saw it as having been composed of three phases. The first was "The Politics of Resurrection," which focused on institutional survival. The second and present phase, he wrote, was "The Politics of Excellence," which focused on the strengthening of the faculty. President Calian's assess-

Transition and the Search for Excellence (1979-2006)

PTS Chapel Service

ment of the phase then beginning and the movement toward the future he called "The Politics of Identity as a Centrist Seminary," asking, "what does it mean to practice being Reformed and Reforming within a Presbyterian heritage seeking to meld diversity and unity in Christ?" He summarized his view of the "Calian legacy" as "an emphasis on *change and innovation* as we process and clarify the complexities of the seminary's community before its wide range of stakeholders." He concluded by speaking of Pittsburgh Seminary's unique position "historically among our Presbyterian seminaries to be known not only as the *oldest and the youngest* seminary of the church, but even more, for its faithfulness to its Reformed Presbyterian heritage and its Reforming innovative spirit within a changing world." [121]

The local newspaper, *The Pittsburgh Post-Gazette,* published an article the day before President Calian's retirement which reflected on his

---

121. Carnegie Samuel Calian, "President Calian's Presidency from 1990 to the Present" (July 2004): 8, 9.

presidency. It pointed out that during his twenty-five year tenure, the seminary's endowment had "skyrocketed from $9 million to $160 million" while enrollment more than doubled to 380 students. This success entailed change and controversy, with the newspaper noting that "some say he saved the future of the oldest seminary in the Presbyterian Church (USA). Others claim he abandoned cutting-edge theology and social ethics to court conservative support."[122]

Calian's response was that, in the writer's words, "he had created a centrist school, that prepares pastors for congregations, not the ivory towers. When he arrived in 1981, ties to local churches were weak, partly because what was taught in class often bore little resemblance to basics learned in Sunday school." Calian said, "I was looking to be faithful to our theological heritage.... I'm a conservative in that I see some basic convictions that are essential to the faith. But I'm open-ended, in that I understand that our day-to-day life often has more questions than answers."

What is agreed on by all, however, is that Calian's success in fundraising enabled the seminary to be put on a more solid financial footing. The endowment of eighteen chairs and fortification of two others, the creation of the new institutes and programs, and the overall improvements to the campus and campus life are all marks of the "Calian legacy." When asked to what he attributed his "golden touch," the outgoing president said, "First and foremost, dependence on God. Only God can create the chemistry in the other person to want to be generous."[123]

Calian also reflected that his "greatest challenge" was "to build a Seminary community of competence, creativity, and compassion." As for the challenges of the twenty-five years, he said,

> Many of the challenges of 25 years ago have been met — improved facilities, stable finances, growth in diversity and number of faculty, administration, and students. Also many new pro-

---

122. Ann Rodgers, "Calian Brought Change, Money to Seminary," *The Pittsburgh Post-Gazette* (January 30, 2006): B1-B2.

123. Rodgers, "Calian Brought Change," B-2. The Fall 2005 issue of the Seminary's *Panorama* highlighted the "Calian Legacy" on campus as including: renovations to the Hicks Chapel; handicap accessible ramp to Barbour Library; library renovations including rare-book and special collections preservation; new Residence (Calian) Hall; renovation and technology installations in Long Hall classrooms; Shakarian Center (former Hungry-I-Thou); on-campus computer labs; expansion of Kelso Bible Lands Museum; and the Renovated Kadel Dining Hall.

Transition and the Search for Excellence (1979-2006)

grams were added — Summer Youth Institute, Metro-Urban Institute, World Mission Initiative, Center for Business, Religion and Public Life, and growth in our Continuing Education events will lead the seminary in new directions.

God has led me through many exciting adventures during my life so far and I trust and expect that there is more to come. I pray that I am faithful to God's leading whatever that may be. And I know also that Pittsburgh Seminary is in God's hands and will continue to grow in many ways.[124]

A Calian Retirement Gala was held on the seminary campus and at the Omni William Penn Hotel in Pittsburgh on January 26, 2006. Nearly three hundred students, staff, faculty, Board, and community members attended. During the meal, Armenian selections in celebration of the Calian family were played by musicians. January 26 was proclaimed "Carnegie Samuel Calian Day in the City of Pittsburgh."

There were two particular highlights of the festivities. One was the announcement that Sam and Doris Calian were to receive a trip to Ethiopia, a country Sam Calian had not visited but which is important for the development of Orthodox Christianity, a lifelong interest of President Calian. The second announcement was that, as noted above, the Board of Directors had indicated that the new residence hall would be known as the "Calian Residence Hall" in tribute to Sam and Doris Calian.

The Calians themselves responded with gratitude. They announced that they would complete the $100,000 Calian Endowment Fund. This fund encourages community service and spirit at Pittsburgh Seminary. Each year an award would be made to the student, staff, and faculty person who most exhibited this type of commitment.[125]

The "Search for Excellence" for which Calian had quested during his quarter-century of service at Pittsburgh Seminary was recognized. In its resolution of thanks to Dr. Calian, the Pittsburgh Seminary Board of Directors elected Carnegie Samuel Calian as President and Professor of Theology Emeritus at Pittsburgh Theological Seminary.[126]

---

124. *Pittsburgh Theological Seminary Panorama*, 45:2 (Fall 2005): 16.
125. *Pittsburgh Theological Seminary Panorama*, 45:3 (Spring 2006): 16.
126. Minutes of the Special Meeting of the Board of Directors, Pittsburgh Theological Seminary (January 25, 2006): 2.

CHAPTER 7

Forming Pastor-Theologians

(2006-2009)

The Presidential Search Committee spent eight months reviewing over 100 applicants for the position of president. At this point in the history of Pittsburgh Seminary, there was no lack of applicants for the presidential position. Seven of the top candidates were interviewed. At a called meeting of the Board of Directors, the Search Committee unanimously nominated the Rev. Dr. William J. Carl III as president and professor of Homiletics at Pittsburgh Theological Seminary. He was to become president-elect on October 1, 2005, and become president on February 1, 2006.

Bill Carl was no stranger to Pittsburgh Seminary. He was born in Broken Arrow, Oklahoma, in 1948 and grew up in Bartlesville, Oklahoma where his father was a Presbyterian pastor. He graduated from the University of Tulsa, (B.S., 1970), Louisville Presbyterian Theological Seminary (M.Div., 1973), and received his Ph.D. degree in Rhetoric and Communication from the University of Pittsburgh (1977). During his years in Pittsburgh, Bill and his wife, Jane Alexander Carl, lived on the Pittsburgh Seminary campus, where Carl studied particularly with homiletician David Buttrick. He also taught on the seminary faculty for one year as an instructor in Homiletics (1975-76).

Carl became an associate professor of Homiletics and Worship and instructor in New Testament Greek at Union Theological Seminary in Virginia from 1976 to 1983. He was ordained in the Presbyterian Church (USA) in 1973 and in 1983 moved to Dallas, where he became pastor of the First Presbyterian Church. During that time the church

President William J. Carl III and Jane Carl

grew significantly in many ways, and Carl actively participated in many community and national religious groups, as well as serving the Presbyterian Church (USA) in a number of significant ways. Among Carl's books are *Preaching Christian Doctrine* (1984), *Waiting for the Lord* (1988), and *The Lord's Prayer for Today* (2006).[1]

The inauguration of President Carl as president of Pittsburgh Theological Seminary was held on May 10, 2006 at the East Liberty Presbyterian Church. The celebration coincided with the seminary's Board of Directors meeting.

---

1. Carl's other books include, with Richard I. Pervo, *Proclamation II, Epiphany, Series C* (Philadelphia: Fortress, 1979); with Bruce Vawter, *Proclamation II, Easter, Series A* (Philadelphia: Fortress, 1981); *Church People Beware!* (Lima, Ohio: C.S.S. Publishing, 1992); *Dancing in Holy Places* (Lima, Ohio: C.S.S. Publishing, 2008); and editor, *Best Advice: Wisdom on Ministry from Thirty Leading Pastors and Preachers* (Louisville: Westminster John Knox Press, 2009).

Forming Pastor-Theologians (2006-2009)

In his first report to the Board, the President indicated there had been a smooth transition in his work with Dr. Calian for four months (October 1, 2005, through January 31, 2006). He then highlighted several items of importance as he began his presidential service: community, financial stability, development, visibility, and vision. During the following months, President Carl initiated discussions with various constituencies in the seminary community to create a new vision statement for the institution from which would also emerge a new mission statement. From these bases, Carl looked toward further developments in areas such as curriculum review, facility improvement, and the feasibility of a new capital campaign.

Faculty representative to the Board Dr. Andrew Purves reported at the May meeting that the faculty was "supportive of one another and not competitive." He also noted that the faculty was "unanimous in its welcome of Bill Carl" and that it was also unanimous in its "appreciation for the special gifts God has given to Barry Jackson as our Dean."[2] Dr. Byron Jackson, longtime professor of Church Education and Director of Field Education, had succeeded Dr. John Wilson and been named interim dean in the final year of Calian's presidency.

The Board met again on November 8, 2006 and heard that the seminary's endowment stood at $157 million. The seminary had ended in a positive financial position for twelve of the last thirteen years. President Carl reported on the various aspects of his work, indicating further steps being taken to develop shared mission and vision statements. Dr. Carl also made a special presentation to the Board on major elements of vision and mission as they currently stood. A Faculty/Board retreat was held in February 2007 for conversations on strategic planning, basic core ideology, mission, values, and an envisioned future for Pittsburgh Seminary.

In the following months, the mission and vision statements emerged and were approved by the Board in May 2007.

Mission

> On a dynamic and challenging global stage
> Pittsburgh Theological Seminary plays its part in
> God's redemption of the world through Jesus Christ

2. Board of Directors Minutes, Pittsburgh Theological Seminary (May 10, 2006): 8-9.

PTS Faculty (2007)

By preparing leaders who proclaim with great joy
God's message of good news in both word and deed!

That's who we have been since 1794 and who we continue to be. It's our core theology and our reason for being. Where do we go now? Read the Vision and you will see!

Vision

The question is not what are we doing on this 13 acre campus, but what is God doing out there in the world and how can we be a part of it. With God as author and director, Christ as protagonist and the Holy Spirit as prompter, we participate in the great drama of salvation history by preparing

Pastor-theologians and **joyful communicators of the Word** who are

- **Inspired by** and **enthusiastic about** the Gospel of Jesus Christ, which points to the One who is the center of our lives and the center of the Church;
- **Engaging preachers and teachers** who interpret both sa-

cred texts and contemporary contexts, and **have the audacity to preach with joy** amidst a broken and hurting world — *theologians-in-residence* who understand history and the constantly changing culture in which we live;
- **Perceptive spiritual directors who "equip the saints"** for ministry by helping people discern their gifts through worship and education, and **helping them see that true joy is no stranger to pain** so that, moved by the Holy Spirit, they can say with confidence, "I care therefore I am";
- **Life-long learners** who **continue seeking wisdom and modeling the faith** knowing that the front line of ministry is not the church building but wherever the people live, work, study and play **"glorifying God and enjoying God forever"**;
- Mission-minded advocates who delight in both **evangelism and social justice ministries**, which are neither conservative nor liberal because Jesus never labeled them that way since both represent the Gospel as in the Luke-Acts tradition;
- **Wise leaders who** demonstrate with integrity how to build **joyful communities** by creating with God's help **positive, happy and healthy cultures** where people "speak the truth in love" and understand that real friendship in Christ means having the right to disagree knowing that mutual respect and affection are not at stake;
- **Responsible stewards who** know how to **raise and manage resources** while **encouraging people to be "cheerful givers."**

Pittsburgh Theological Seminary — we are more than stately buildings and nice classrooms nestled in an urban setting of pathos and hope. "Surprised by joy," we are a transient community of scholars and learners who rejoice at the opportunity to share in God's redemptive work in the world. We prepare students of the Word who, called by God, committed to Christ and empowered by the Holy Spirit, bear witness to the joy of the Gospel. We join the Church through the ages in affirming Christ as Savior and Lord and, following his ancient commission that is new every morning, our graduates and program participants proclaim with great gladness God's grace-filled message of healing and shalom. To God be the glory!

Pittsburgh Theological Seminary Logo (2008)

PITTSBURGH THEOLOGICAL SEMINARY

At the November 2007 Board meeting, "Suggested Elements of a Strategic Plan for Pittsburgh Theological Seminary" was shared with the Board of Directors. These seven elements expanded on the seven parts of the vision statement and became key elements in the production of the strategic plan to guide Pittsburgh Seminary into the future.[3]

This Board meeting also featured a report on the seminary endowment. The seminary was debt-free, and on May 31, 2007, the endowment stood at $170,489,161. In historical perspective, this marked a $69 million increase from December 31, 1996, when it stood at $101,424,862. Three valuation dates in the last ten years had been marked by a negative

---

3. Board of Directors Minutes, Pittsburgh Theological Seminary (November 14, 2007).

Forming Pastor-Theologians (2006-2009)

percentage change or loss (2000, 2001, 2002). Twenty-five years earlier, the endowment had been worth only $13,827,000.[4]

To support the new mission and vision statements, the Board adopted a strategic plan at its special meeting on February 23, 2008.[5] The five areas that plan addressed were: 1) improving programs of study; 2) raising admissions standards for students and support levels during their education and their transition to positions of leadership; 3) strengthening service to those already in ministry and to lay leaders through improvements in continuing education programs; 4) continual commitment as a community of scholars to being formed through worship, hospitality, and joyful service; and 5) the practicing and modeling of stewardship through careful guardianship, planning, and fundraising.

The strategic plan, vision statement, and mission statement were all designed to work together to carry out the institutional purposes and ministries of Pittsburgh Theological Seminary. The emphasis of the seminary in the presidency of William Carl moved toward "preparing pastor-theologians and joyful communicators of the Word."[6] In this way, Pittsburgh Theological Seminary has moved from "ever a frontier" to "ever a vision," seeking foremost the glory of God.

---

4. Board of Directors Minutes, Pittsburgh Theological Seminary (November 14, 2007).

5. Board of Directors Minutes, Pittsburgh Theological Seminary (February 23, 2008). This document is included as Appendix A.

6. See William J. Carl III, "Pastor-theologians for the 21st Century," *Panorama* 47:2 (Spring 2008): 8-9. This issue is devoted to "Perspectives on Pastor-Theologians."

POSTSCRIPT

Ever a Vision!

Pittsburgh Theological Seminary has faced many challenges during its five decades of existence. These have been both internal and external. The consolidation of Pittsburgh-Xenia and Western Seminaries in 1959 brought into sharp relief a number of the tensions inherent in the relationships of the new denomination the seminary would serve. The traditions of the "old UP's" and the "Presbyterians" brought heritages with different emphases and styles of Christian life. Approaches to theology and to theological education at variance with each other became features of the new Pittsburgh Seminary, even as the legacies of the past lived on for a number of years. In its early years, the seminary had to find ways to navigate these differences while seeking to provide the kind of theological education needed by those who would serve churches in the United Presbyterian Church in the United States of America.

The growing pains of the "two become one" were supplemented by the difficulties of the impinging cultures of the 1960s, in which cultural and societal unrest presented a host of new problems and issues for theological education in general and for Pittsburgh Seminary in particular. Struggles over the seminary's curriculum were difficult at Pittsburgh Seminary; the traditional approaches of emphasizing the classical disciplines conflicted with desires for freedom of choice by students to plan their own studies and for the seminary to offer courses that could speak directly to the upheavals in church and society. The "Freedom to Learn" approach was coupled with a governance style that invited broad and open participation by the community. When it became apparent that some core elements were required for solid theological education and that the demands of the open community on time and energies of faculty and administration were severe, the structures of governance for the seminary were changed.

Some effects of the seminary's path in the view of many were a loss of focus and direction and a feeling that the institution was out of touch with the needs of the church constituencies it was trying to serve in the surrounding region. The Rea Report was a wakeup call that led to stronger efforts by the seminary to initiate more structure, accountability, and opportunities for interaction with surrounding pastors and churches through continuing education programs.

The establishment of the seminary's vision as it evolved in the second half of this time period brought the institution into a stronger financial position (particularly through the growth of its endowment), increased student enrollment, created new and vital programs for pastors and laity, and emphasized assembling an excellent faculty who would be scholars also committed to the church and its mission and to providing theological education to meet the needs of churches year in and year out.

The vision of Pittsburgh Seminary as it has emerged and continues to develop now emphasizes the proclamation of the gospel of Jesus Christ in word and deed and the formation of "pastor-theologians." The vision calls for the education of "engaging preachers and teachers who interpret both sacred texts and contemporary contexts, and have the audacity to preach with joy amidst a broken and hurting world." The challenges continue to be many, but the vision guides the way.

Pittsburgh Theological Seminary builds on the richness of its past heritage. It draws on the resources it receives in the present. It dreams toward a future in which the church of Jesus Christ is served as women and men engage in the ministries to which God calls them. Through all the challenges of culture and church and through the vicissitudes of human life itself, Pittsburgh Theological Seminary seeks to be faithful to the gospel of Jesus Christ entrusted to it. The seminary looks to serve Jesus Christ, to follow where it is led, and to carry out its mission and ministry by living out God's vision in the world.

APPENDIX A

Strategic Plan for Pittsburgh Theological Seminary, 2008

February 23, 2008

In order to be faithful to our mission, we who are part of Pittsburgh Theological Seminary commit our energies and resources to achieving this Strategic Plan —

1.0 **We will strive for a new, higher level of academic excellence in service of the Church**

    1.1 *Improving our Programs of Study*

        1.1.1 In order to improve our academic programs, we will implement a plan for their assessment. Through the leadership of the Faculty, we will engage in a deliberative process that will examine our faithfulness to our purpose as it is expressed in the mission statement and the fruitfulness of our work as it is exhibited in our teaching, our students, and graduates. The Faculty will consider all areas being taught in our programs, with attention to how these are linked directly or indirectly to preparing students to be pastor-theologians.

            1.1.1.1 This process will consider the full scope of the objectives of the academic programs, with special attention to the goal that graduates be effective leaders in congregations and other settings in teaching the Bible and theology, proclaiming the Gospel in word and deed, and interpreting contemporary contexts.

1.1.1.2 Throughout this process, we will strengthen our commitment to academic programs that focus on the preparation of leaders for ministry and on our conviction that this preparation best occurs through intensive, campus-based educational encounter. As a part of this commitment, we will determine the optimal class sizes for course instruction.

1.1.1.3 We will promote the use of a cross-cultural immersion experience as a part of degree programs, more clearly defining the nature of the experience and its place in the curriculum. In addition, we will promote international partnerships, for instance between our seminary and similar schools in other parts of the world (like Trinity Theological College in Singapore, Trinity Theological Seminary in Ghana, and St. Tihon's Seminary in Moscow), asking how these relationships can enhance our programs while being of service to others.

1.1.1.4 In this context, we will review special programs focusing on their objectives and outcomes within the broader mission of the Seminary. We will focus especially on the Metro Urban Institute to consider how its social justice objectives might be more fully integrated across the curriculum.

1.1.1.5 We will review the place of field education within the curriculum and consider ways to strengthen the practical component of the educational experience through supervised apprenticeship on site, and a classroom experience that presents best practices in ministry.

Strategic Plan for Pittsburgh Theological Seminary, 2008

      1.1.1.6 We will consider how increased use of cohort groups might enhance the educational experience.

      1.1.1.7 Benchmark: In order to demonstrate progress toward the continuing improvement of our educational programs and to meet the requirements of accrediting agencies, we will have an established procedure for measuring our faithfulness to our purpose and the fruitfulness of our mission in place by 2010.

  1.1.2 As we learn by this process, we will consider the possibility of other degree or special programs that focus on areas such as mission studies, science and theology, urban studies, new church development, a Ph.D. program, or other initiatives.

      1.1.2.1 Benchmark: In 2008, we will reach a conclusion regarding a certificate program in Spiritual Direction and Leadership, taking both interest in and resources for the program into consideration when making this decision.

      1.1.2.2 Benchmark: In 2008, we will plan a D.Min. track that is focused on Science, Technology, and Pastoral Ministry.

      1.1.2.3 We will continue to explore opportunities for distance learning and off-campus programs while protecting faculty time and our commitment to campus-based programs.

      1.1.2.4 Should we go forward in any of these areas, part-time and short term faculty, guest lecturers, administrators, and support staff will be added as needed.

  1.1.3 We will continue to increase our use of technology to enhance on-campus educational programs and to help students gain skills in information technology as tools for ministry. We will develop a plan that addresses the development of more "smart" classrooms, a media lab for students, web-enhancement for courses, a preaching classroom, and training and staff to support them. Benchmark: comprehensive plan by November 2008.

1.2 *Strengthening the Faculty*

1.2.1 As we make progress in our assessment of the academic programs, we will plan for future needs in faculty appointments, leading to recommendations for new positions or endowed chairs as needed. Benchmark: By April 2008, the faculty will offer its assessment to the President about the need for endowed chairs for new positions in theology and world Christianity. By April 2009, the faculty will offer its preliminary assessment of the need to endow already existing faculty positions in areas of the curriculum such as homiletics, church history, biblical studies, and social or cultural studies in religion.

1.2.2 As positions become available and new faculty members are sought, we will give special attention to the global, ethnic, racial, and gender diversity of the church.

1.2.3 We will strengthen the current faculty through the development of policies and resources, such as the Kelley Fund, that support scholarship, publication, teaching, and public presence.

1.3 *Building on the Strength of our Library*

1.3.1 We will maintain the status of the Barbour Library as a premier research facility, continuing to build its resources while taking into account various changes in infrastructure in light of digital resources.

1.3.2 We will improve the library building in order to maintain its quality and to create more inviting spaces for reading and for scholarly conversation.

Strategic Plan for Pittsburgh Theological Seminary, 2008

    1.3.3 We will more fully integrate the library into the teaching and learning community of the seminary.

2.0 **We will continue raising the admission standards for students and the support we provide them during their education and their transition to positions of leadership.**

    2.1 *Recruiting Outstanding Students*

        2.1.1 We will continue to strengthen our efforts to recruit and select the strongest possible candidates for study in preparation for leadership in the church.

        2.1.2 We will set a target for the ideal student body size consistent with our educational standards, the availability of applicants, and the needs of the church. Benchmark: By May 2008, we will have in place a provisional decision on the number of students to be admitted each year and the optimal size of individual classes for instructional purposes. We will review this decision in light of changes in circumstance or based on our assessment of our academic programs.

        2.1.3 We will increase our efforts to recruit students who are women, racial or cultural minorities, persons with disabilities, and students from international settings.

        2.1.4 We will evaluate our current staffing and admission resources.

    2.2 *Providing Stronger Student Support*

        2.2.1 We will increase available scholarships and student financial aid, including need and merit based funding and funds for international students. Benchmark: a 50% increase by 2011.

        2.2.2 We will review the needs of students for pastoral care and psychological services, and address needs as they are identified.

        2.2.3 We commit ourselves to assessing needs and making

APPENDIX A

substantial improvements to student housing, particularly married student apartments. These needs will be addressed as part of the master plan for the campus.

2.2.4 We will continue to look for ways to support all our students through the placement process and, as appropriate, continue to provide encouragement and support during their early years in ministry.

3.0 **We will strengthen our service to those already in ministry and to lay leaders in the church through improvements to our continuing education programs.**

3.1 *Assessing the Needs and Opportunities for Improvement of our Programs of Continuing Education:* We will engage our continuing education constituencies and our ecumenical and judicatory partners in a study of the needs and the objectives of our program, including how continuing education should flow from the M.Div. degree through an intentional program of life-long education.

3.2 *A Plan for Stronger Programs:* Based on this assessment, we will review our programs, including goals, staffing, budget, institutional support, faculty involvement, and develop a plan for the future. Benchmark: adopt plan by May 2009.

4.0 **As a community of scholars who seek to grow in grace and in the knowledge of God, we will increase our commitment to be formed through worship, hospitality, and joyful service.**

4.1 *Worship:*

4.1.1 We will increase our focus on worship and the spiritual disciplines in our personal and communal life, including a greater emphasis on the role of corporate worship.

4.1.2 We will assess the need for architectural modifications to the chapel building, including issues of accessibility.

4.2 *Hospitality:*

- 4.2.1 We will increase the sense by all on campus that they are welcome to join us here as part of an educational community.

- 4.2.2 We will create a campus free of physical barriers.

- 4.2.3 We will consider architectural modifications to enhance hospitality, such as a welcome center.

- 4.2.4 We will improve the culture of hospitality by increasing the availability and helpfulness of campus personnel.

4.3 *Service:*

- 4.3.1 We will create opportunities for service together in the local community or in other settings.

- 4.3.2 We will consider a co-curricular requirement that all students be involved in some form of local ministry or service.

5.0 **As a community blessed by God and the support of many friends, we will practice and model stewardship through careful guardianship, planning, and fundraising.**

5.1 *We will take care of our buildings, land, and endowment as a trust for the future.*

- 5.1.1 We will continue to draw prudently from our endowment while increasing our unrestricted giving to the annual fund to at least 10% of the Seminary's annual operating budget.

- 5.1.2 We will develop a master plan for the seminary campus, taking into consideration current spaces, new construction, and partnerships that might assist us to achieve institutional goals.

- 5.1.3 We will develop a plan to become an environmentally "greener" campus.

APPENDIX A

5.2 *We will develop a plan for a capital campaign based on needs that are identified through careful planning in all areas outlined in this Strategic Plan.*

    5.2.1 We will undertake a process of institutional or program assessment. In light of what we learn, we will revise our Strategic Plan. This process of assessment and planning will inform the development of a comprehensive financial campaign. Benchmark: Assessment completed by November, 2008.

    5.2.2 We will assess the resources of the advancement program to support the financial campaign and provide adequate funding for staff, marketing, and communications.

APPENDIX B

Historical Roll of Professors
Pittsburgh Theological Seminary

James Leon Kelso (Xenia)	1923-1963
William F. Orr (Western)	1936-1974
Theophilus Mills Taylor (Pittsburgh-Xenia)	1942-1962
Jarvis M. Cotton (Western)	1944-1961
Frank Dixon McCloy (Western)	1944-1967
Walter R. Clyde (Western)	1945-1975
Addison Hardie Leitch (Pittsburgh-Xenia)	1946-1961
David Noel Freedman (Western)	1948-1964
Gordon Edmund Jackson (Pittsburgh-Xenia)	1949-1983
John H. Gerstner (Pittsburgh-Xenia)	1950-1980
Clifford E. Barbour (Western)	1951-1962
Bessie M. Burrows (Pittsburgh-Xenia)	1953-1971
James Arthur Walther (Western)	1954-1983
Sidney O. Hills (Western)	1954-1975
Robert Lee Kelley, Jr. (Pittsburgh-Xenia)	1955-1997
Robert Clyde Johnson (Western)	1955-1963
Howard M. Jamieson, Jr. (Pittsburgh-Xenia)	1955-1970
John M. Bald (Pittsburgh-Xenia)	1957-1977
Elwyn Allen Smith (Western)	1957-1966
Walter E. Wiest (Western)	1957-1987
Malcolm S. Alexander (Pittsburgh-Xenia)	1958-1966
Harold E. Scott (Pittsburgh-Xenia)	1959-1978
Howard L. Ralston (Western and Pittsburgh-Xenia)	1960-1972

APPENDIX B

William A. Nicholson (Western)	1960-1975
James Sheppard Irvine	1960-1966
J. Gordon Chamberlin	1960-1979
Gayraud S. Wilmore	1961-1965
Arlen P. Dohrenburg	1961-1964
Edward D. Grohman	1961-1964
David G. Buttrick	1961-1975
Donald G. Miller	1962-1970
George H. Kehm	1962-1996
Dietrich Ritschl	1963-1970
Markus Barth	1963-1972
Edward Farley	1963-1969
Lynn Boyd Hinds	1963-1972
Iain G. Wilson	1963-1968
Douglas R. A. Hare	1964-1993
Donald E. Gowan	1965-1999
Jared J. Jackson	1965-1997
H. Eberhard von Waldow	1966-1993
Dikran Hadidian	1966-1985
Peter Fribley	1966-1970
Robert S. Paul	1967-1977
Ford Lewis Battles	1967-1978
Neil R. Paylor	1968-1982
Paul W. Lapp	1968-1970
Robert M. Ezzell	1969-1999
Ronald H. Stone	1969-2003
John Wiley Nelson	1971-1979
William H. Kadel	1971-1978
Arthur C. Cochrane	1971-1975
John S. Walker	1971-1972
David T. Shannon	1972-1978
M. Harjie Likins	1973-1998
Samuel K. Roberts	1973-1976
Gonzalo Castillo-Cardenas	1977-2004
Ulrich W. Mauser	1977-1990
Marjorie Suchocki	1977-1983
Charles B. Partee	1978-2009
Richard J. Oman	1979-1999

Historical Roll of Professors

Carnegie Samuel Calian	1981-2006
Andrew Purves	1983-
Ronald H. Cram	1983-1985
John E. Wilson, Jr.	1984-
Susan Nelson	1984-2006
Byron H. Jackson	1986-
Martha A. Robbins	1986-
Stephen D. Crocco	1987-1997
Keith F. Nickle	1990-1994
Ronald Peters	1991-
Robert A. J. Gagnon	1994-
Scott W. Sunquist	1994-
Linda M. Day	1995-2004
Bonnie Bowman Thurston	1995-2002
Ronald Cole-Turner	1996-
Dale Allison	1997-
Richard A. Ray	1997-2001
Ron E. Tappy	1997-
John P. Burgess	1998-
Steven C. Perry	1999-2006
Richard Curtis Chapple	2000-2008
Jerome F. D. Creach	2000-
Fred Douglas Smith	2000-2003
Teresa Lockhart Stricklen	2000-2008
M. Craig Barnes	2002-
Edith M. Humphrey	2002-
Timothy D. Son	2004-
Deirdre King Hainsworth	2005-
Steven S. Tuell	2005-
William J. Carl III	2006-
Sharon A. Taylor	2007-
Susan L. Kendall	2007-
George E. Tutwiler	2007-
Edwin Chr. van Driel	2009-

APPENDIX C

Deans of the Faculty

Gordon E. Jackson   1960-1970
Professor of Christian Education and Pastoral Theology

Howard M. Jamieson Jr.   1970
Professor of New Testament

John M. Bald   1970-1971
Associate Professor of Christian Ethics

Robert M. Ezzell   1971-1972
Assistant Professor of Homiletics

David T. Shannon   1972-1978
Associate Professor of Old Testament

Douglas R. A. Hare   1979-1981
Professor of New Testament

Ulrich W. Mauser   1981-1990
Professor of New Testament

Keith F. Nickle   1990-1993
Professor of New Testament Studies

Deans of the Faculty

Richard J. Oman 1993-1999
  Professor of Homiletics

John E. Wilson 1999-2005
  Professor of Church History

Byron H. Jackson 2005-
  Associate Professor of Church Education

APPENDIX D

Board of Directors

2008-2009

Officers

Chair	John S. Isherwood
Vice Chair	Sandra A. Lamb
Secretary	Peter Y. Herchenroether
Treasurer	Roger E. Wright
Asst. Secretary/Treasurer	Patrick Cunningham
Legal Counsel	Peter Y. Herchenroether

Members

Harold W. Burlingame	Peter Y. Herchenroether
William J. Carl III	W. Allen Hogge
Lawrence R. Chottiner	David R. Hosick
James W. Craig	John W. Hoyt
Ronald D. Dickel	Leslie Huff
Earnest J. Edwards	John S. Isherwood
W. Craig Esterly	Robert L. Kelly Jr.
Kimberly Tillotson Fleming	Sandra A. Lamb
James M. Gockley	Donald K. McKim
Wendy Myers Heinz	James E. Mead

PTS Board of Directors, 2008-2009

Kimberly R. Merrell
Bryan Miller
James D. Miller
Roberta Lemons Miller
Sue Sterling Montgomery
Norman M. Pritchard
Michael S. Rawlings
Thomas M. St. Clair
Stephanie K. Simmons

William L. Standish
Alan H. Staples
Robert J. Starck
F. David Throop
Susan E. Vande Kappelle
Jack van Hartesvelt
Brian Wallace
Roger E. Wright

Index of Names

Anderson, John, 2, 44

Bald, John M., 75, 76, 78, 142
Ballantyne, Agnes, 40
Barbour, Clifford E., 9, 14, 18, 19, 21, 22, 27, 28, 35, 40, 42, 77
Barnes, M. Craig, 217
Barth, Karl, 38, 42
Barth, Markus, 38, 39, 42, 143, 149
Battles, Ford Lewis, 39, 143
Berger, Peter, 61, 66
Bogan, Louise, 64
Bower, Debbie, 211
Buttrick, David G., 28, 63, 64, 112, 113, 133, 143, 225

Calian, Carnegie Samuel, 152-70, 172, 177, 180, 181, 184, 202, 205-8, 212, 214, 216, 217, 220-23, 227
Calian, Doris, 152, 153, 216, 223
Carl III, William J., 225-27, 231
Carl, Jane Alexander, 225
Carnegie, Andrew, 153
Castillo-Cardenas, Gonzalo, 142
Chamberlain, J. Gordon, 28
Clasper, Douglas N., 163
Clyde, Walter R., 8
Cochrane, Arthur C., 142

Cole-Turner, Ronald, 209
Cram, Ronald H., 176
Crocco, Stephen D., 188, 209
Cushman, Robert, 54

Dahhrenburg, Arlan P., 28
Darrow, Clarence, 8
Davison, James E., 215
Dawson, Donald, 217
Dunstan, G. R., 62

Elligan, Michael, 158
Elliott, David, 7n
Ezzell, Robert M., 40, 87

Fairman, Edwin, 158
Fairman, Marion, 158
Farley, Edward, 39
Fisher, George, 29
Foster, Lisa Dormire, 179
Freedman, David Noel, 8
Fribley, Peter, 40
Frost, Randall, 112

Gerstner, John H., 147
Gittings, James, 104n
Gowan, Donald E., 39, 178, 186
Griggs, Milton, 45

Index of Names

Hadidian, Dikran Y., 39, 43
Hainer, Frank, 142
Halsey, Luther, 6
Hambrick-Stowe, Charles, 215
Hanna, Dwight C., 120, 129
Hare, Douglas R. A., 39, 141, 156, 201
Harper, Robert T., 220
Herchenroether Jr., Henry C., 14n, 19n, 37n, 81n
Herron, Francis, 5
Hicks, Lewis W., 44-46
Hicks, Wenham A., 44
Hills, Sidney O., 142
Hinds, Lynn B., 39, 143
Hinsey, J. Rowe, 68
Hitler, Adolf, 42
Hodge, Archibald Alexander, 8
Hodge, Charles, 6, 8
Holland, Robert Cleveland, 151, 162

Irvine, James, 40, 41, 43
Isherwood, John, 220

Jackson, Byron H., 201, 227
Jackson, Gordon, 16, 21, 25, 26, 28, 50, 53, 58, 75, 87, 88, 103, 106, 164
Jackson, Jared J., 39
Jacobus, Melanchthon W., 8
James, Beverly W., 154
Jamieson, Howard, 75, 76
Johns, Mary Eleanor, 210
Johnson, Robert Clyde, 16

Kadel, William H., 76-83, 85-89, 93-95, 105, 110, 112, 113, 120-22, 124, 129-31, 134-36, 140-43
Kehm, George, 103
Kelley Jr., Robert L., 186, 206
Kennedy, Robert, 72
Kenyon, Walter Wynn, 147
King Jr., Martin Luther, 58, 72, 73, 109, 188

Kurtzman, David H., 38

Lapp, Nancy, 213
Lapp, Paul W., 40
LeFevre, Perry, 54
Lehmann, Paul L., 47
Leitch, Addison H., 4, 5, 14, 15, 18, 29, 32
Likens, M. Harjie, 142
Lockhart, Charles, 4
Long, George A., 4, 5
Ludwig, W. Paul, 140, 151

Marx, Karl, 62
Mason, Henry Lee, 4
Matheson, George, 141
Mauser, Ulrich W., 142, 156, 159, 164, 171, 186
McCloy, F. Dixon, 7n, 8
McGahey, Frank, 133
McKim, LindaJo H., 147
McMillan, John, 44
McNaugher, John, 3, 4
McNaugher, William, 15
Mehl, John E., 178, 215
Meneilly, Robert H., 183
Miller, Donald G., 35-40, 42, 44, 45, 47, 48, 53, 54, 58-63, 66-68, 73, 75, 77, 94, 102, 103, 143
Morse, Herman N., 17
Moule, C. F. D., 44

Nelson, John Wiley, 142
Nelson, Susan, 177
Nelson, Thomas, 220
Nevin, John Williamson, 6
Nickle, Keith F., 187, 194, 201
Nicolson, William A., 142
Niemöller, Martin, 42, 43

Oman, Richard J., 141, 201
Orr, William F., 8, 201

Partee, Charles B., 142, 189

INDEX OF NAMES

Paul, Robert S., 39, 143
Paylor, Neil R., 40
Peters, Ronald H., 187
Phillippe, William, 142
Plumer, William S., 8
Purves, Andrew, 176, 227

Ralston, Howard L., 142
Ramsay, James, 2
Rapp, Jeannette, 142, 158, 187
Rapp, Richard J., 142, 158
Ray, Richard A., 211
Rea, William, 111, 114, 139
Ricoeur, Paul, 44
Riesman, David, 65
Ritschl, Dietrich, 38
Robbins, Martha Bowman, 209
Roberts, F. Morgan, 158
Roberts, Samuel K., 142
Rogers, Fred, 147

Schaff, David, 8
Schaff, Philip, 6, 60
Scharfe, Howard C., 85
Scott, Harold E., 83, 89, 110, 143, 183
Scott, Mary Ellen, 188
Serovy, Mary, 209
Shannon, David T., 88, 106, 151
Sharp, H. Parker, 189
Shoemaker, G. Albert, 183, 186, 201, 209

Shoemaker, Mercedes, 186, 209
Small III, Joseph D., 142
Snowden, James H., 8
Speakman, Frederick, 39
Stone, Ronald H., 40, 189
Suchocki, Marjorie, 142
Swift, Elisha Pope, 6

Talbot, Mary Lee, 187, 215
Tappy, Ron E., 219
Taylor, Theophilus Mills, 8, 12, 17
Torrance, T. F., 60
Tutweiler, George, 142

Vogelsang, Robert, 102
von Waldow, H. Eberhard, 39, 201

Waits, James, 207
Walker, John S., 142
Walther, James Arthur, 23n, 29n, 164, 204
Warfield, Benjamin B., 8
Wells, Ronald V., 152, 154
White, John E., 158, 182, 183, 213
Williams, Sharon L., 182
Wilmore, Gayraud S., 28
Wilson Jr., John E., 177, 213, 227
Wilson, Iain G., 39
Wilson, Samuel Jennings, 8
Wolfe, Marianne L., 111, 137
Wren, Christopher, 45

www.ingramcontent.com/pod-product-compliance
Lightning Source LLC
Chambersburg PA
CBHW031350230426
43670CB00006B/498